Australia:
Great Southern Pictorial

Australia: Great Southern Pictorial

Rob Benton

Esotericom®

All photographs by Rob Benton

ISBN 978-0-9980682-5-1

He turns a desert into pools of water,
a parched land into springs of water.

And there He lets the hungry dwell,
and they establish a city to live in;

they sow the fields, and plant vineyards,
and get a fruitful yield.

By His blessing they multiply greatly;
and He does not let their cattle decrease.

Psalms 107: 35-38

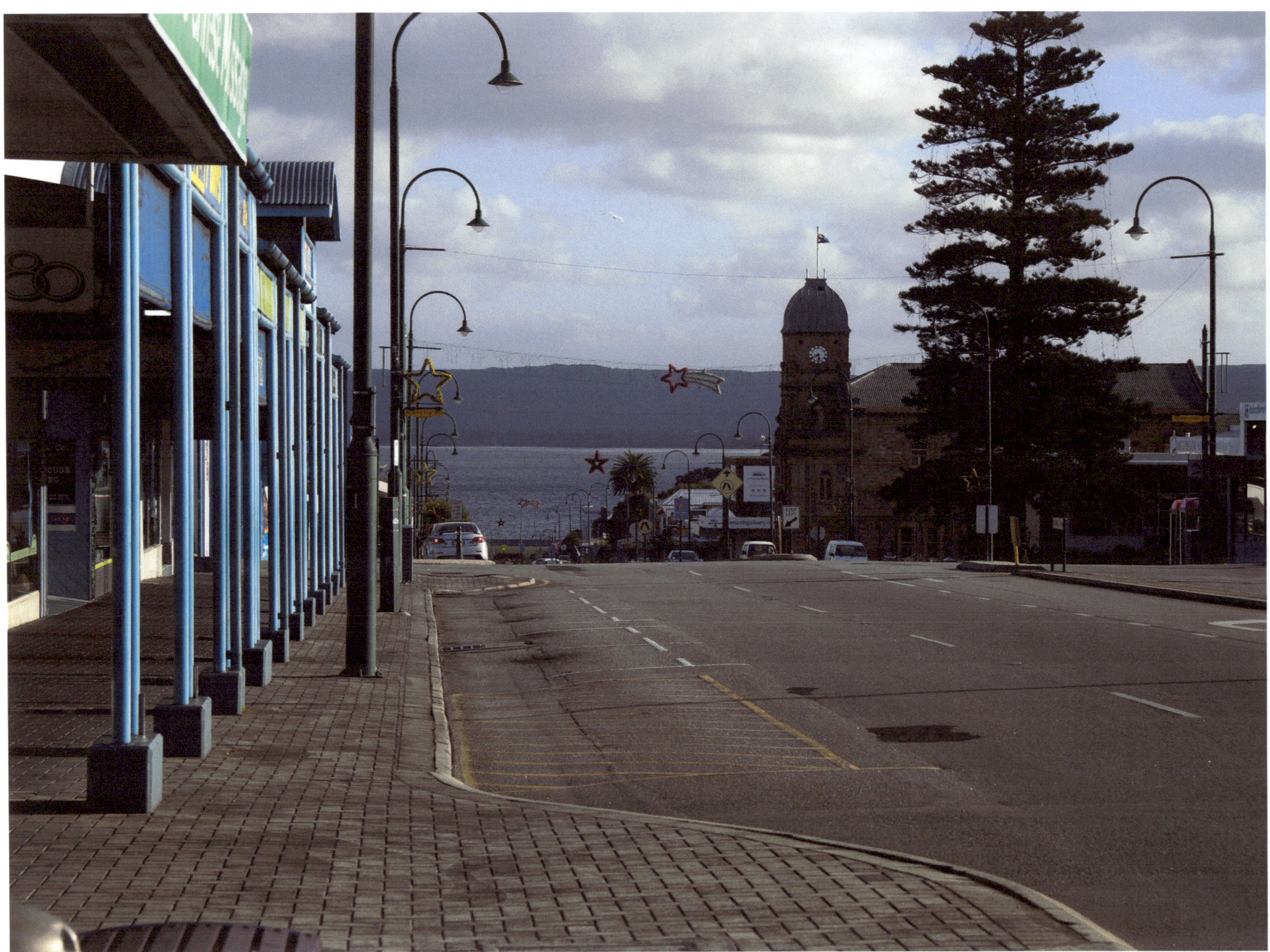

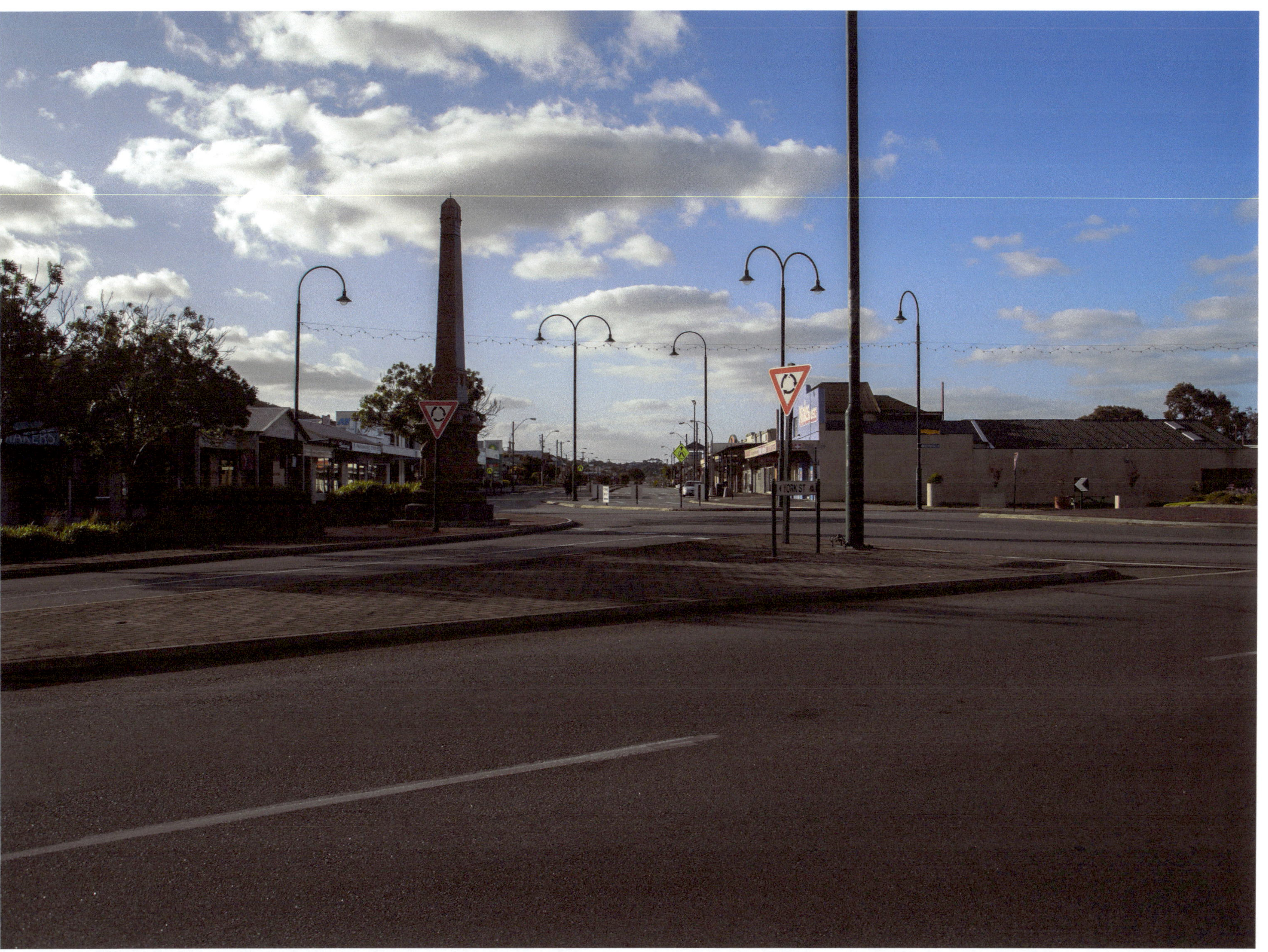
YORK ST

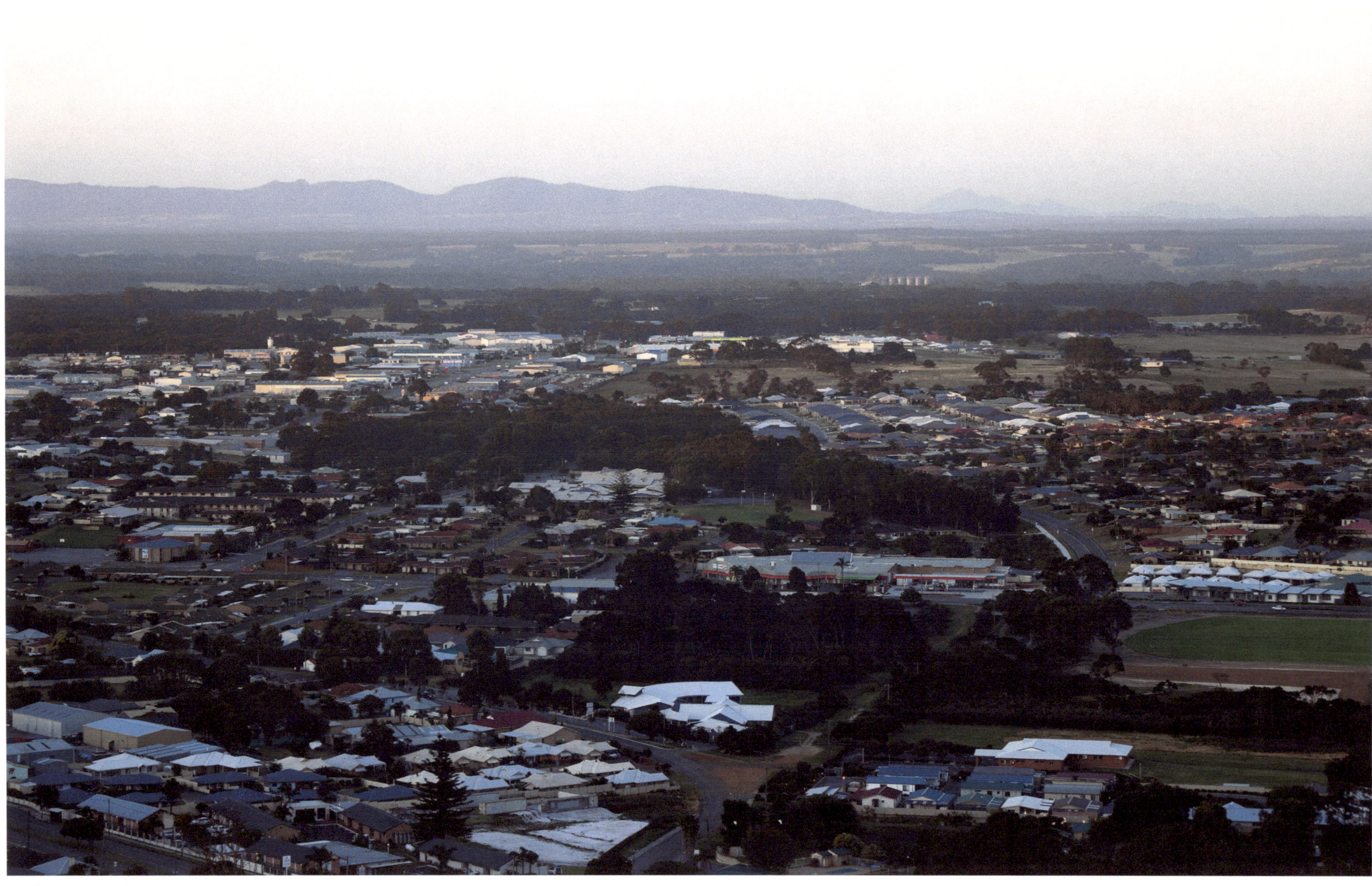

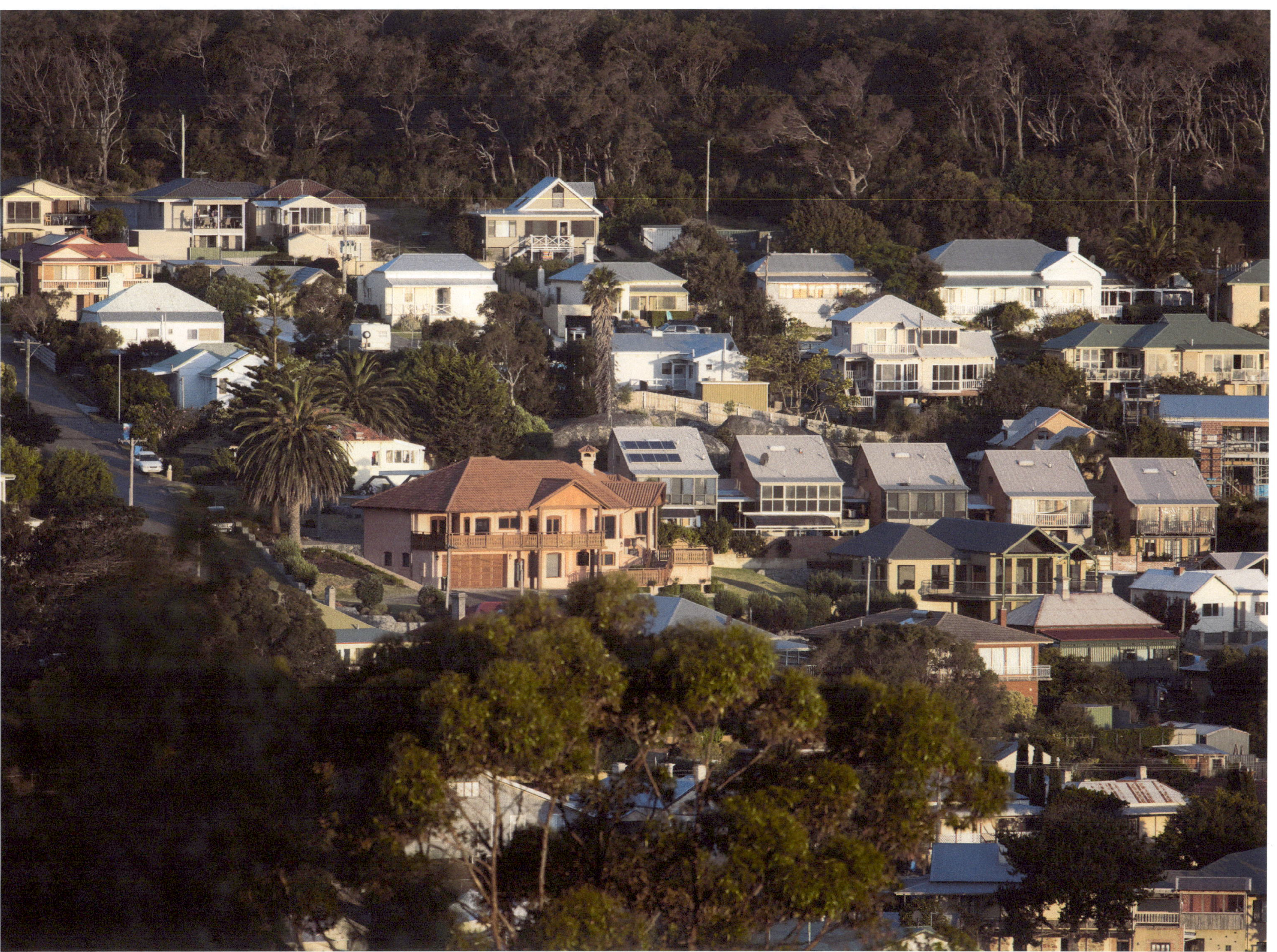

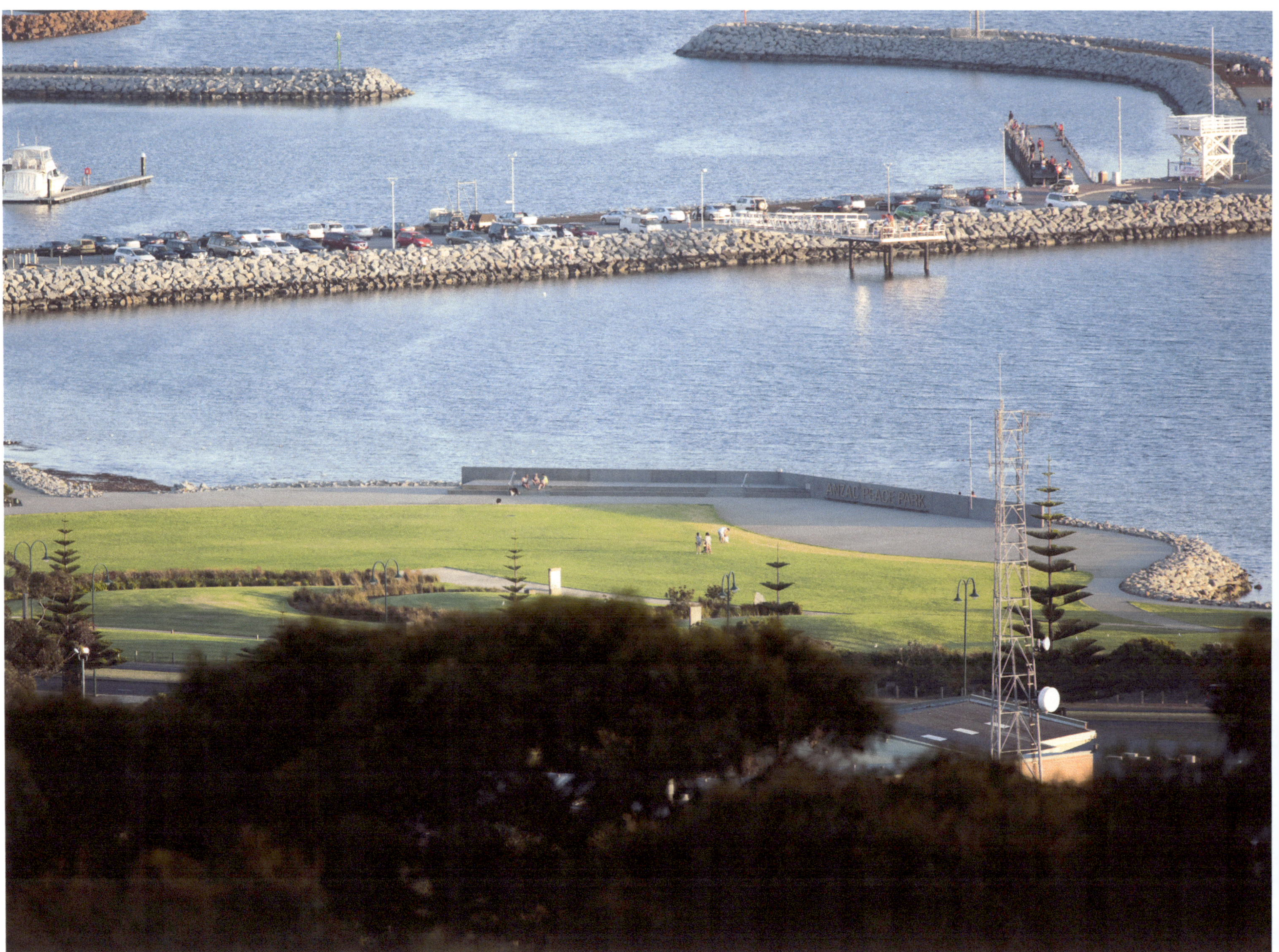
ANZAC PEACE PARK

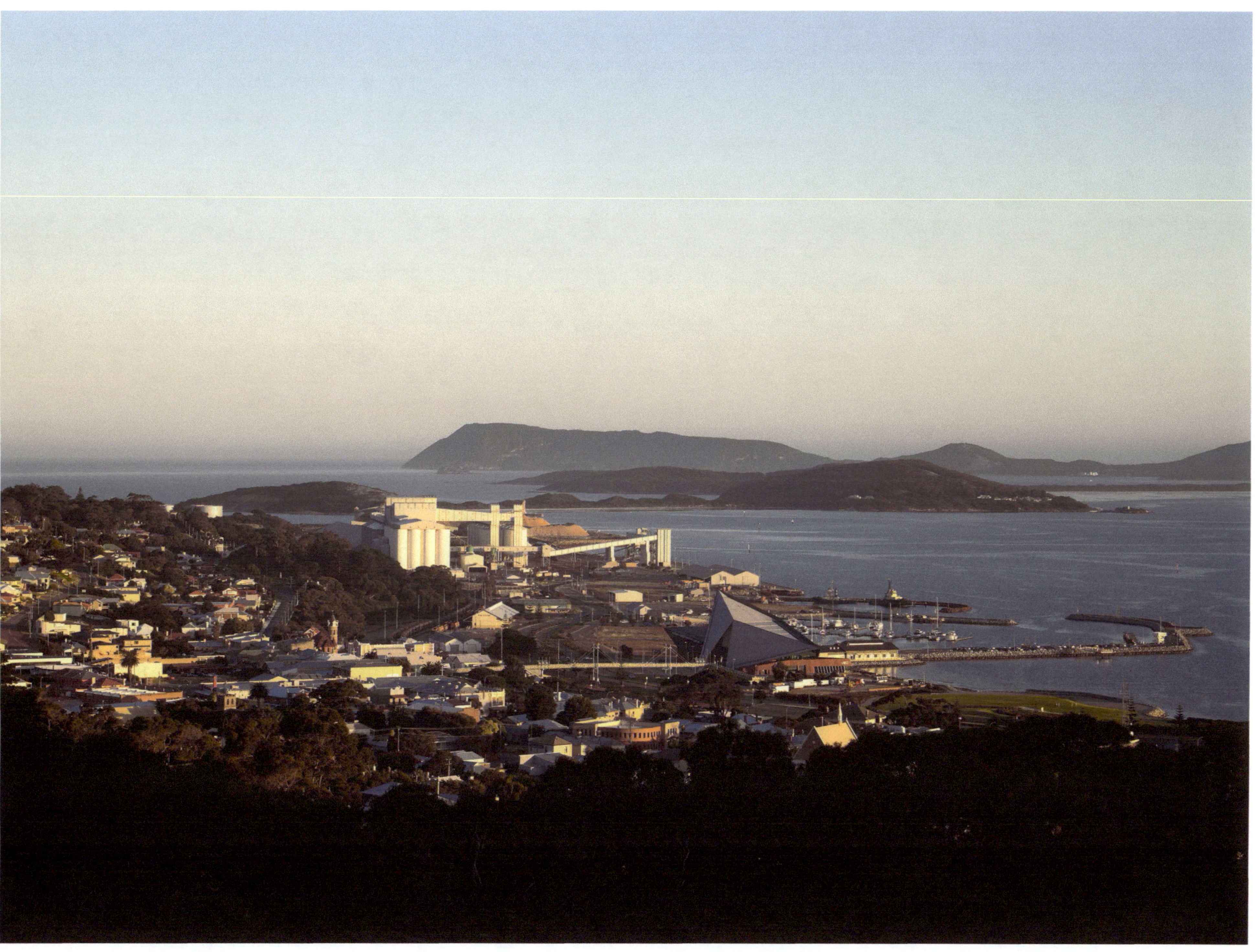

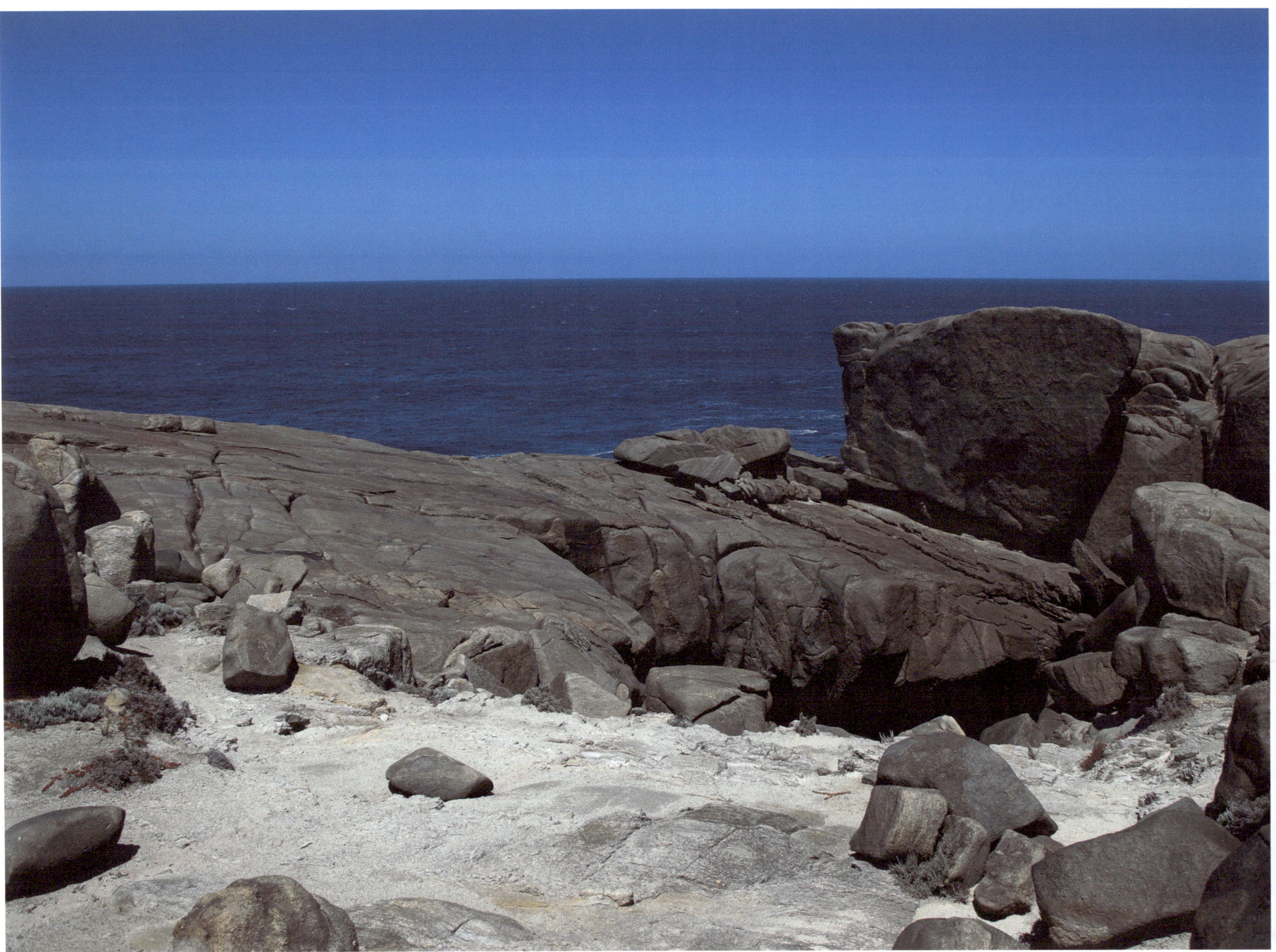

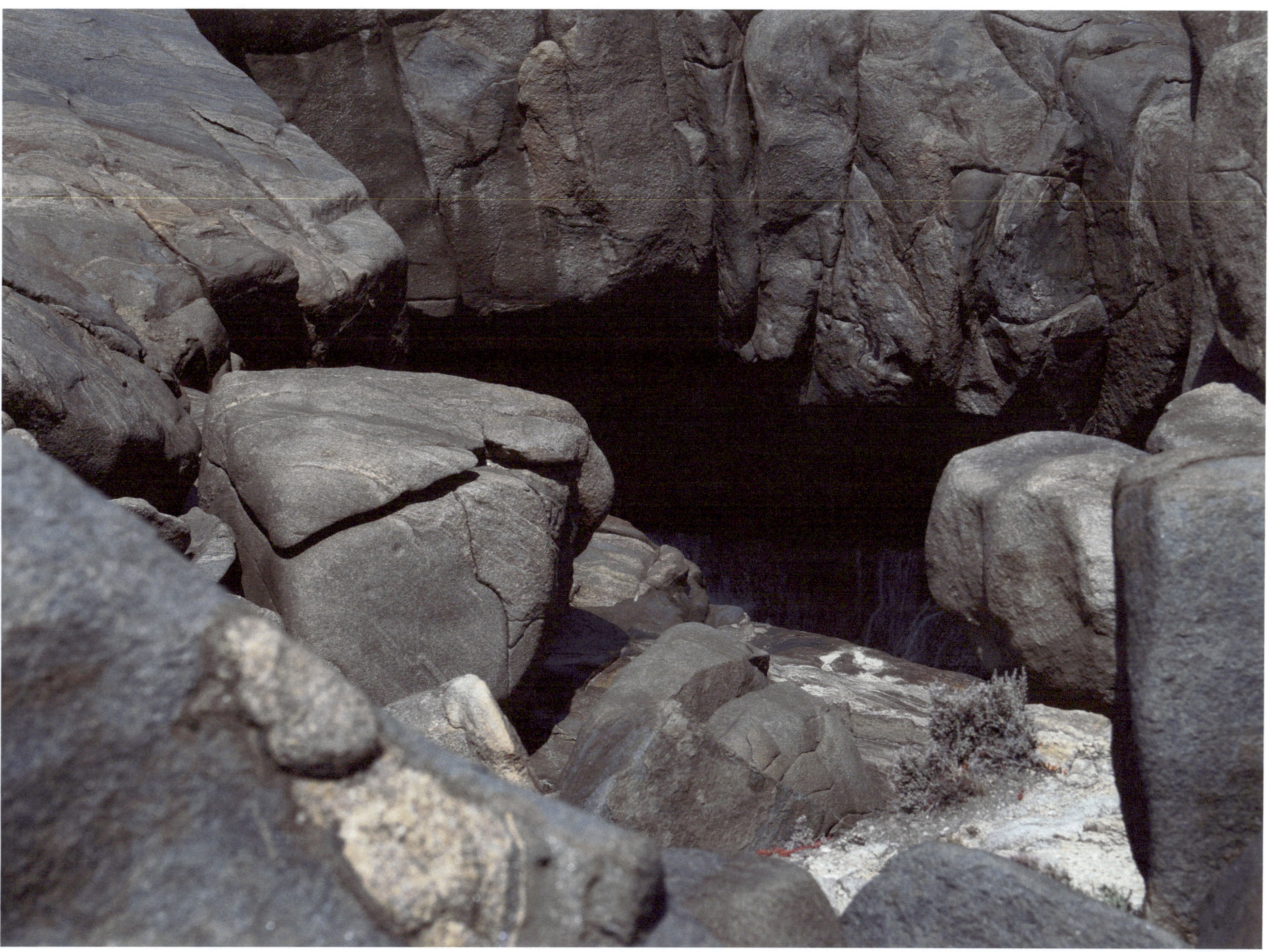

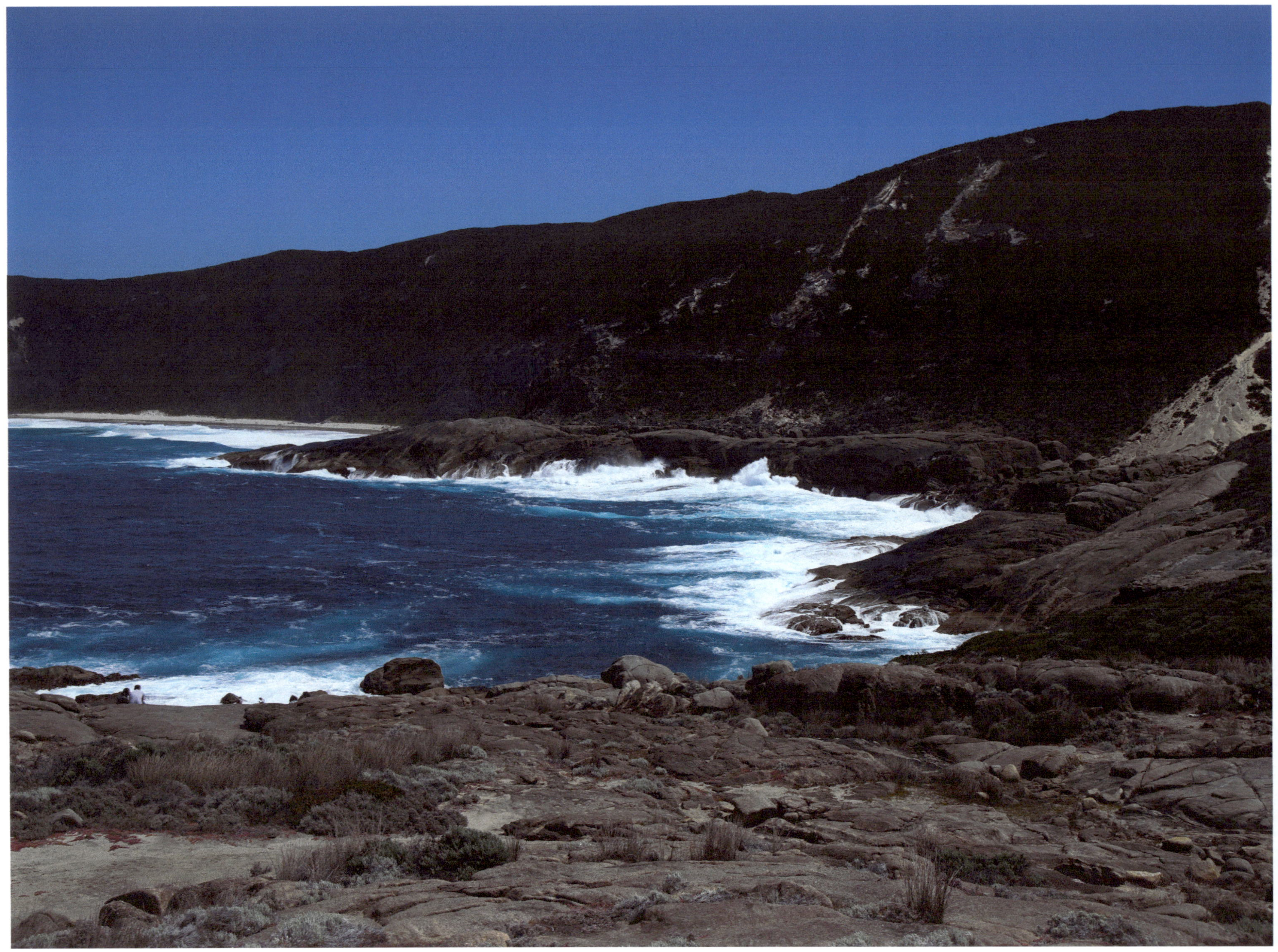

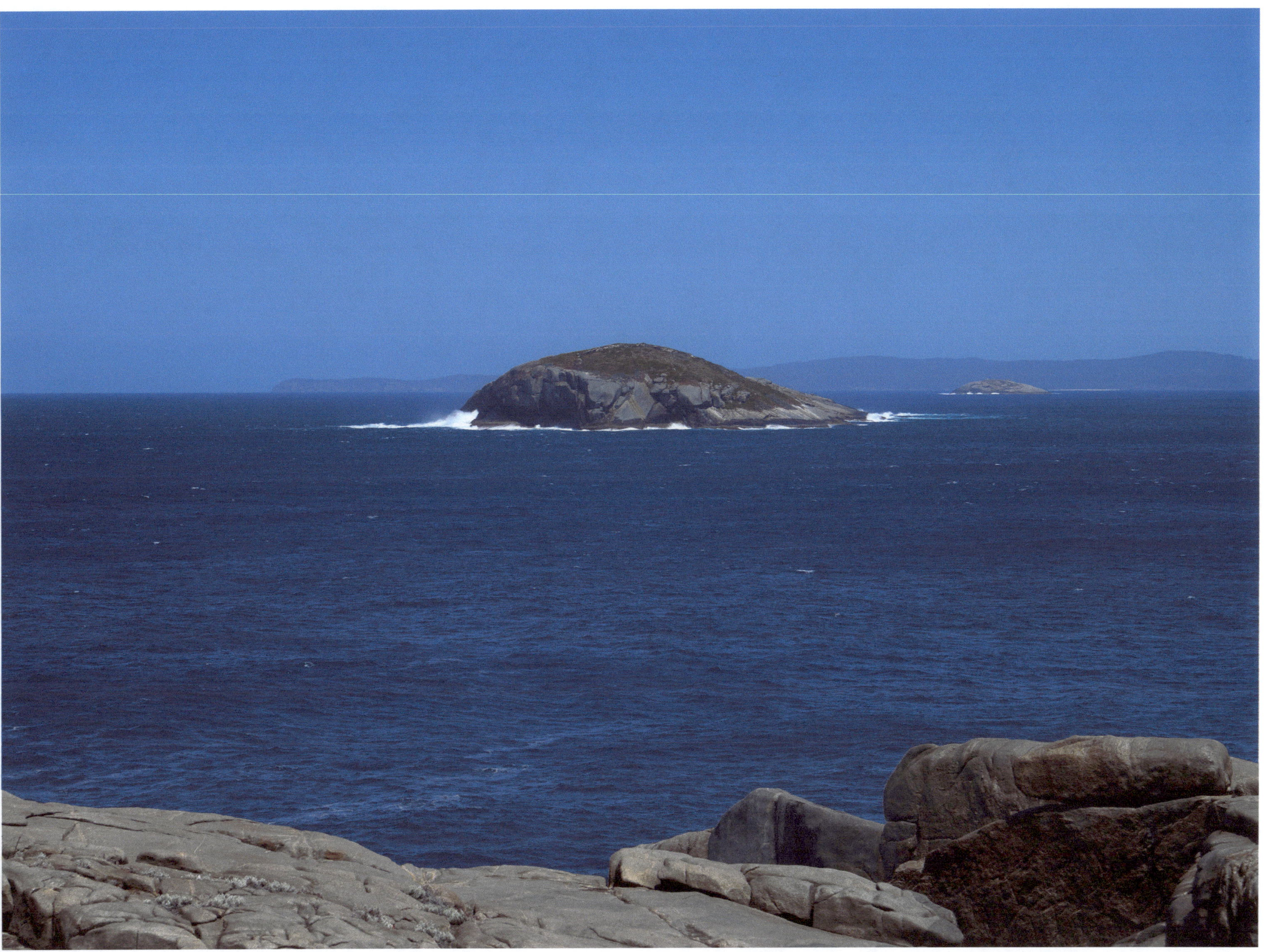

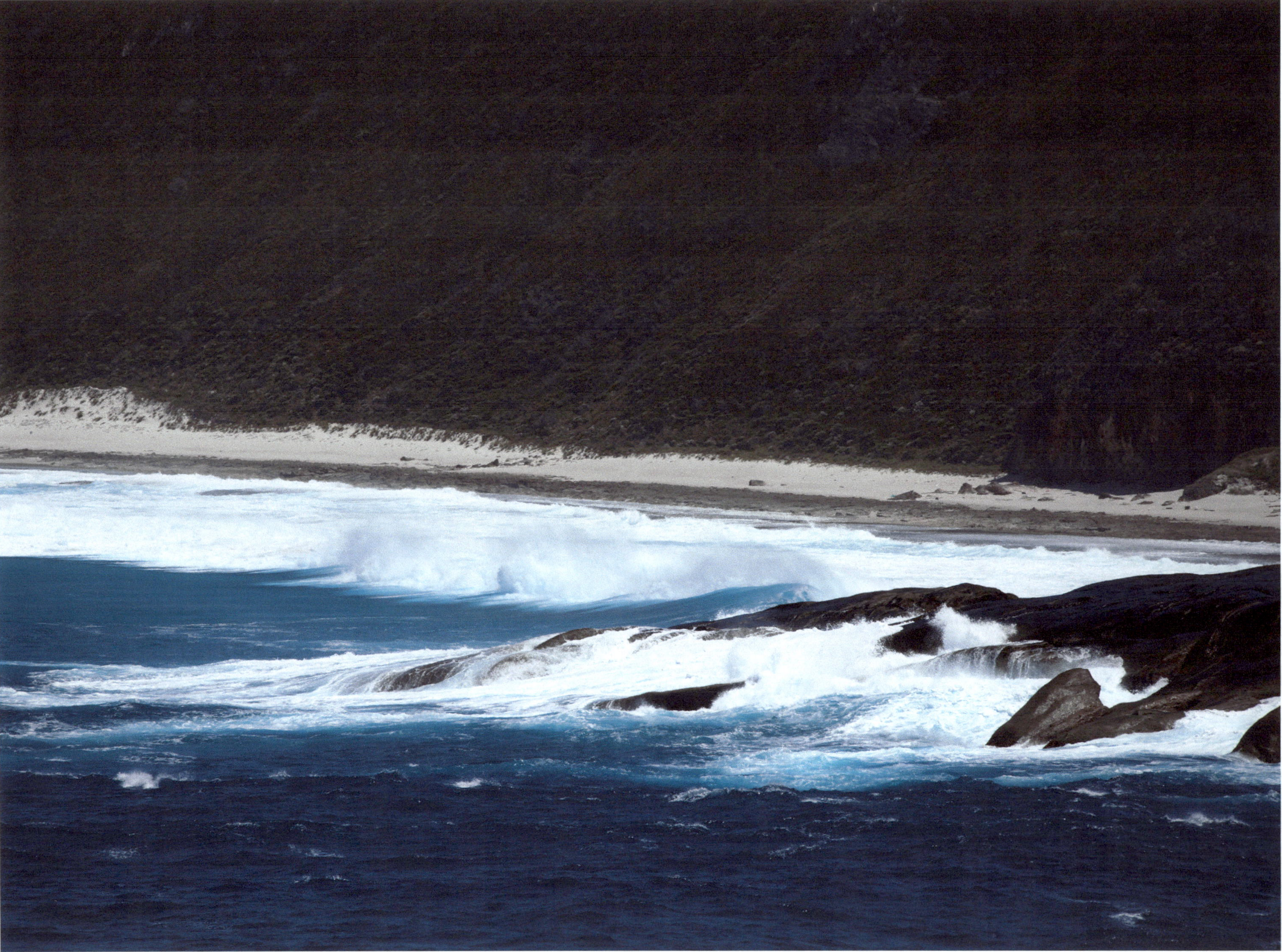

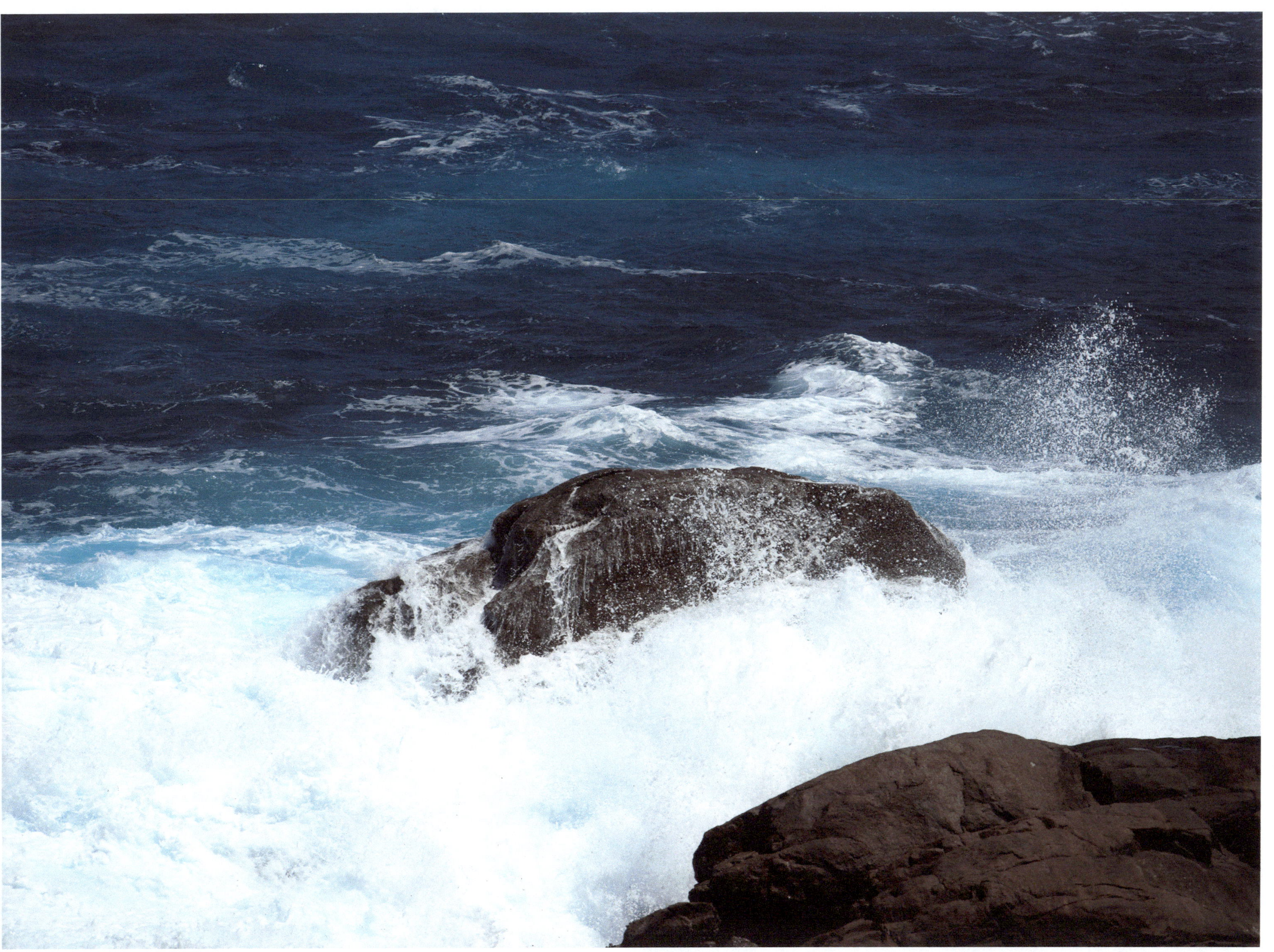

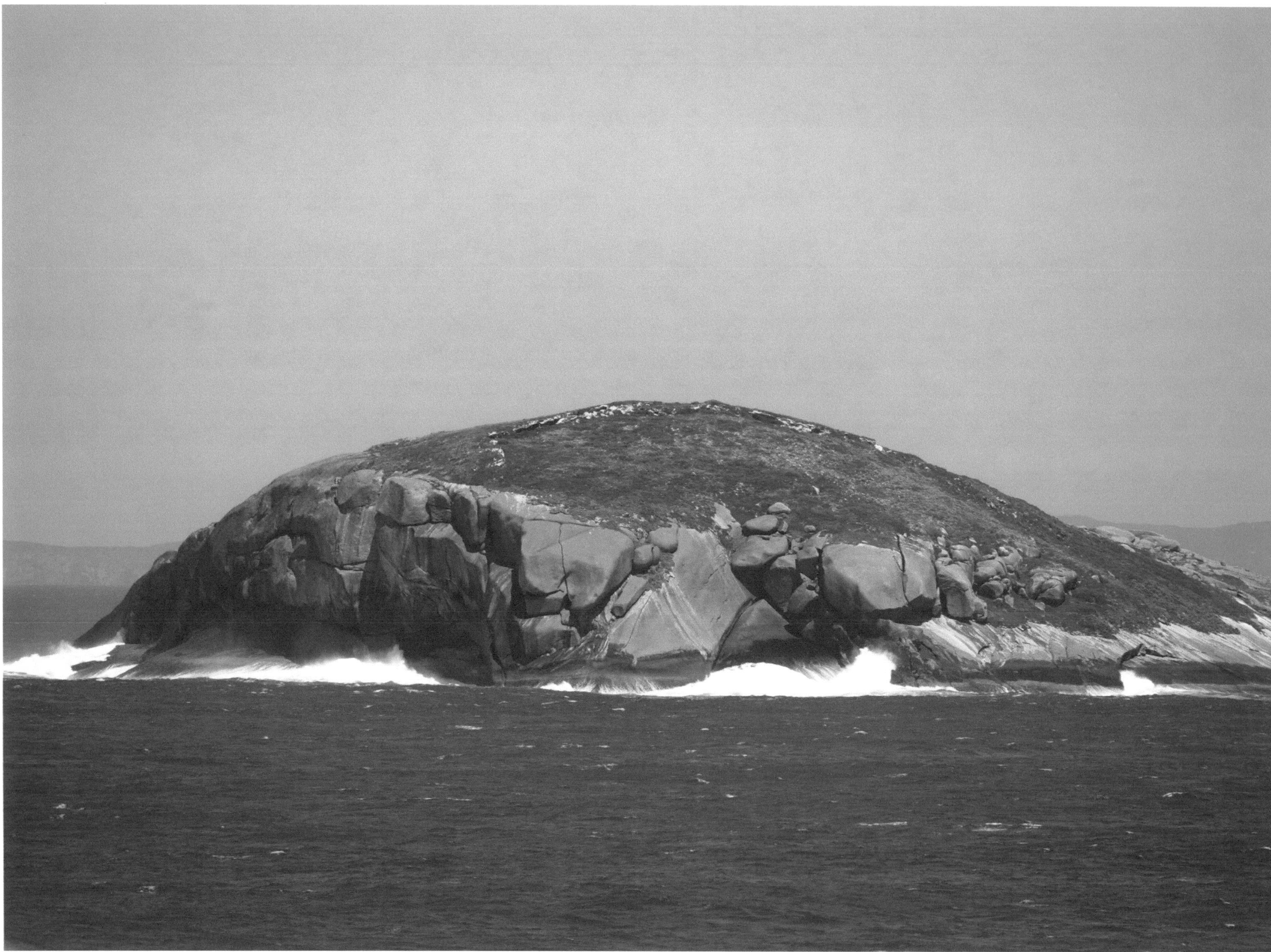

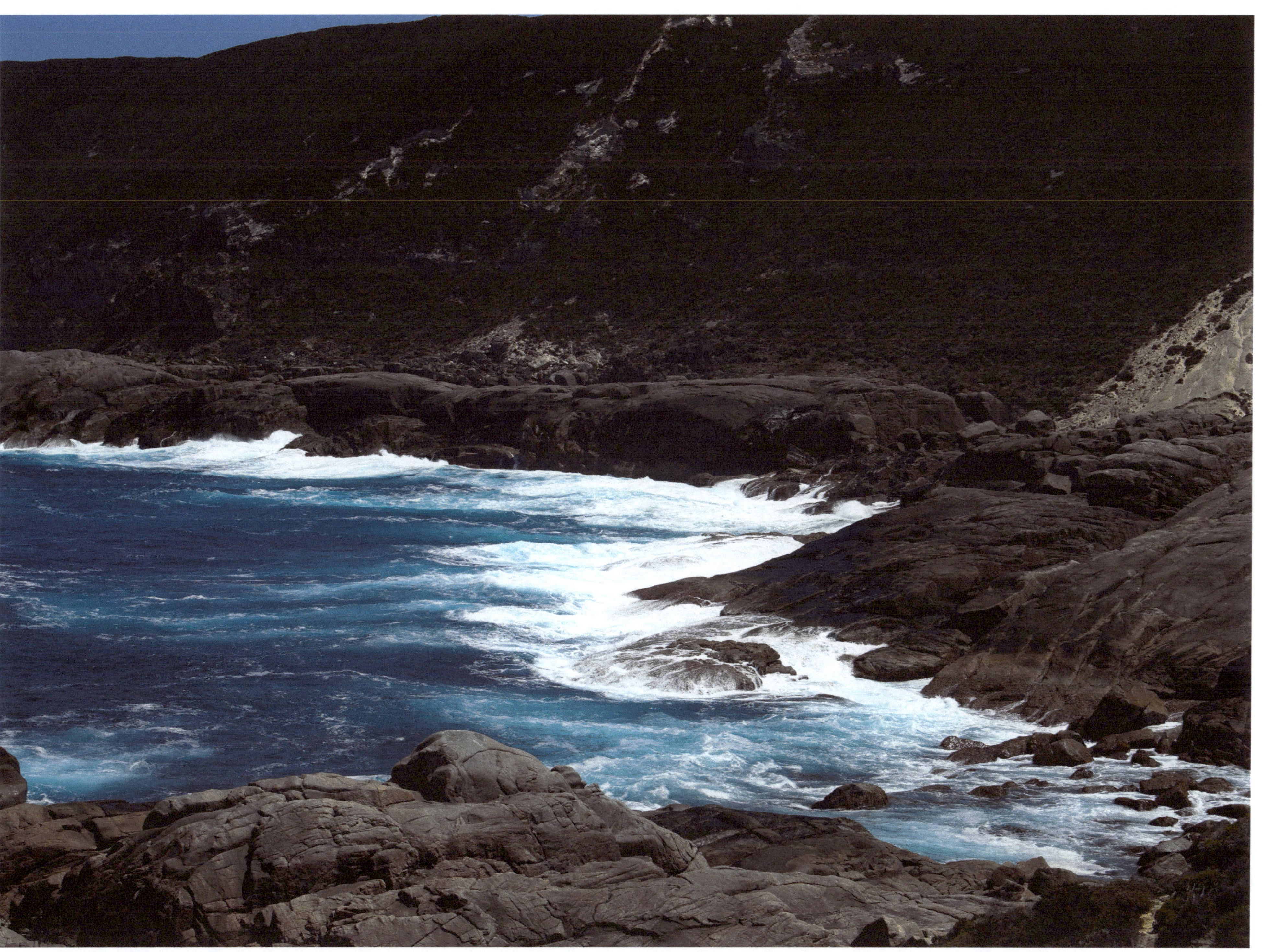

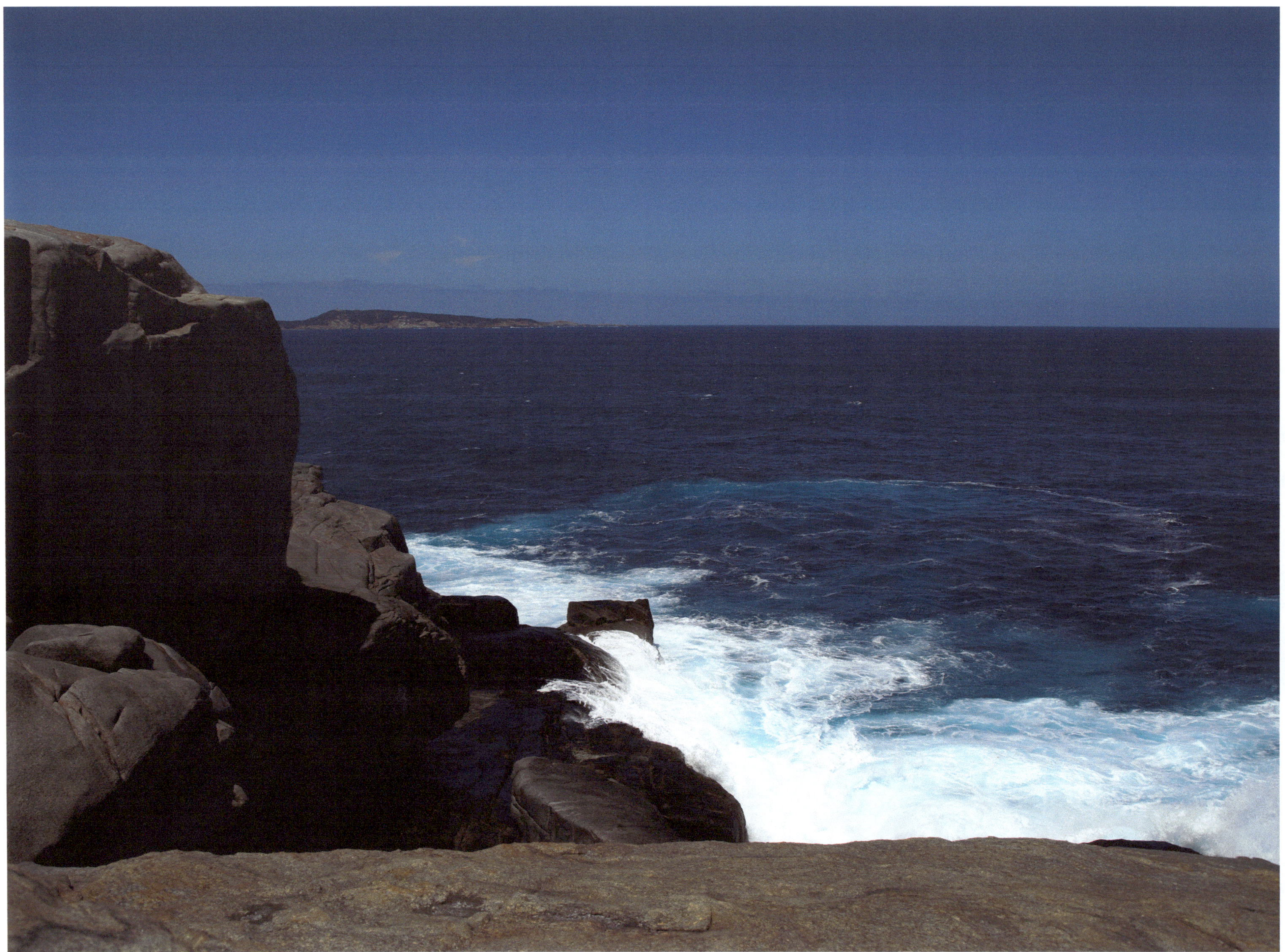

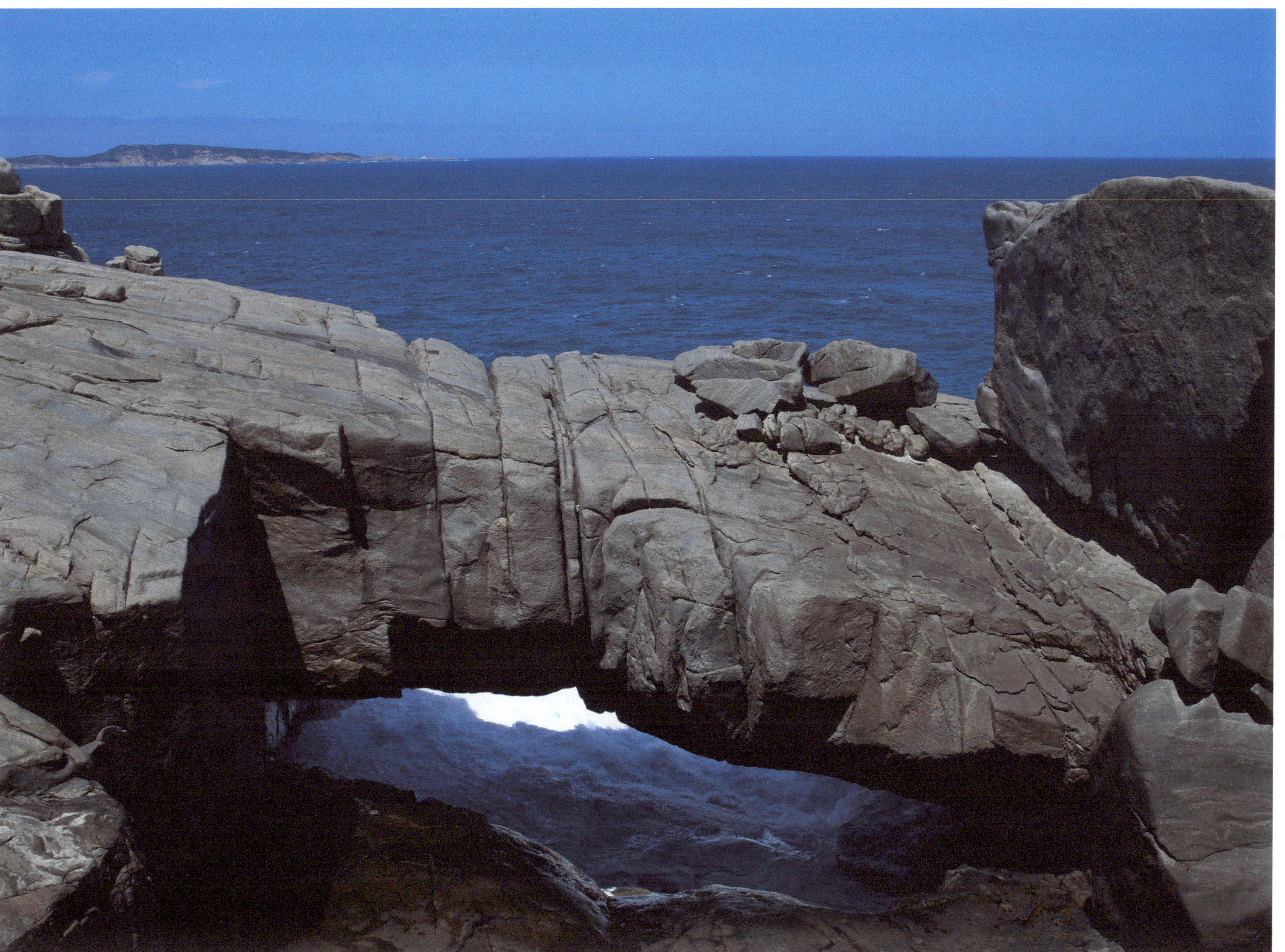

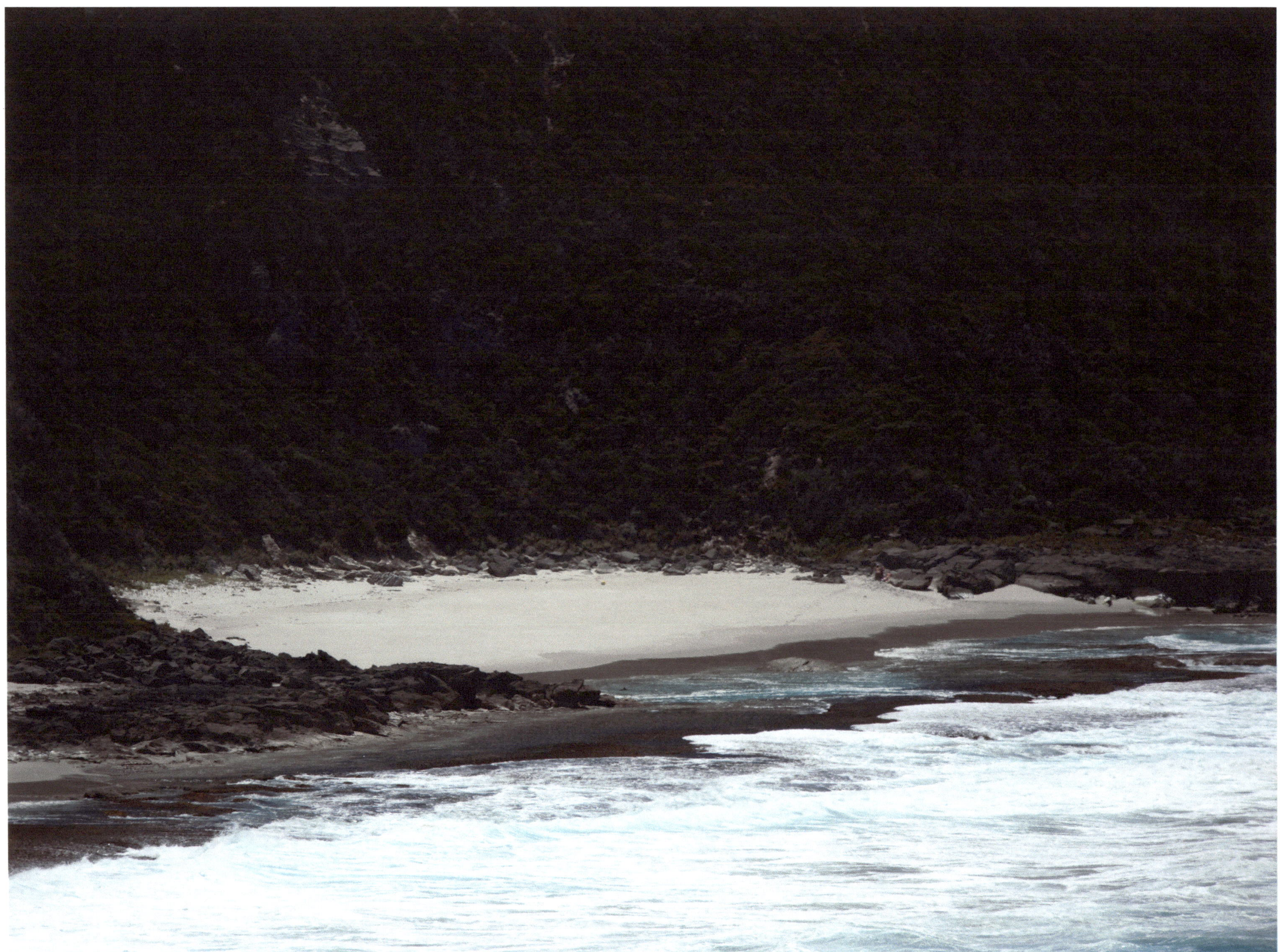

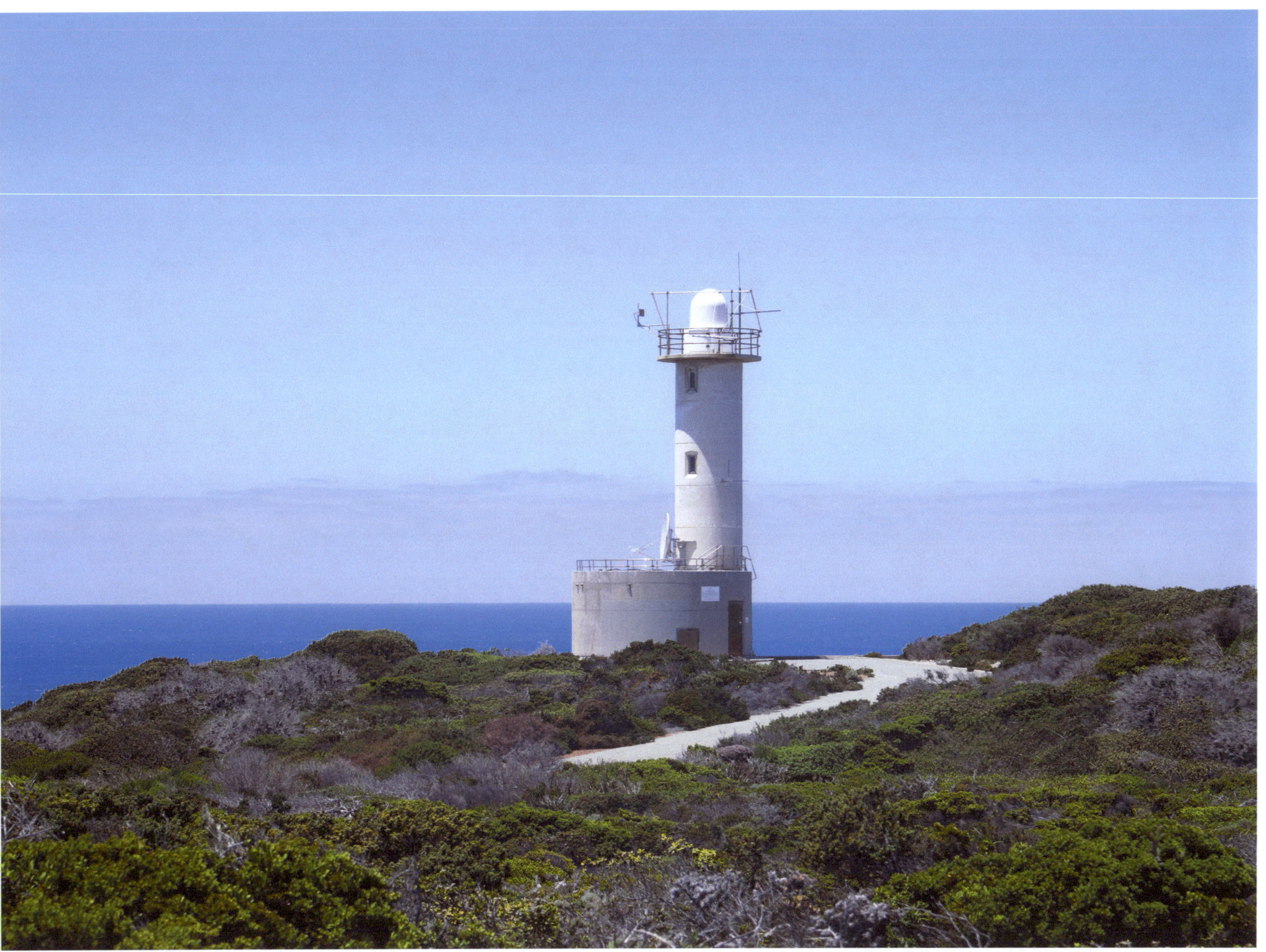

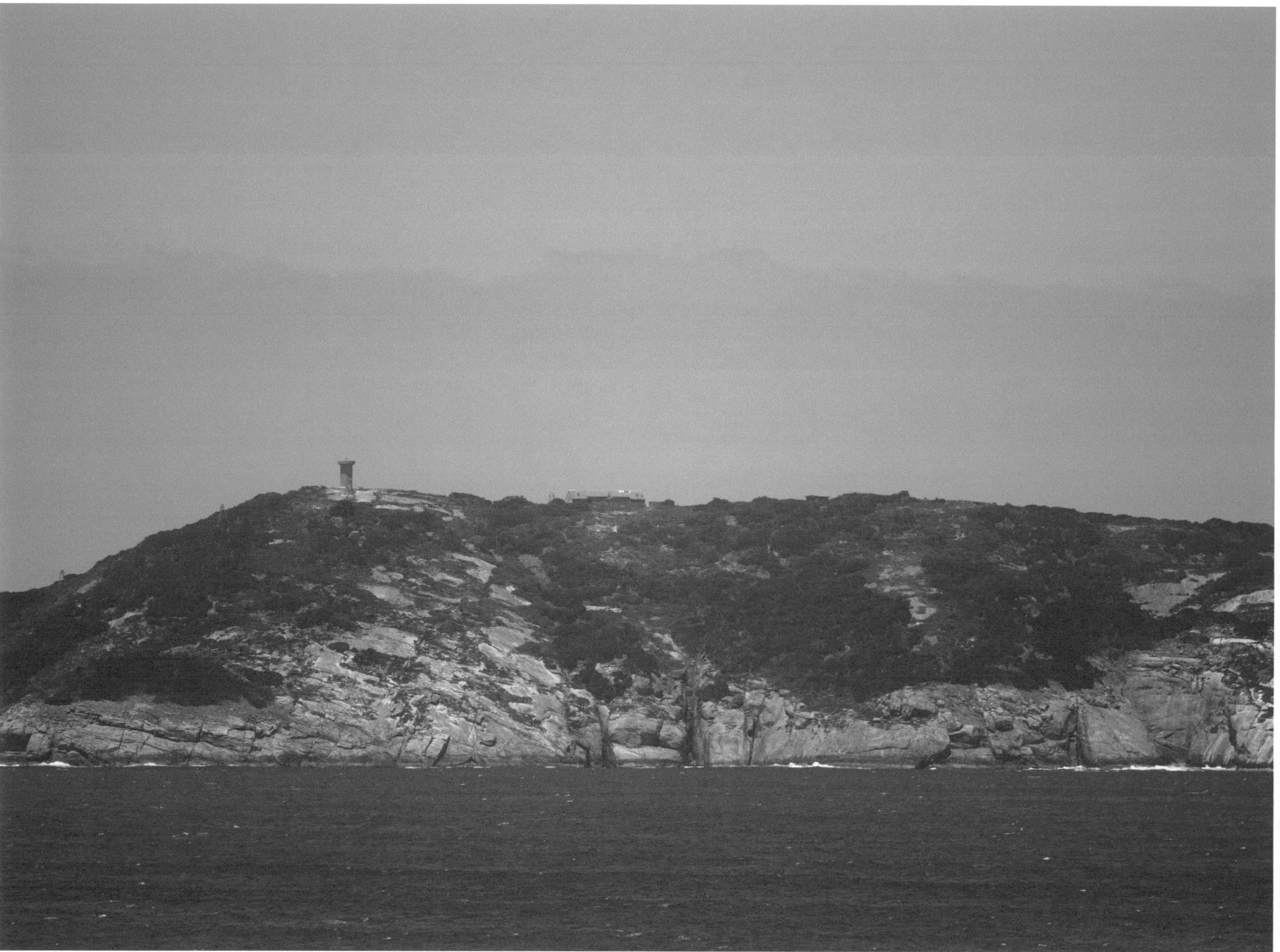

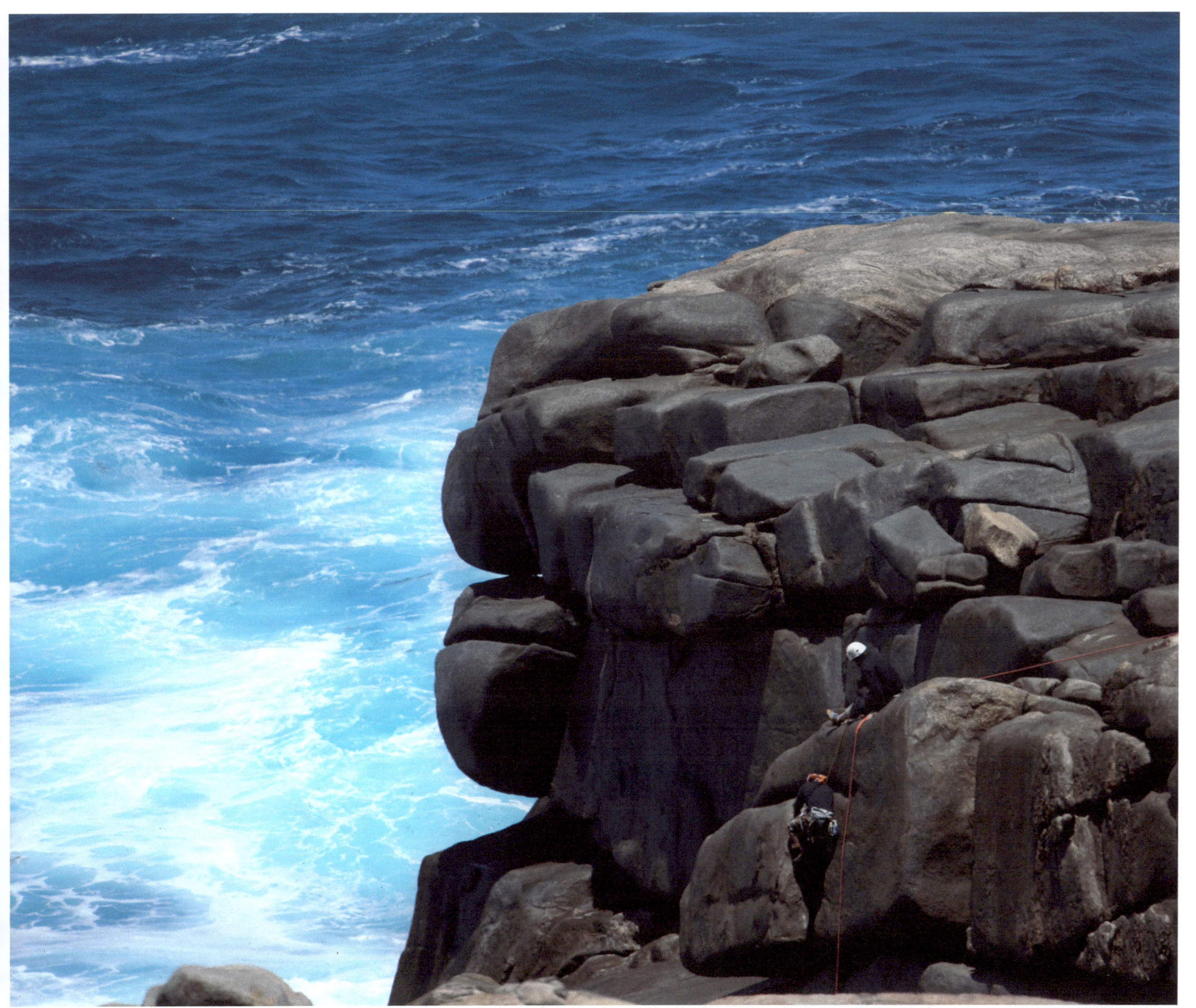

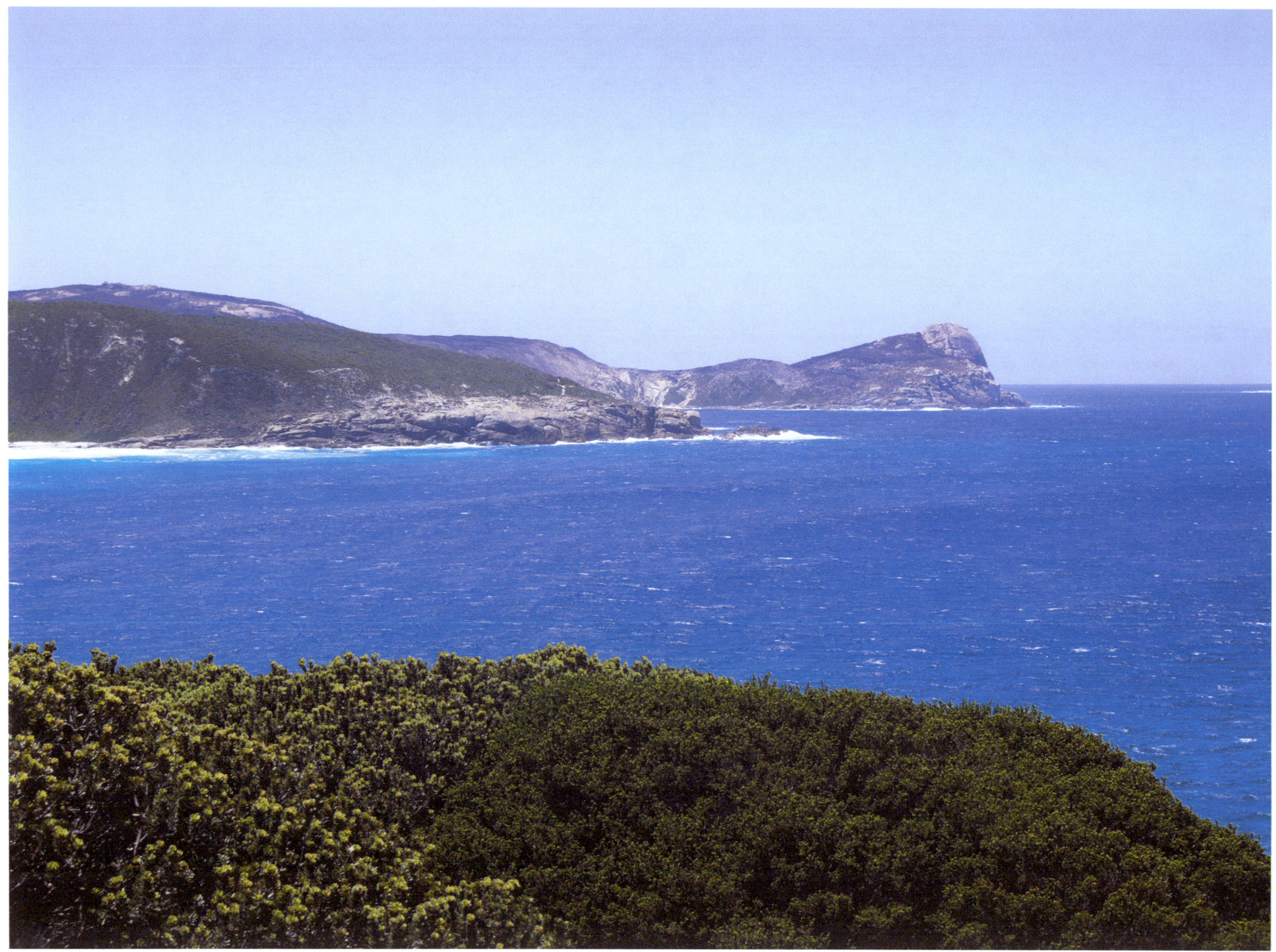

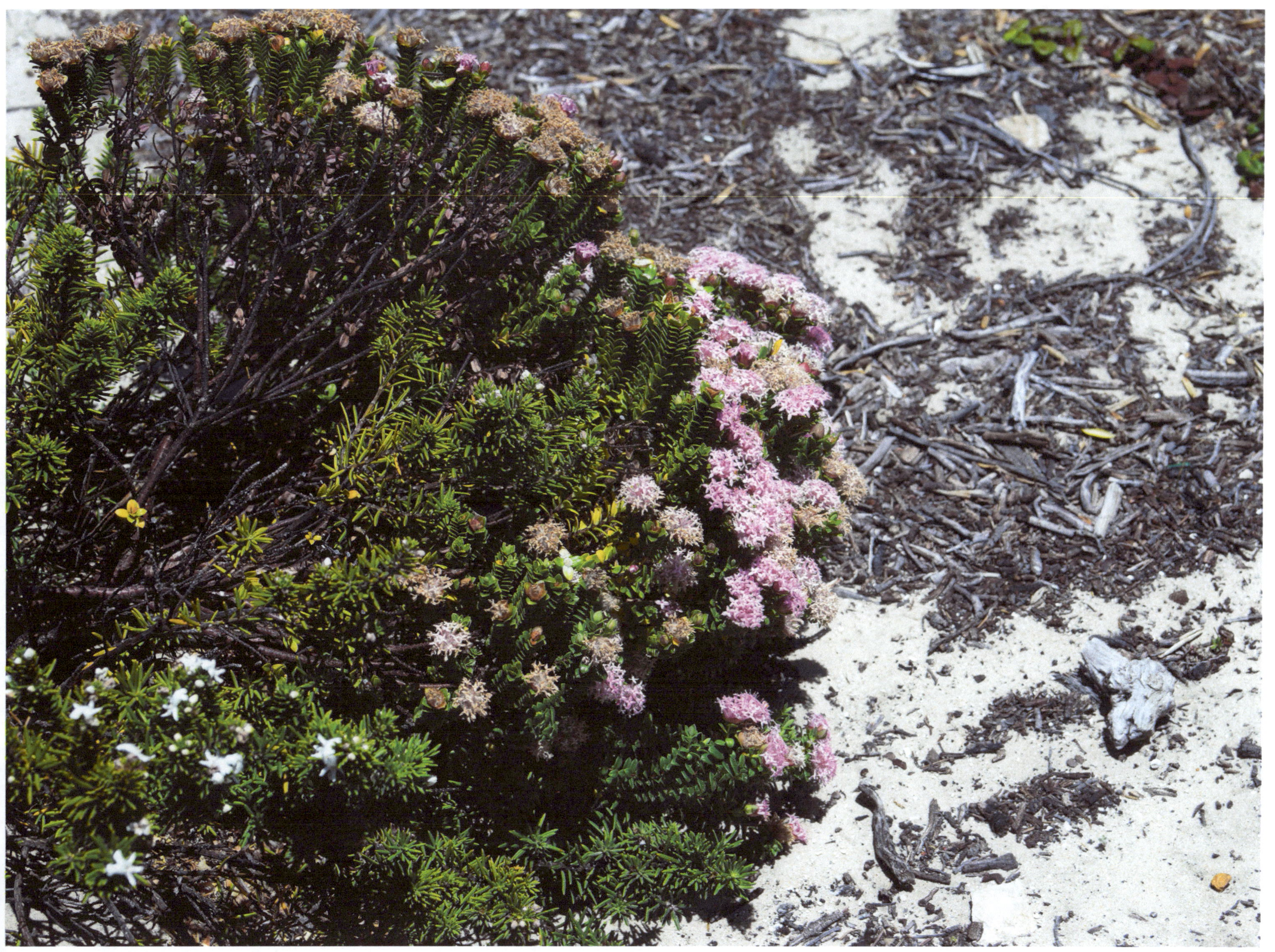

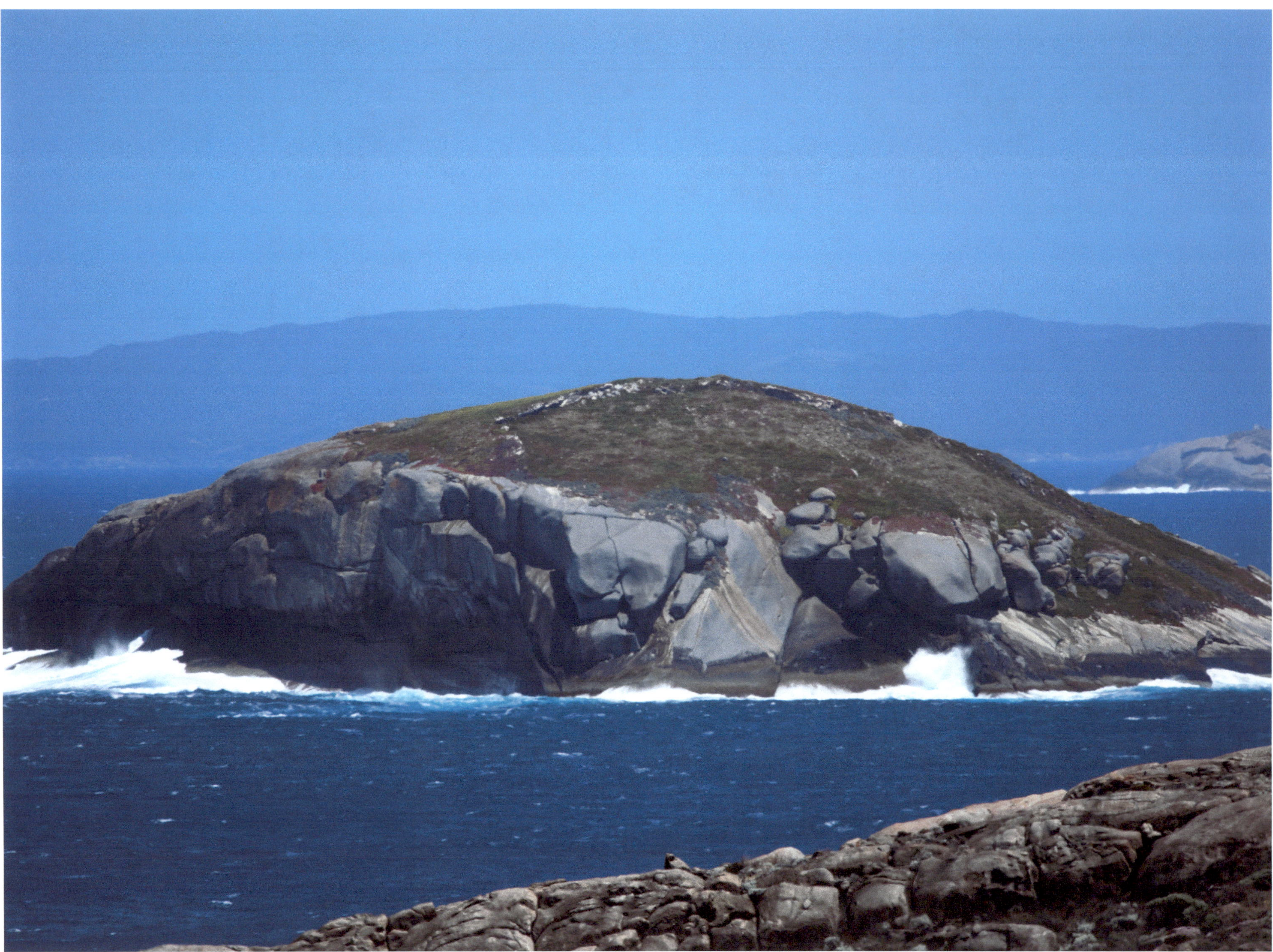

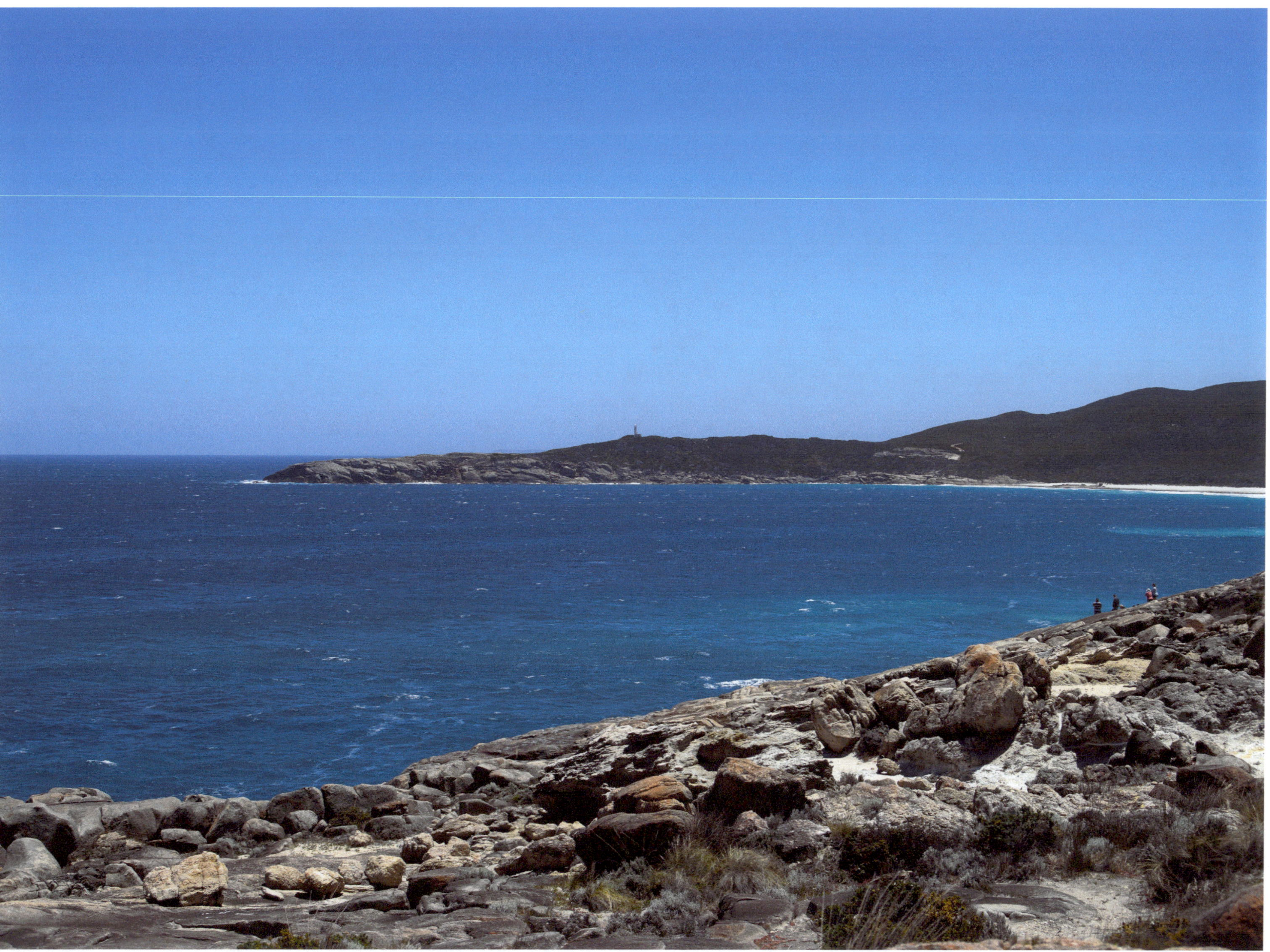

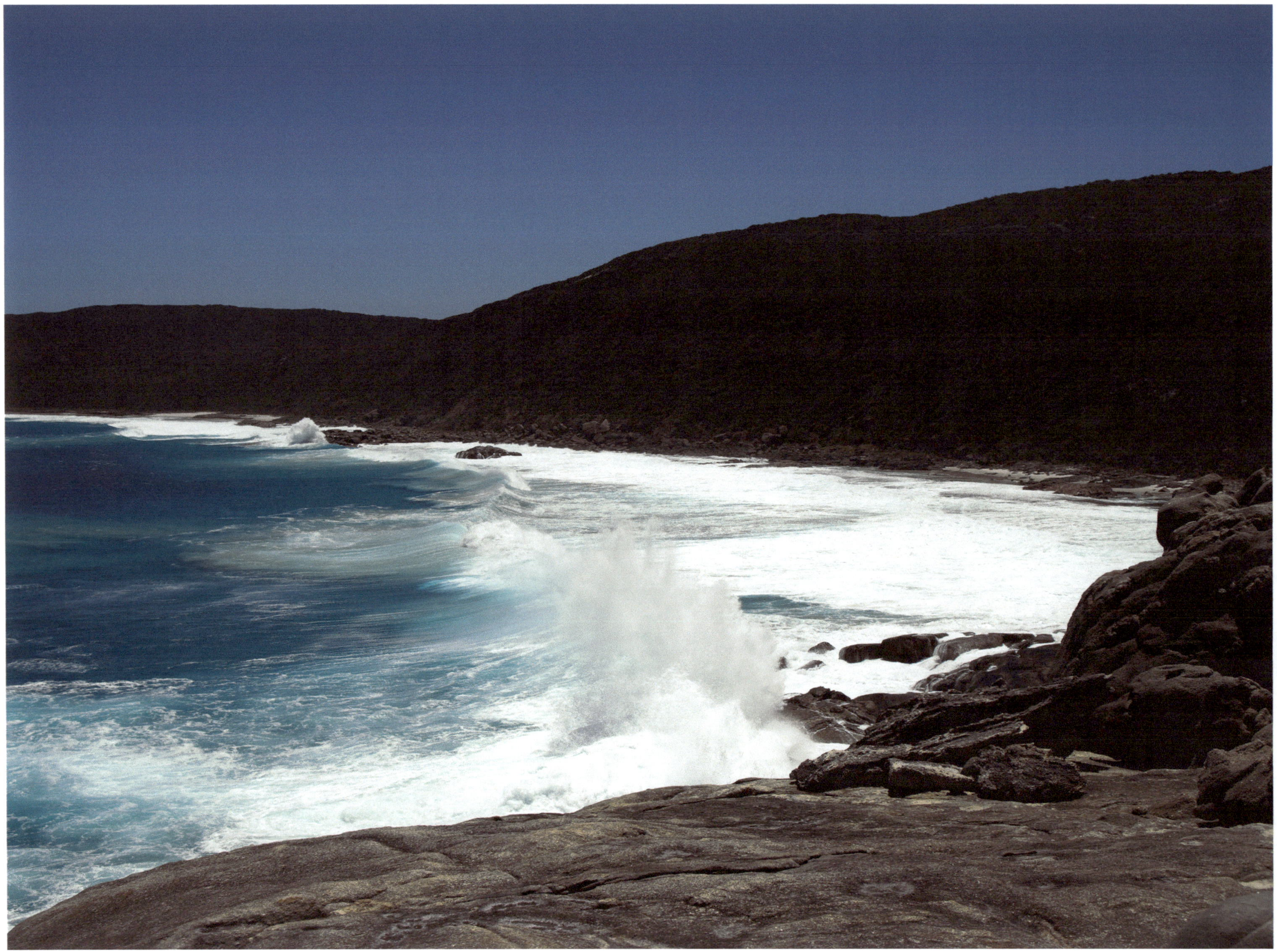

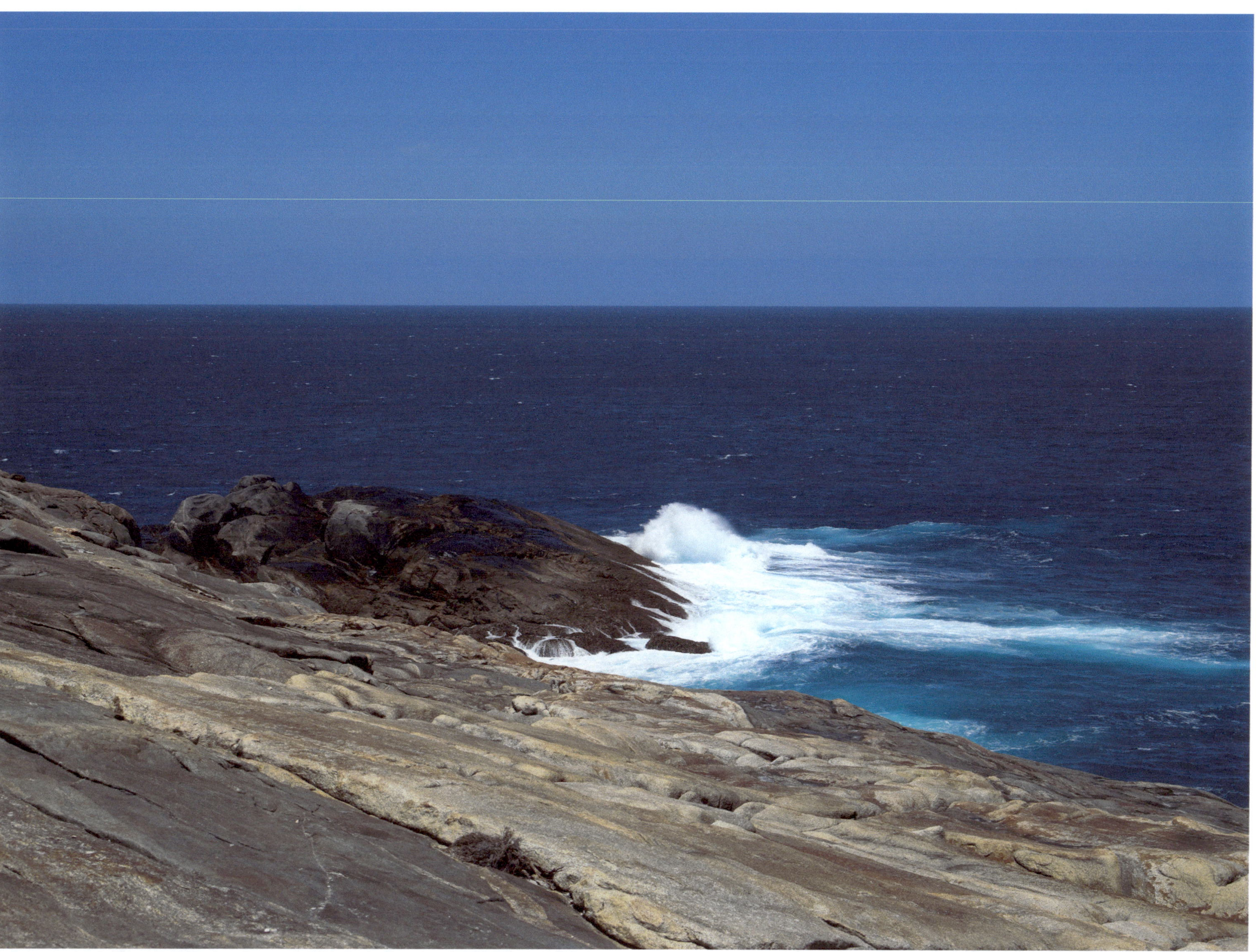

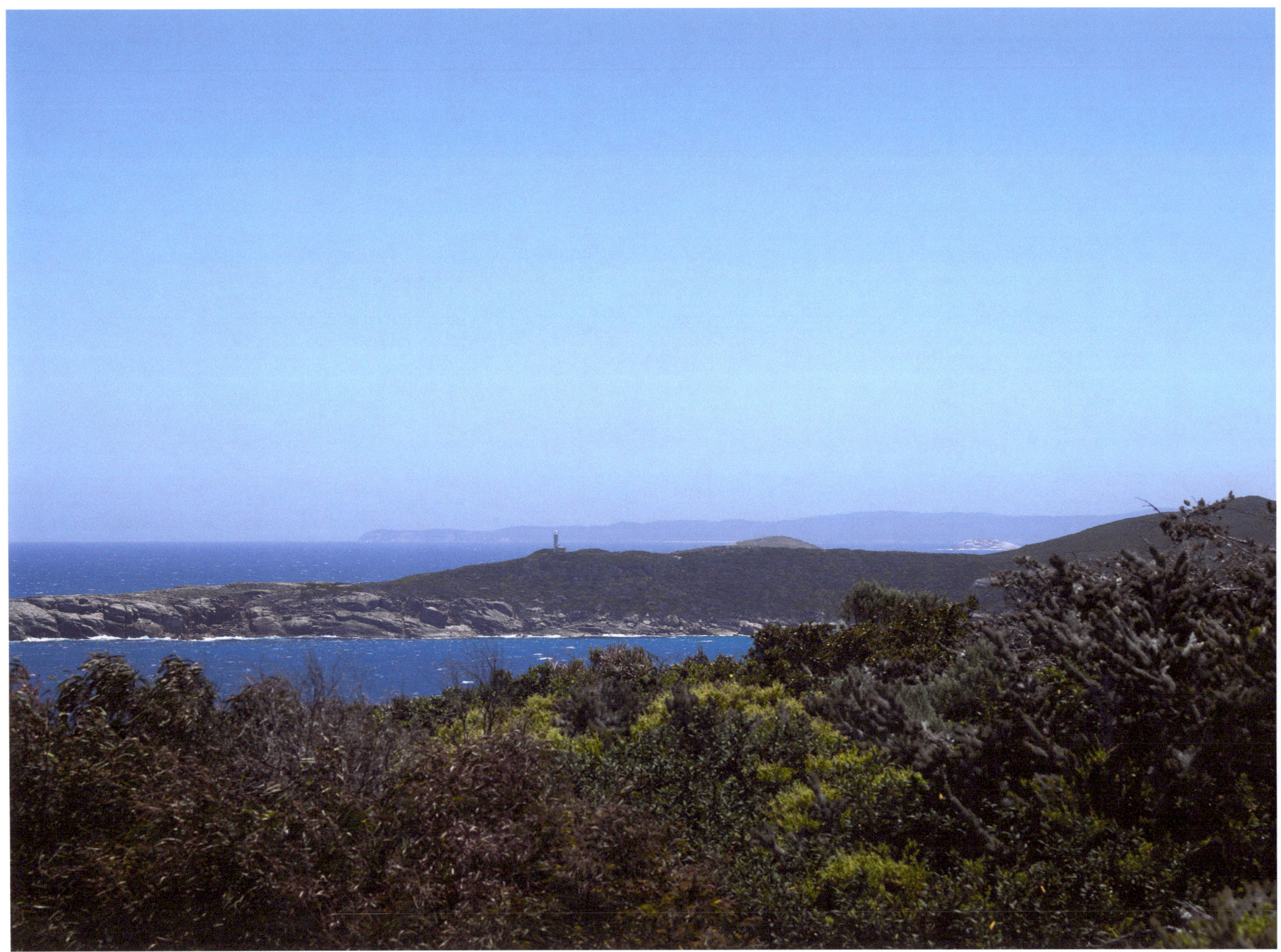

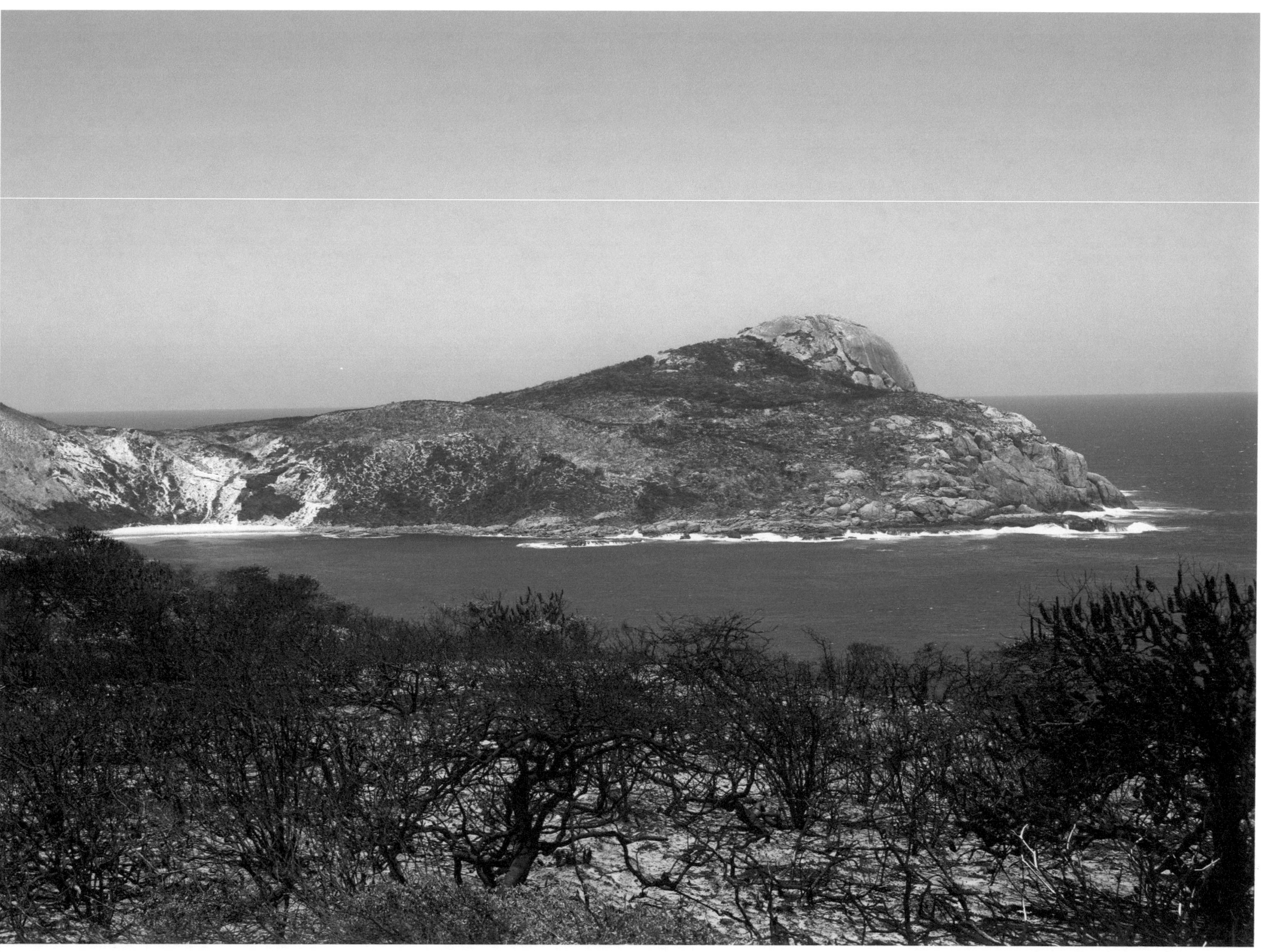

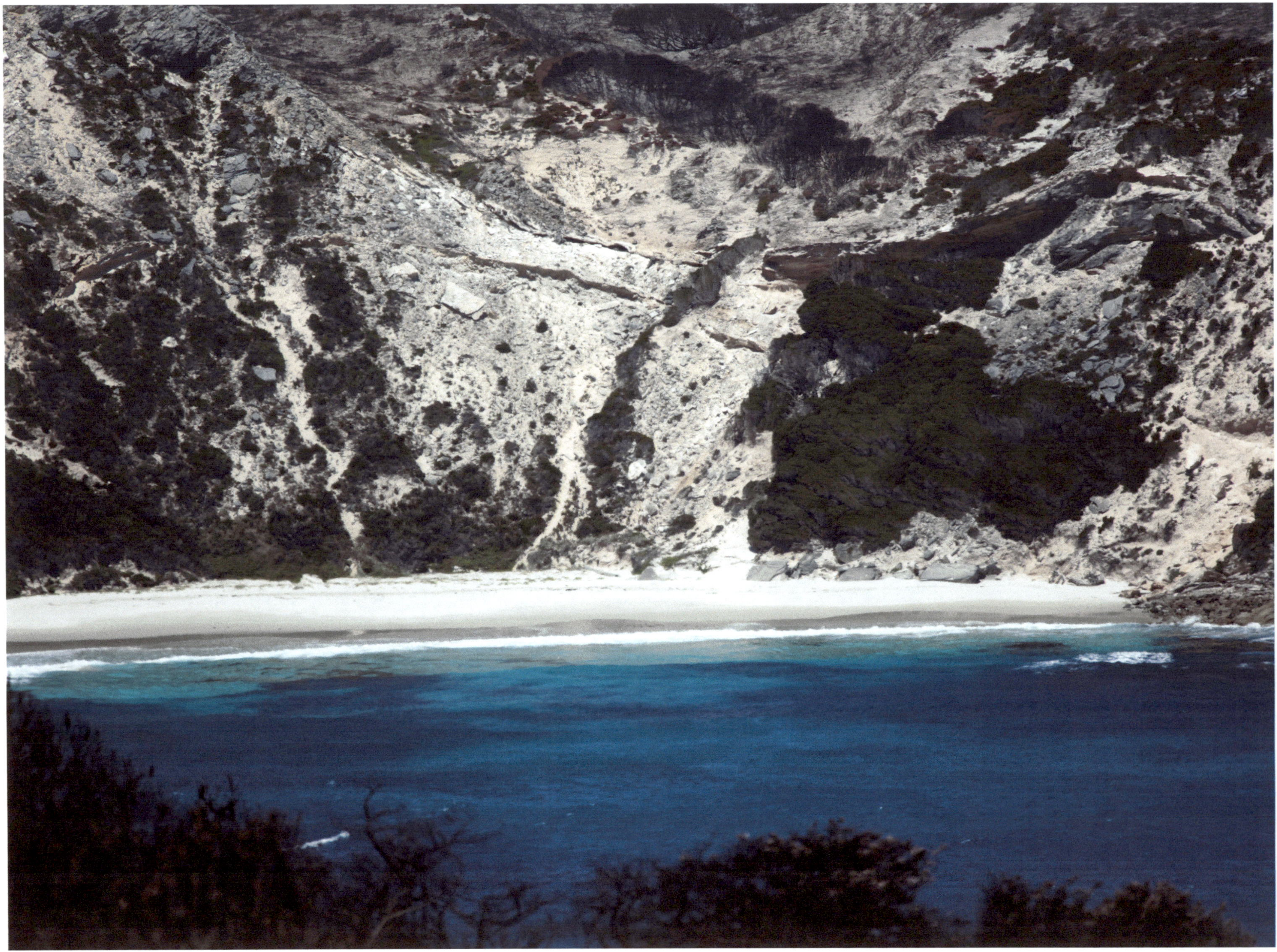

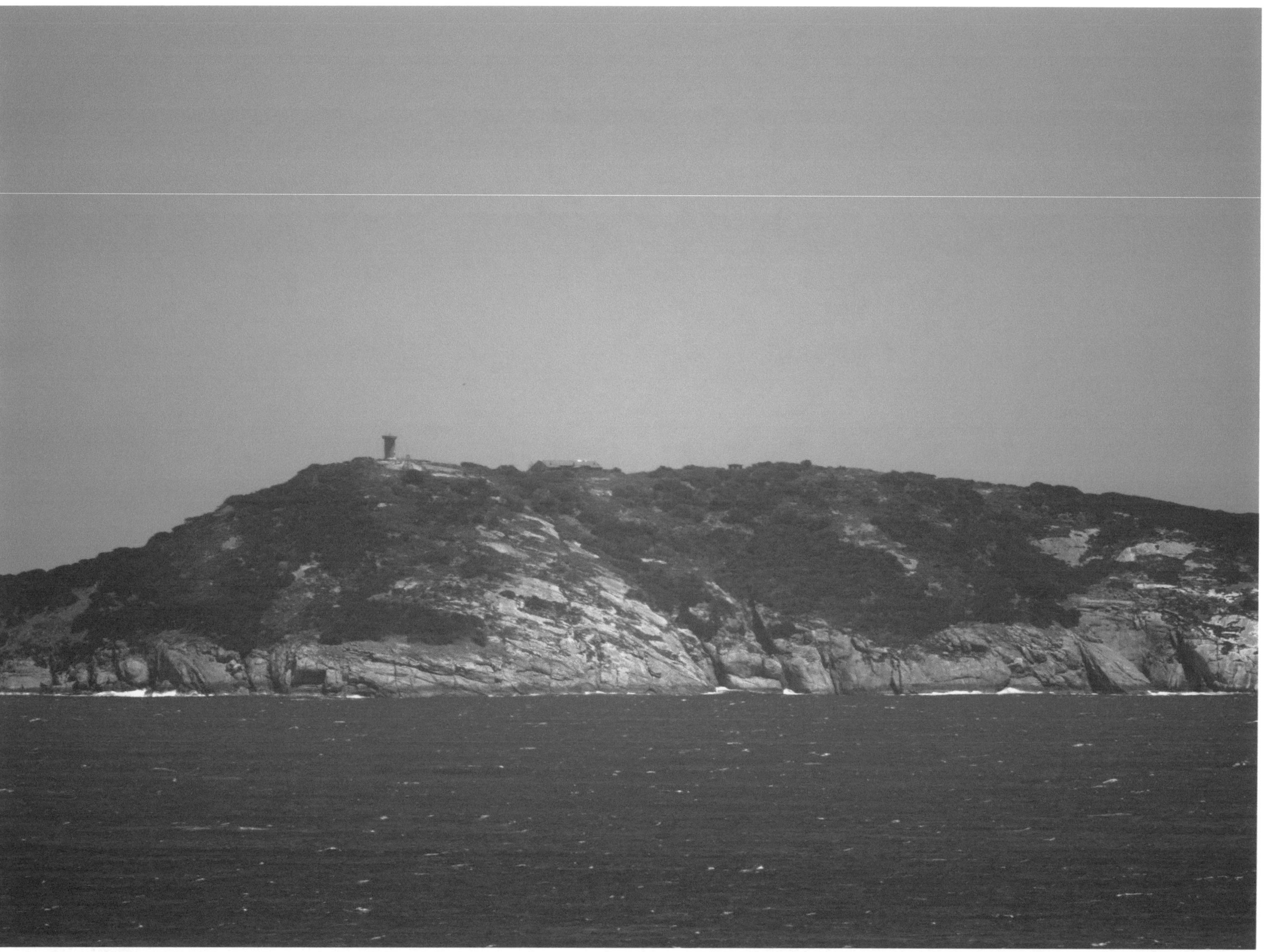

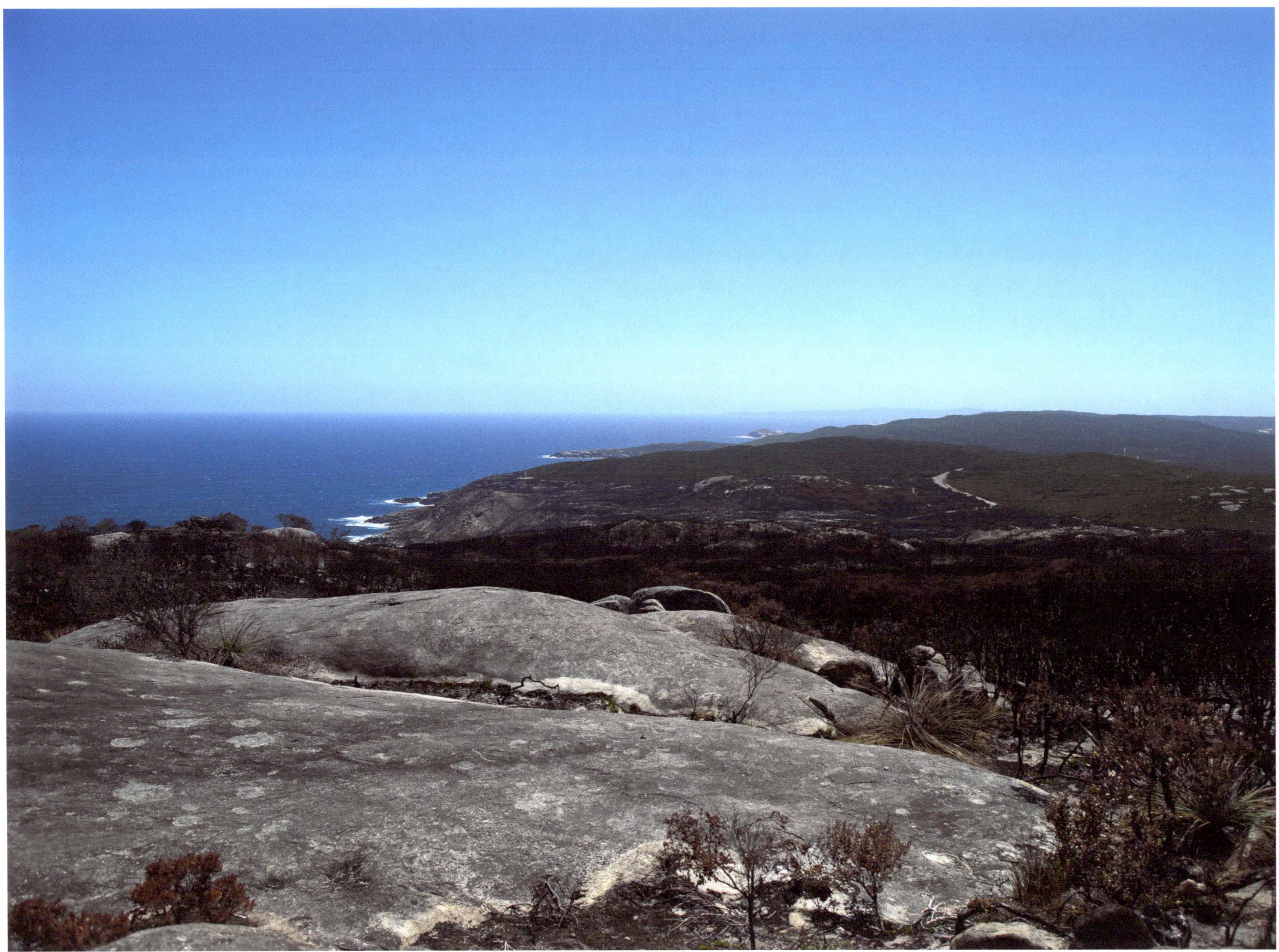

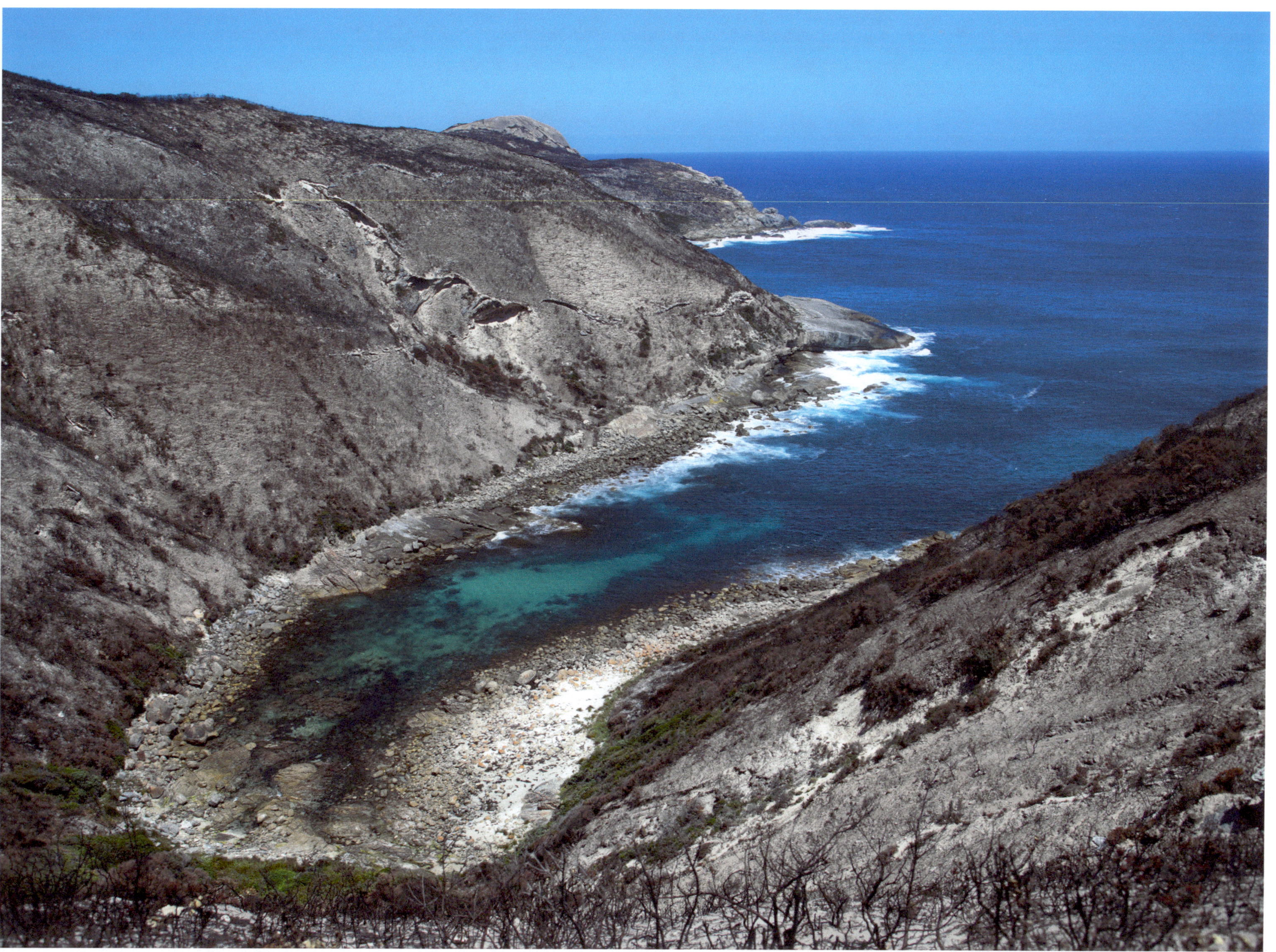

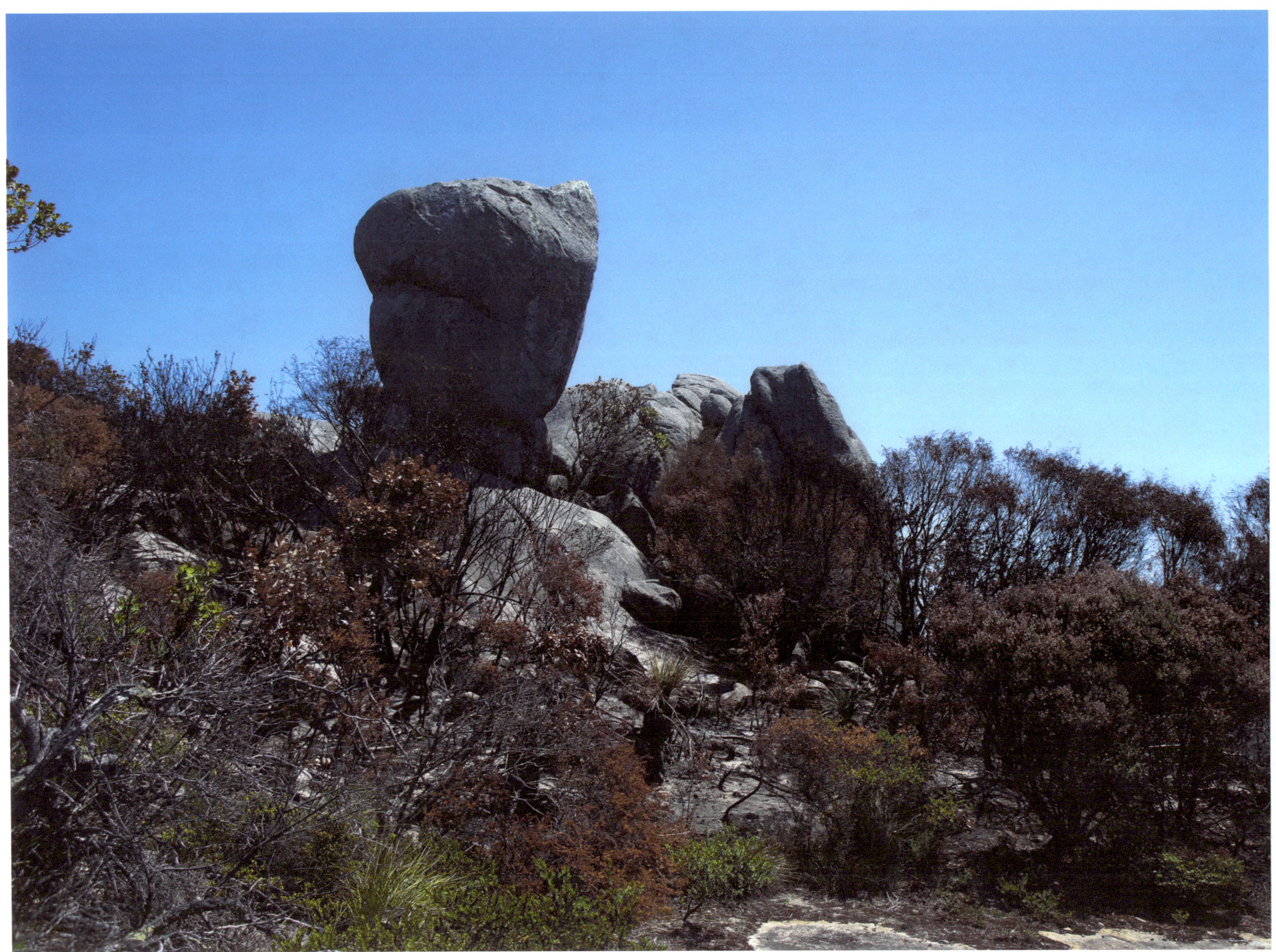

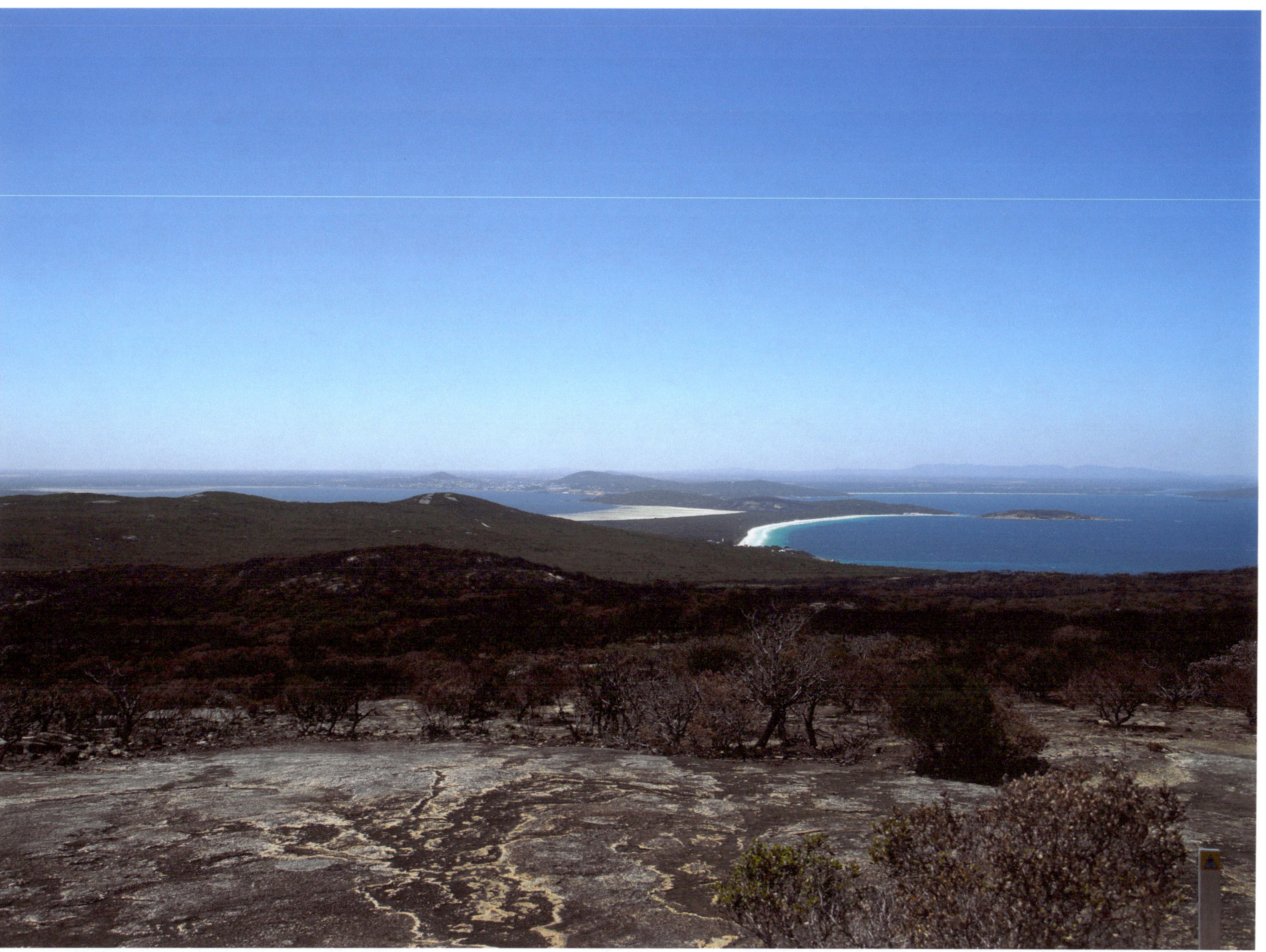

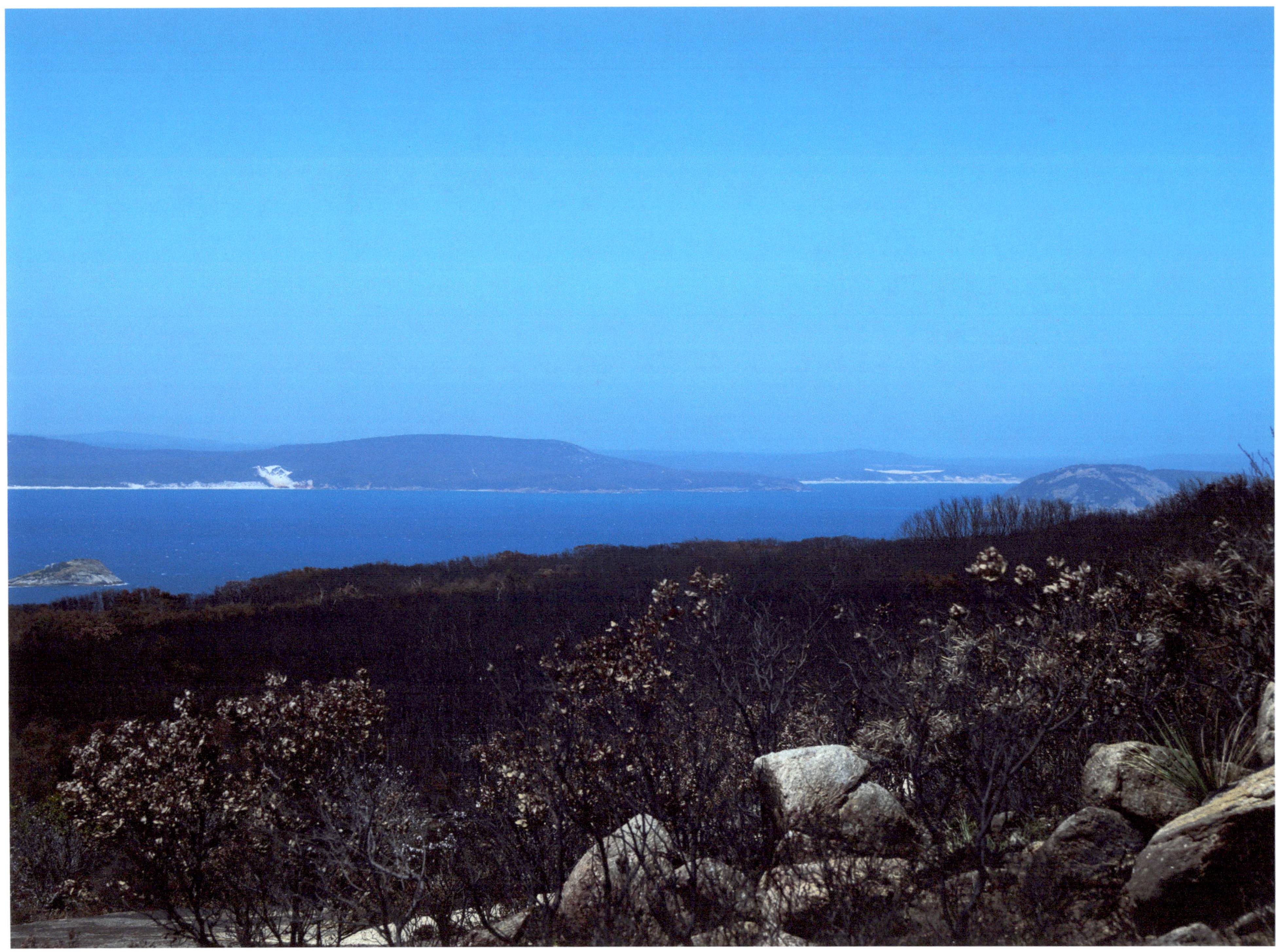

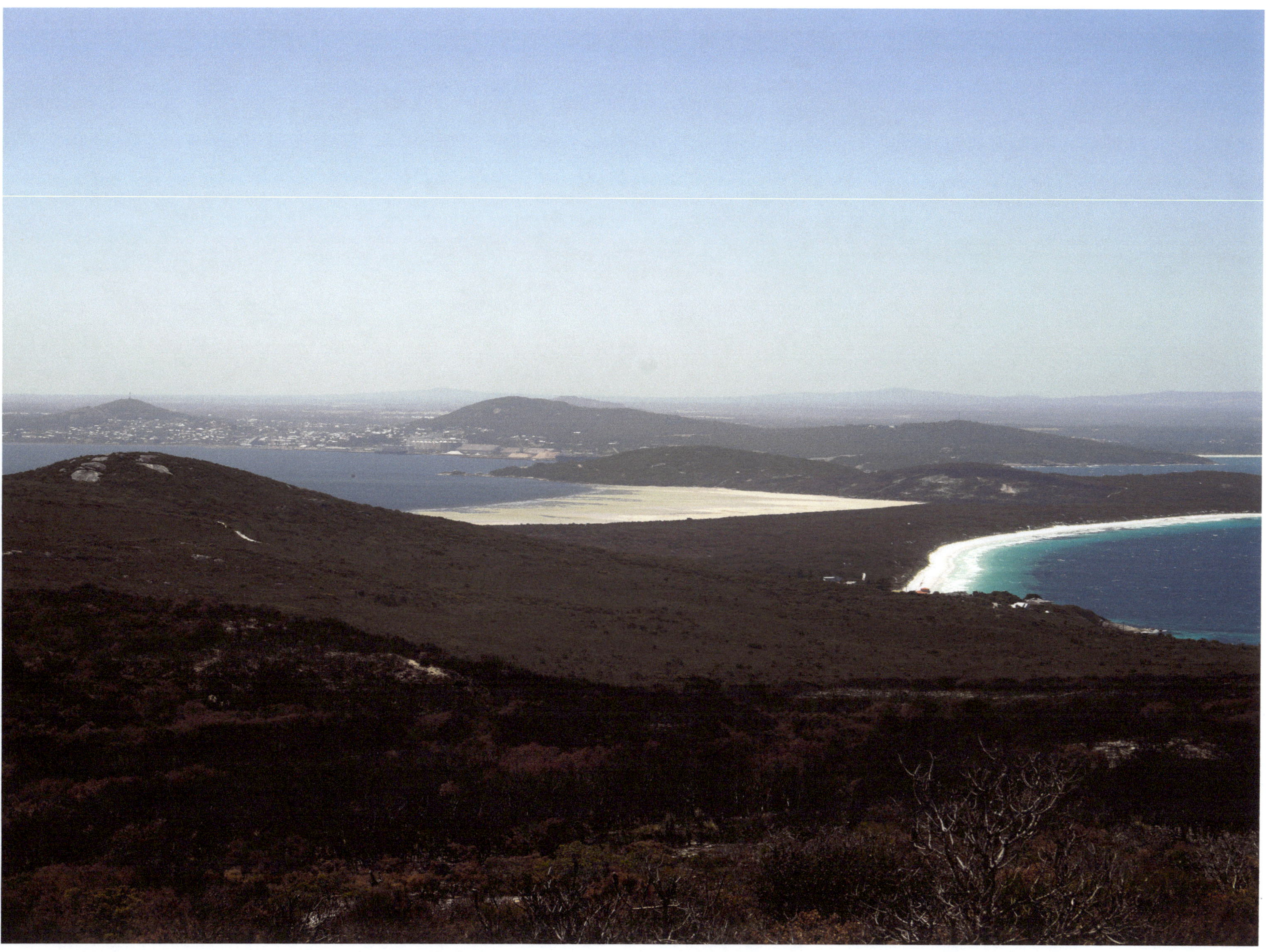

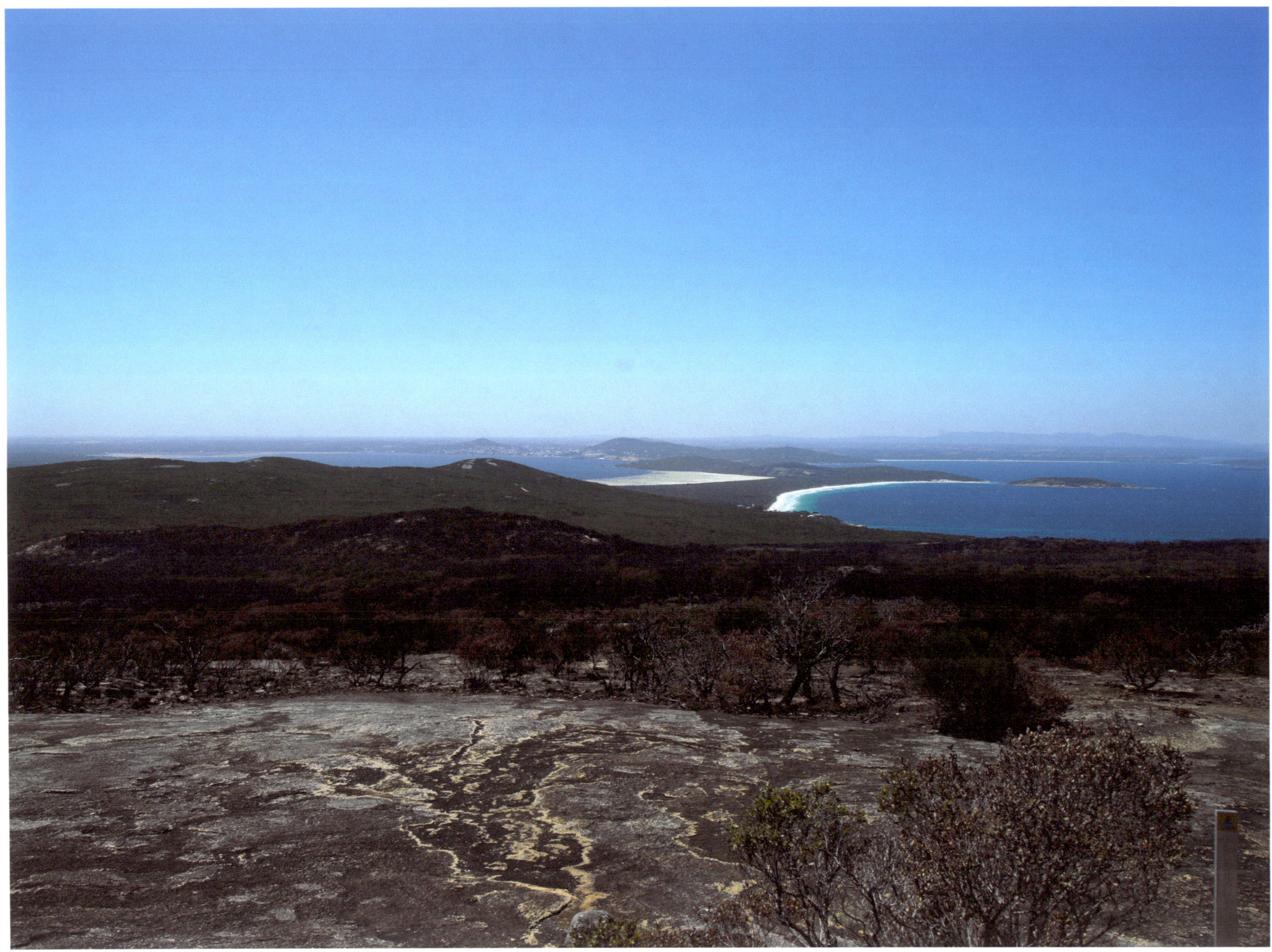

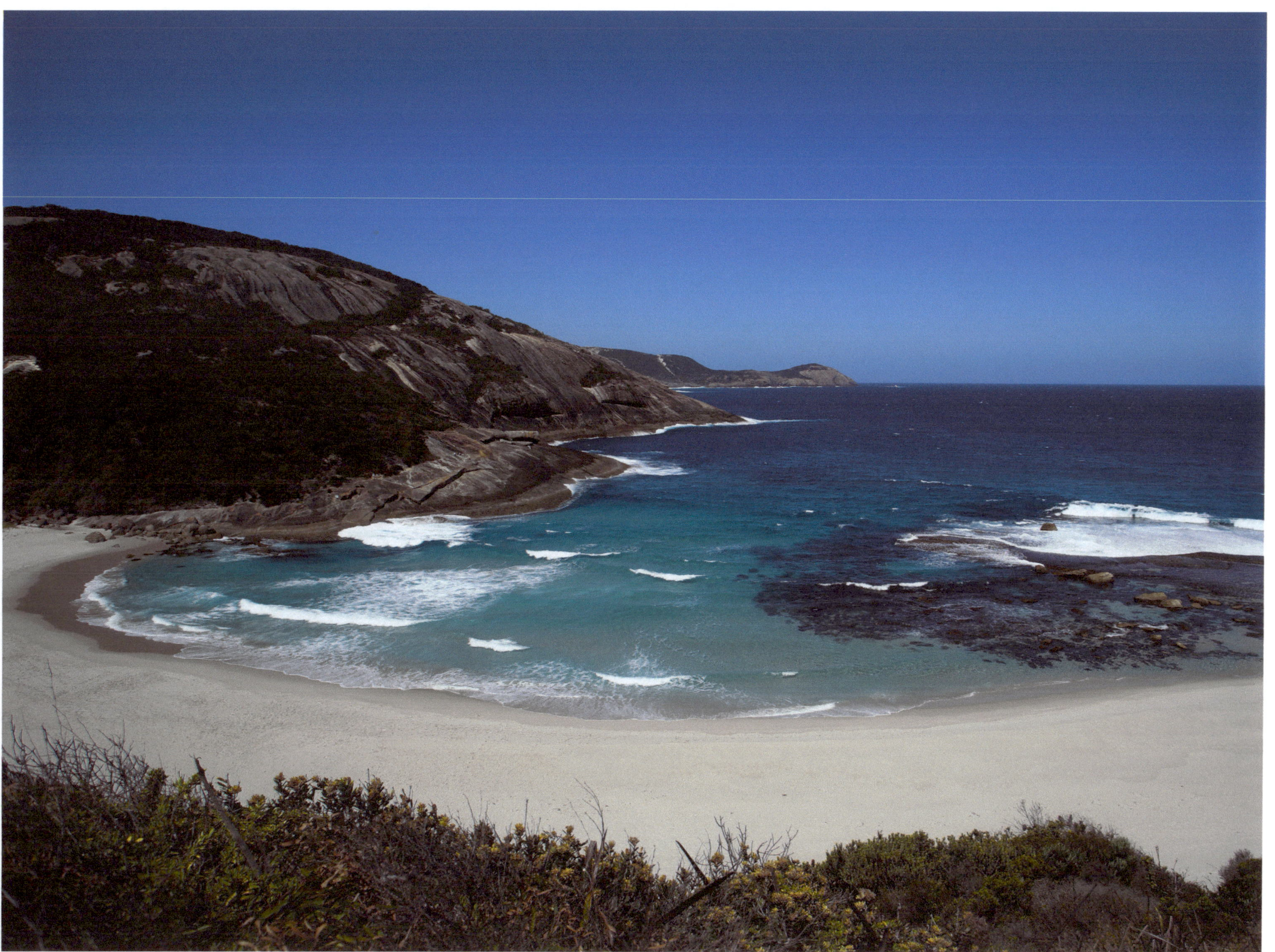

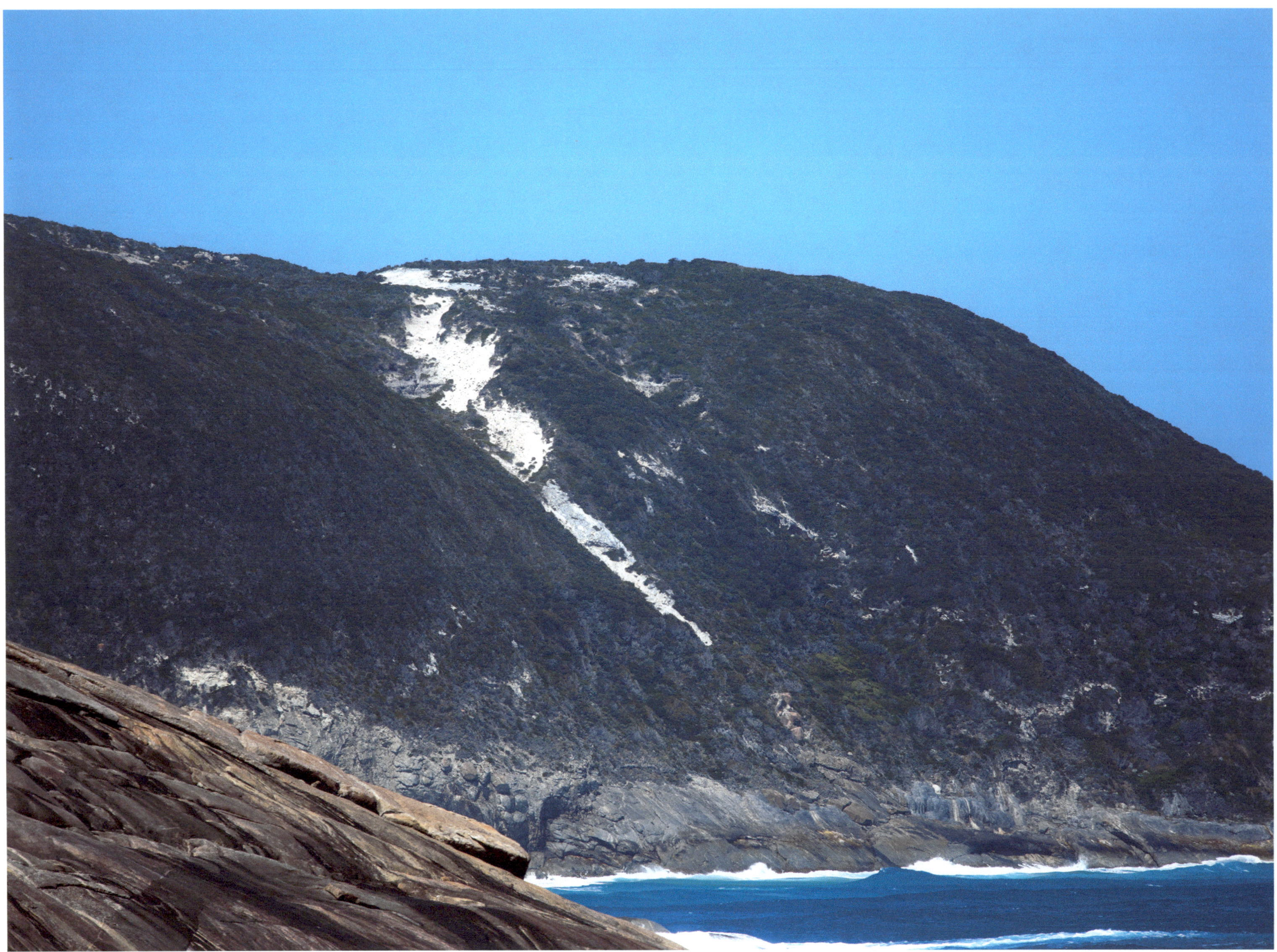

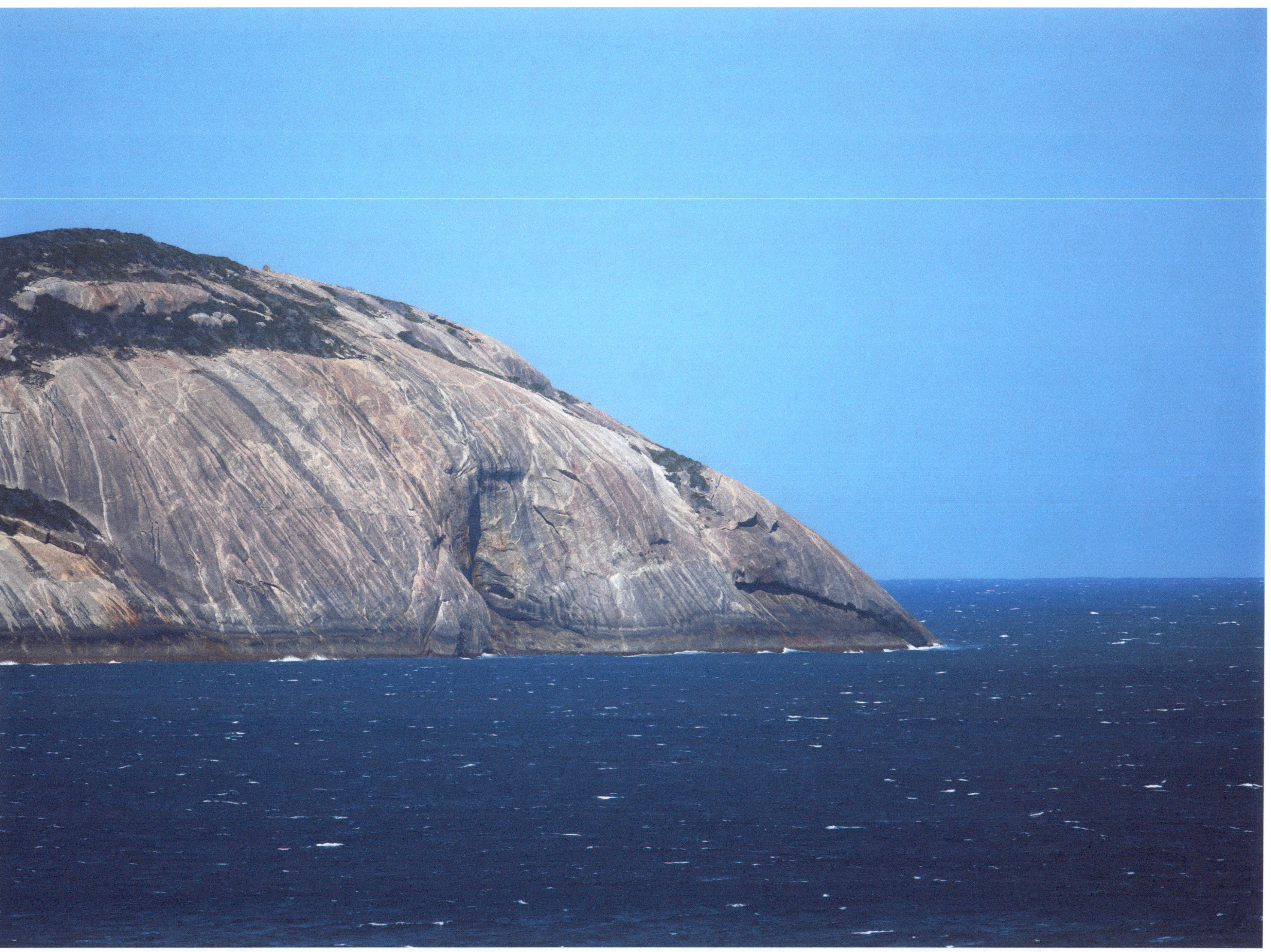

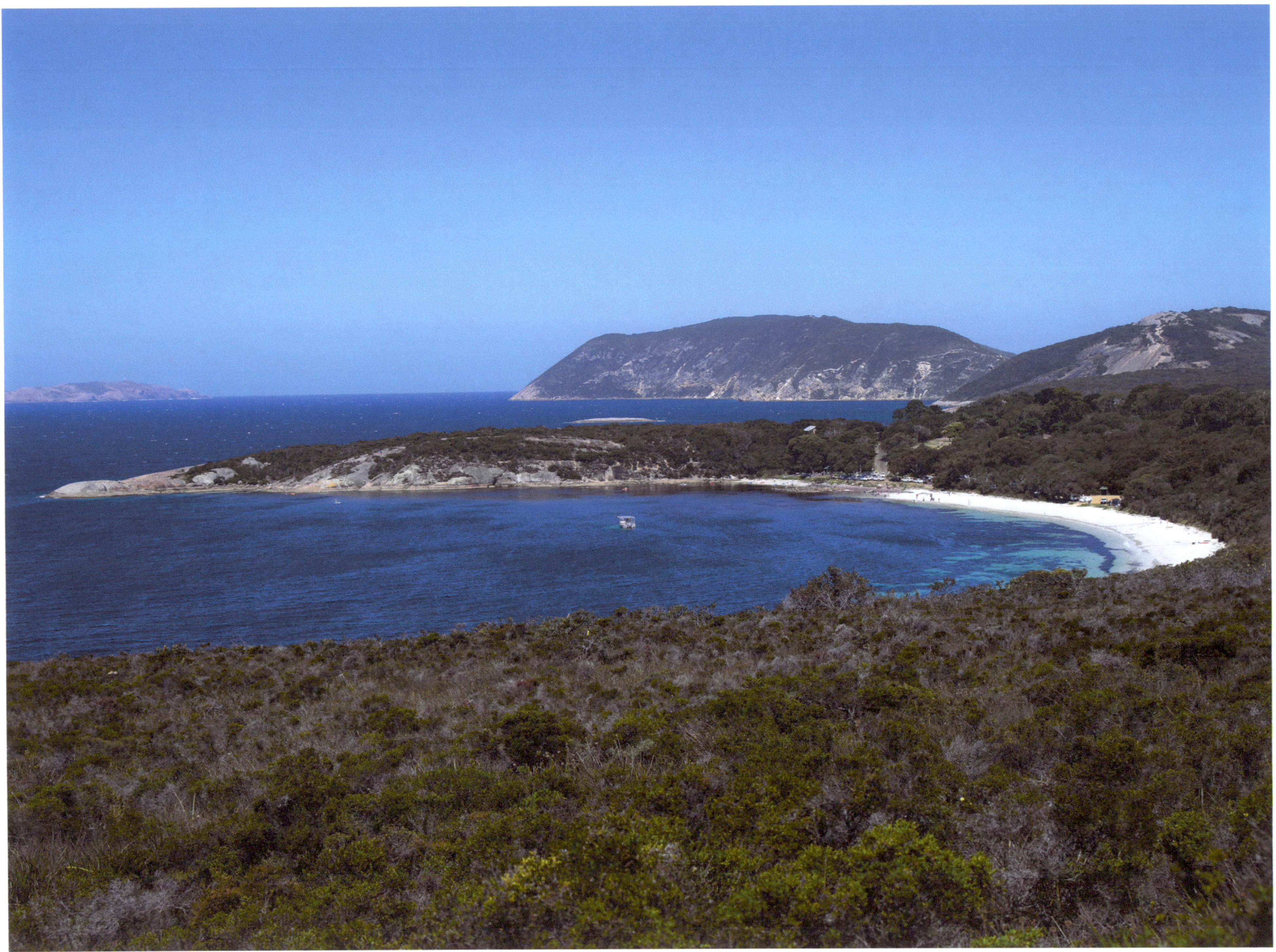

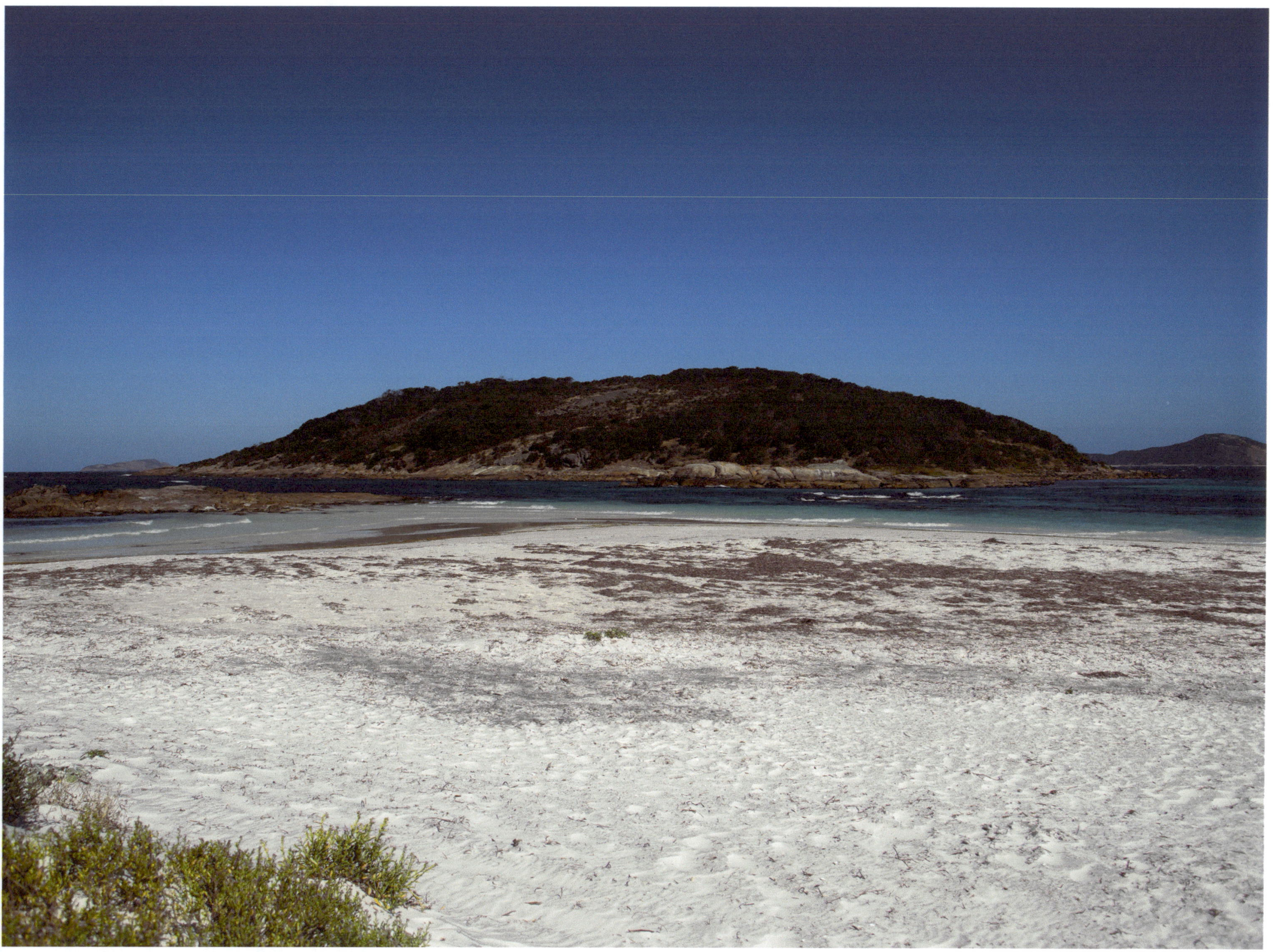

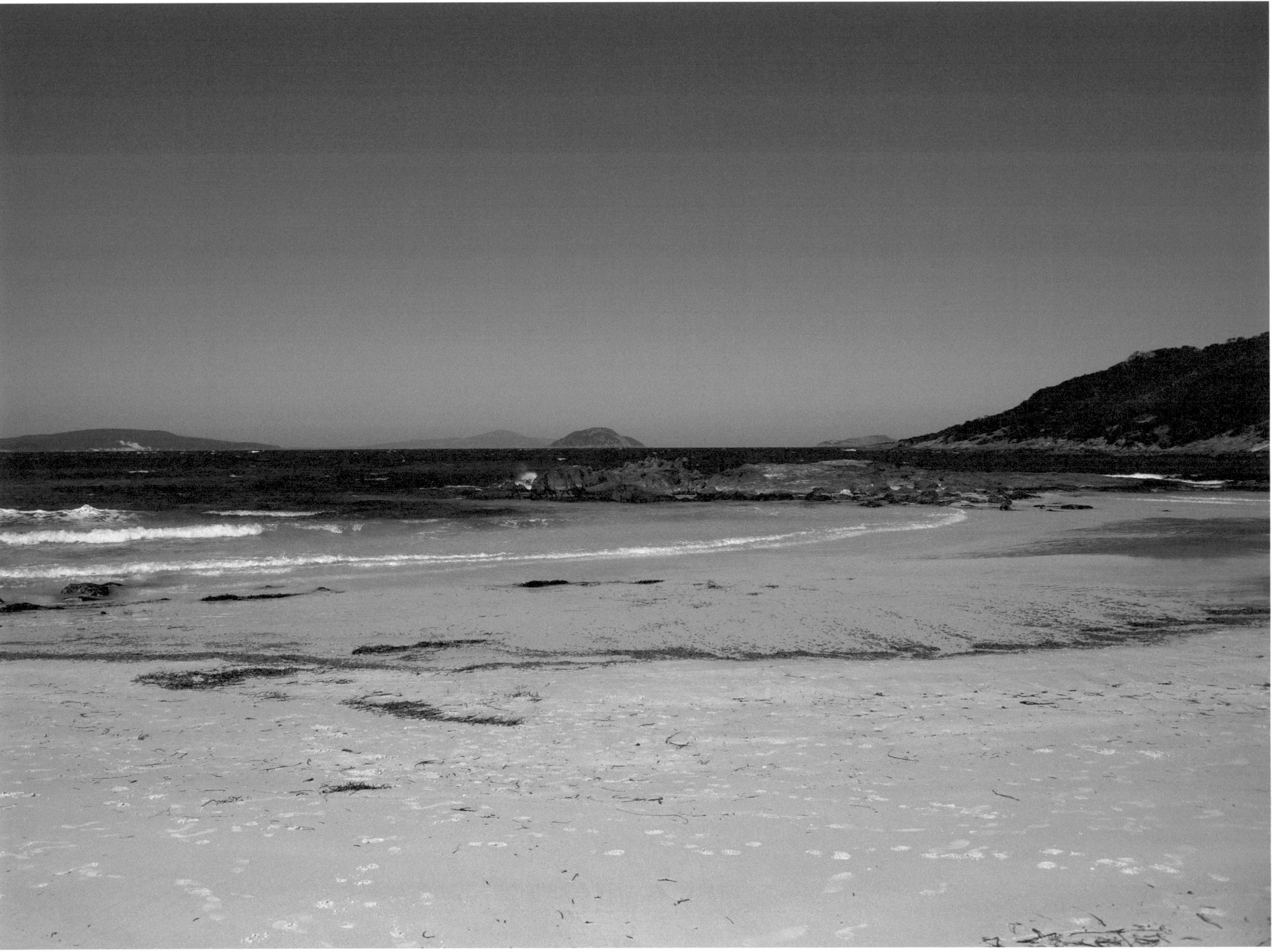

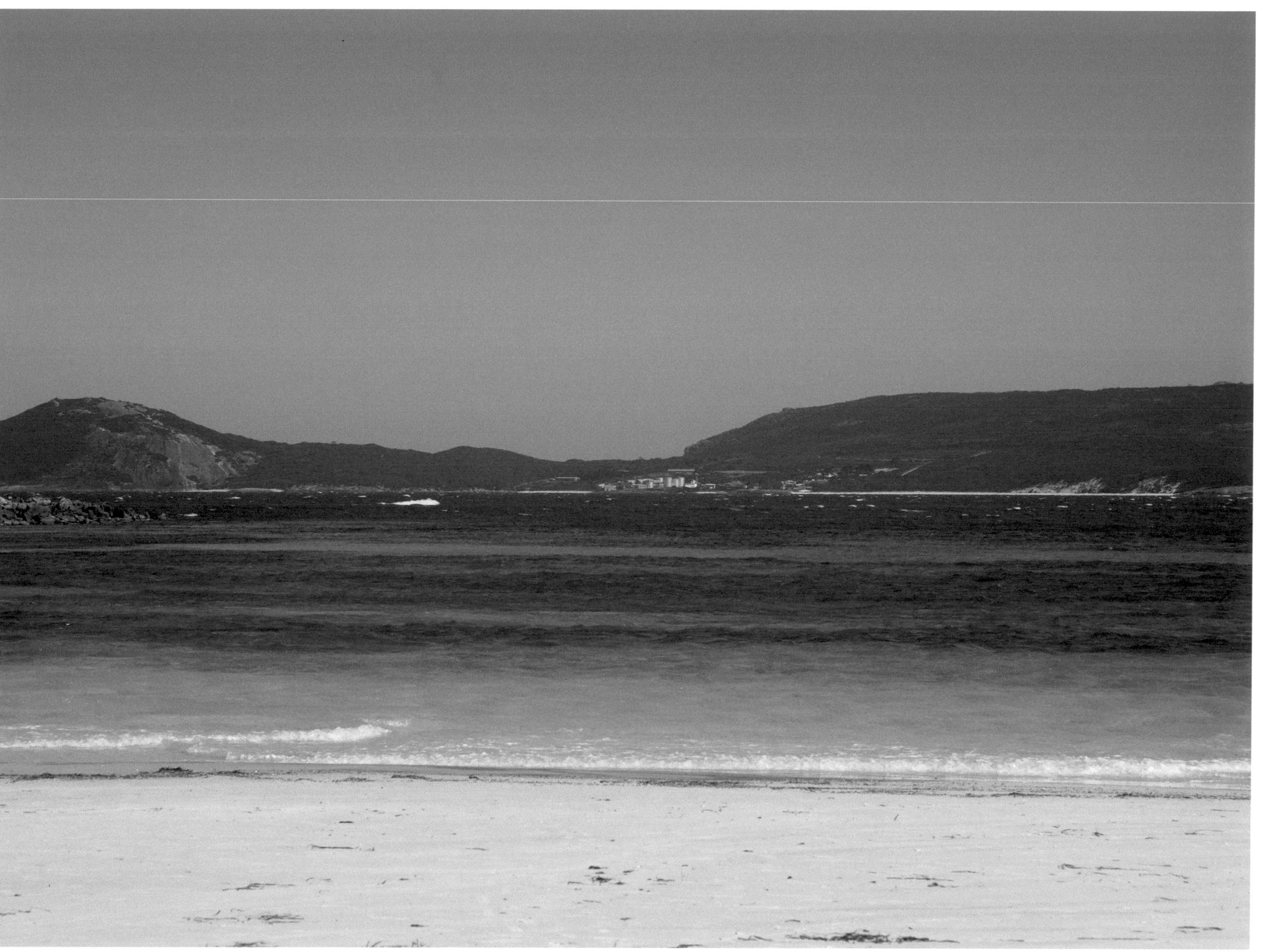

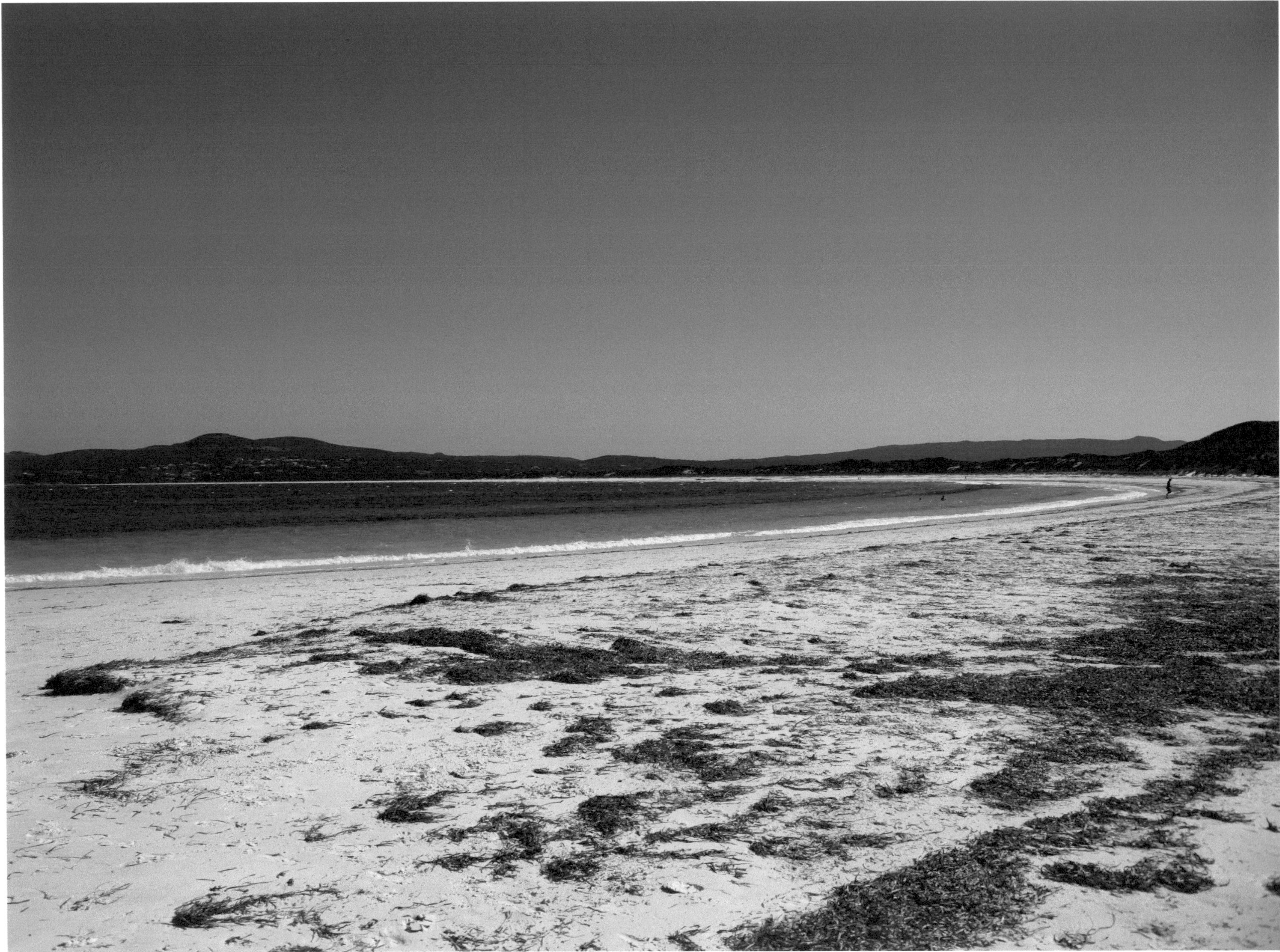

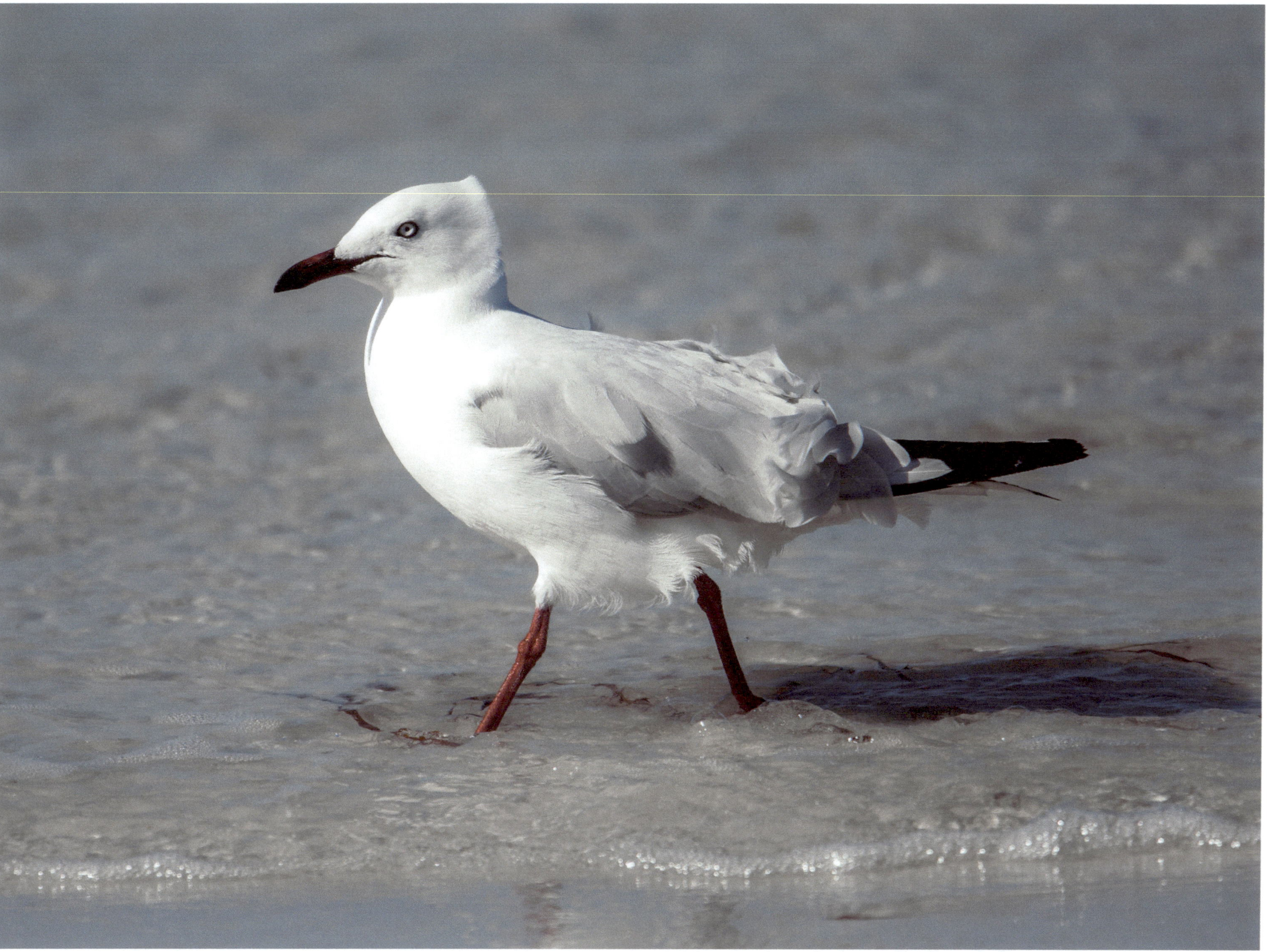

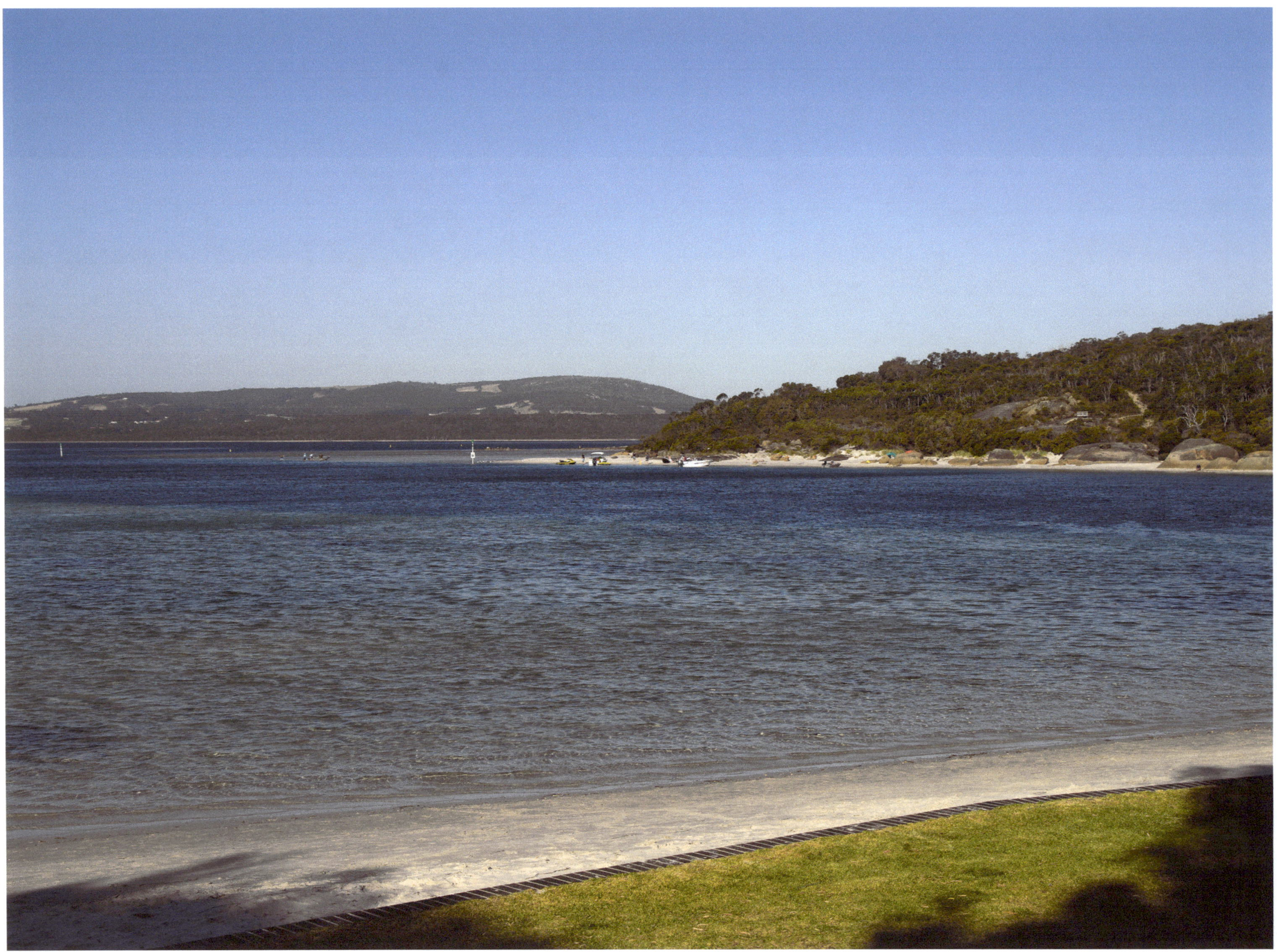

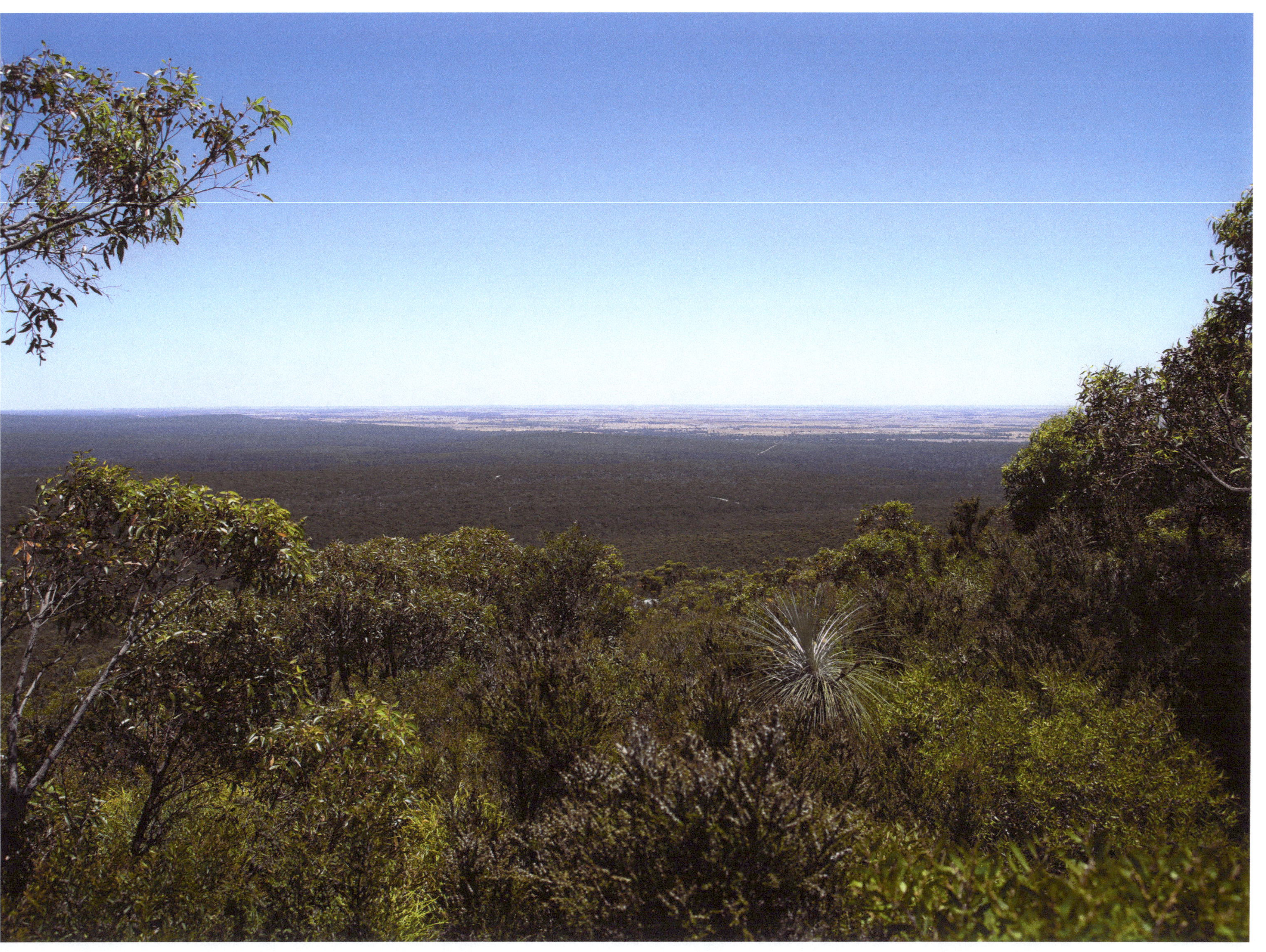

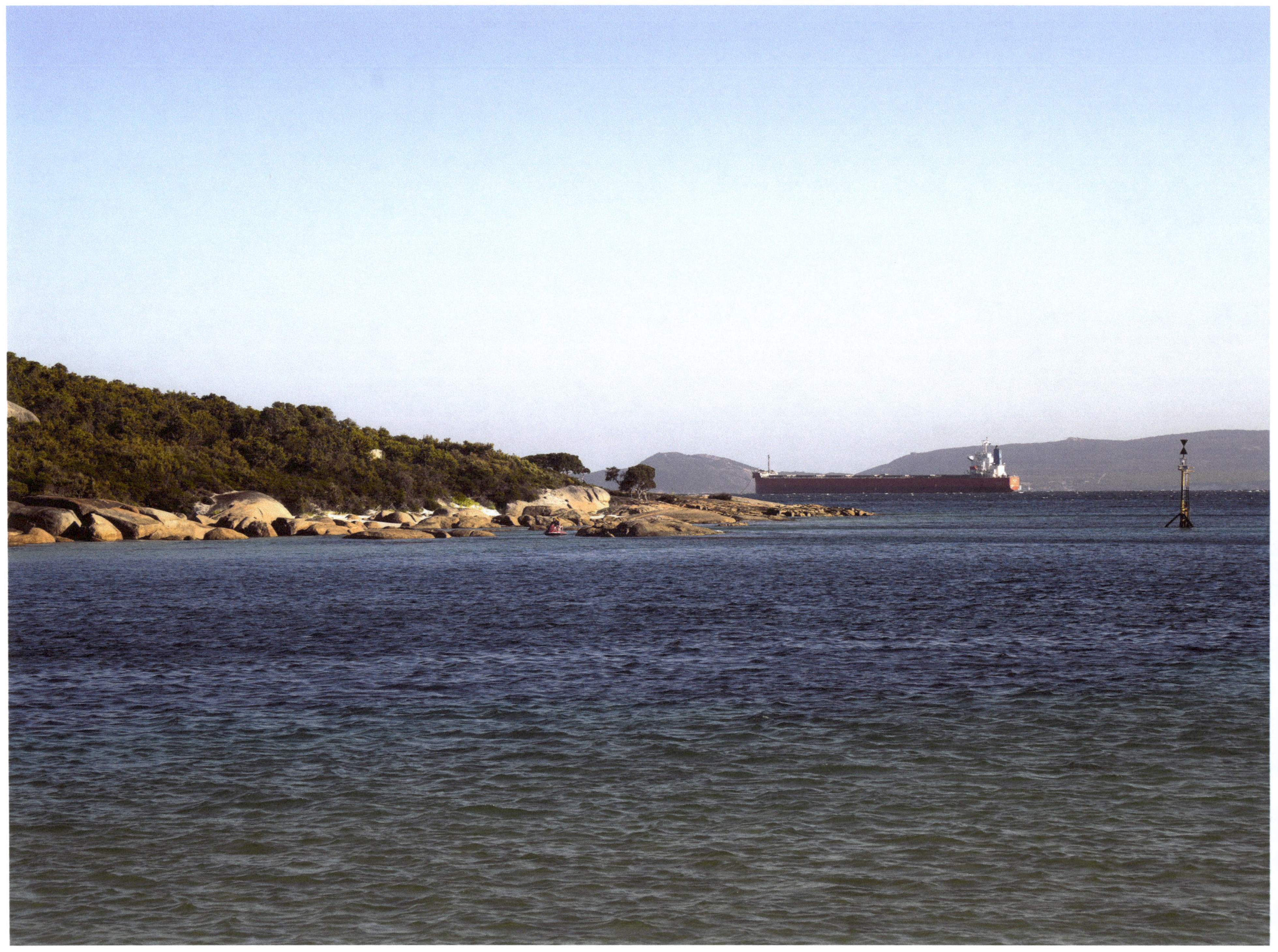

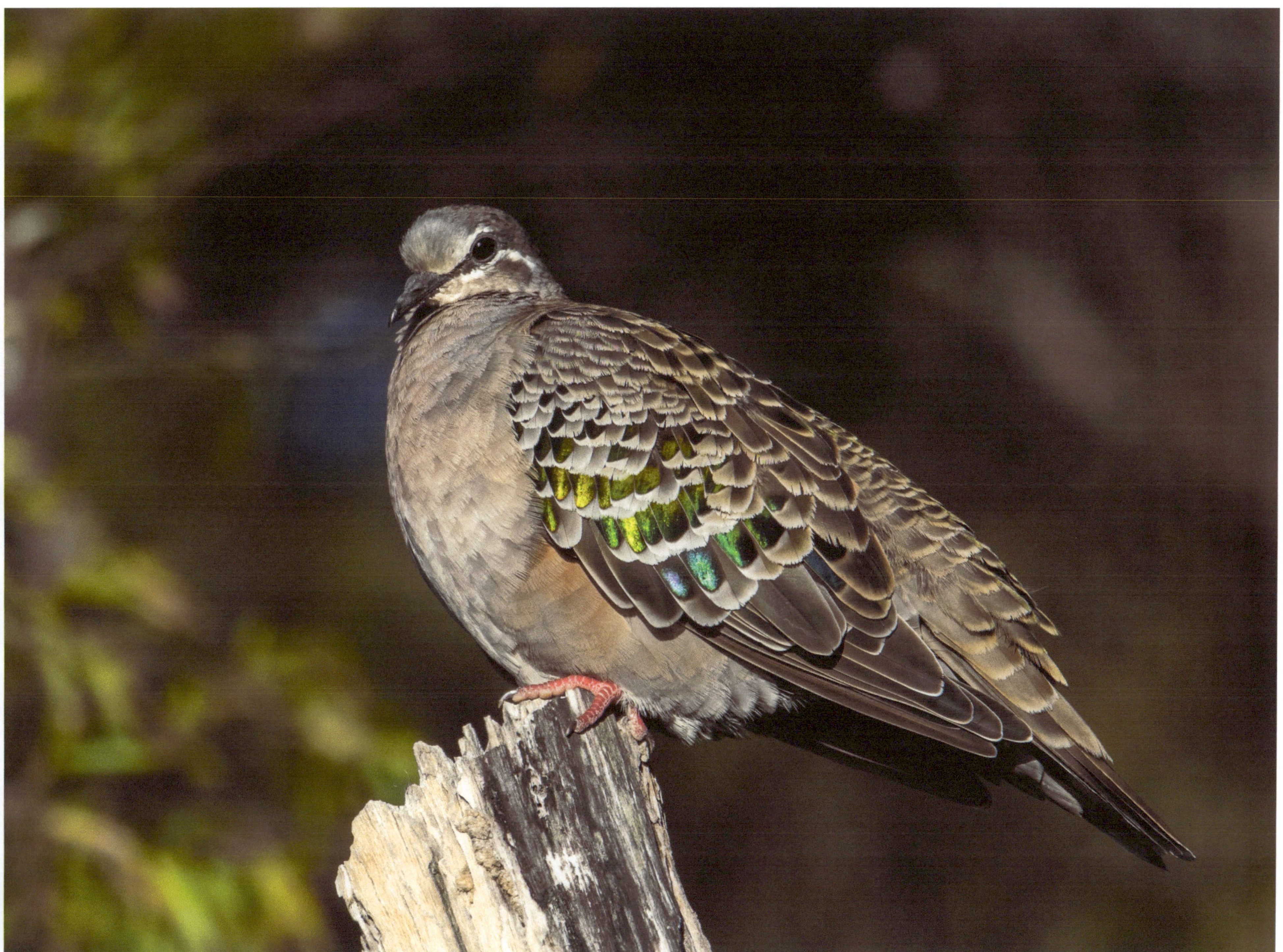

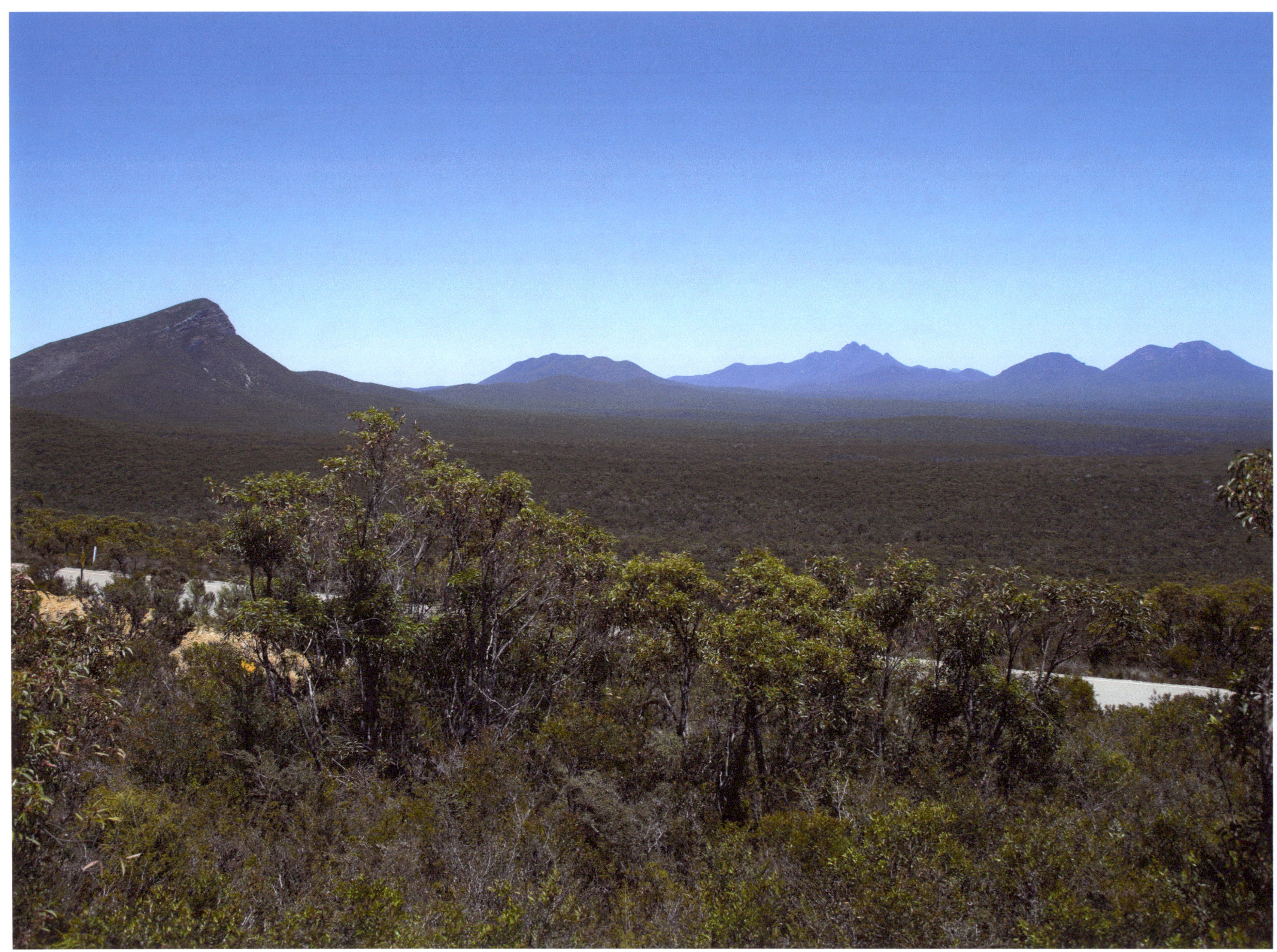

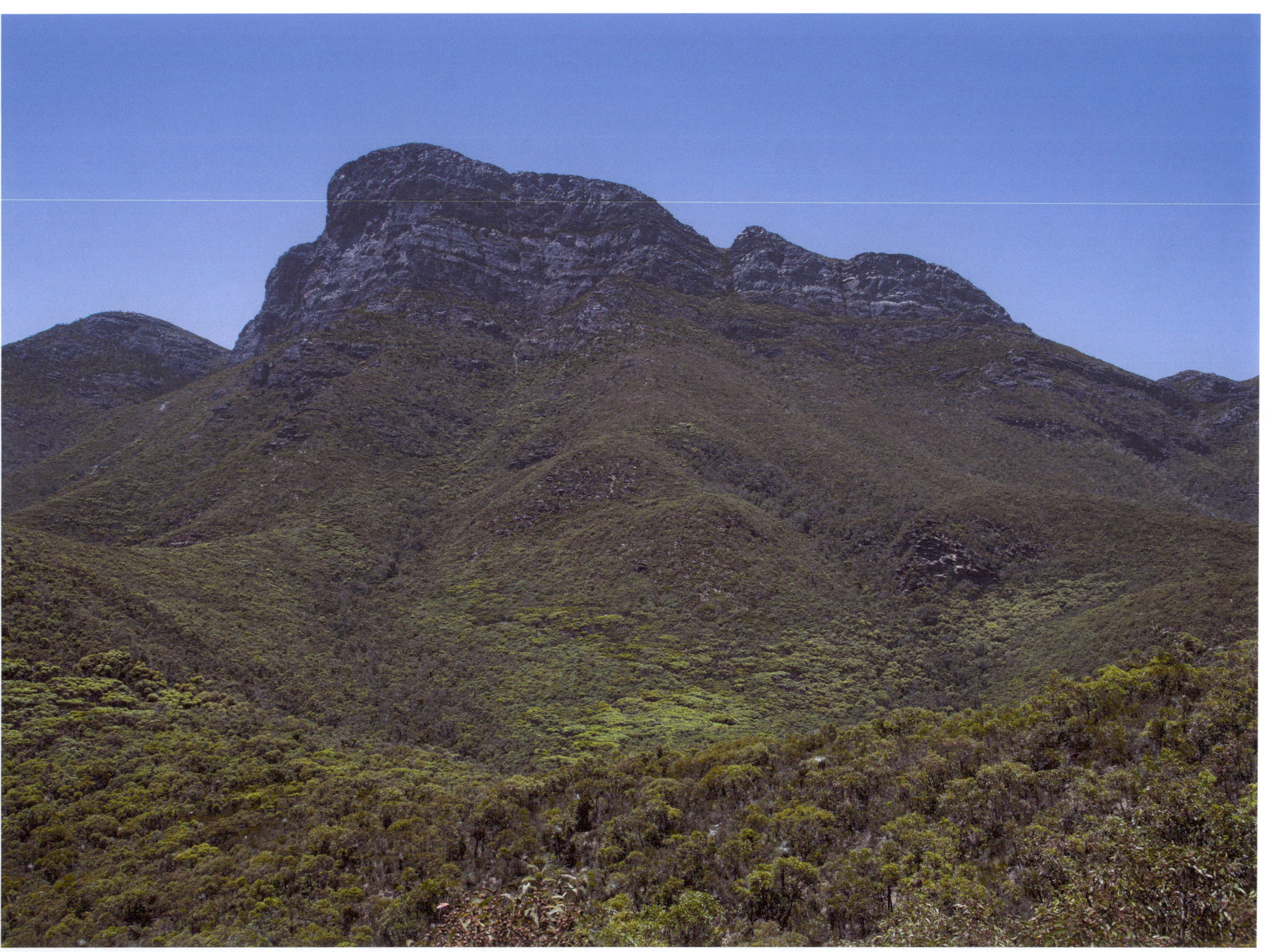

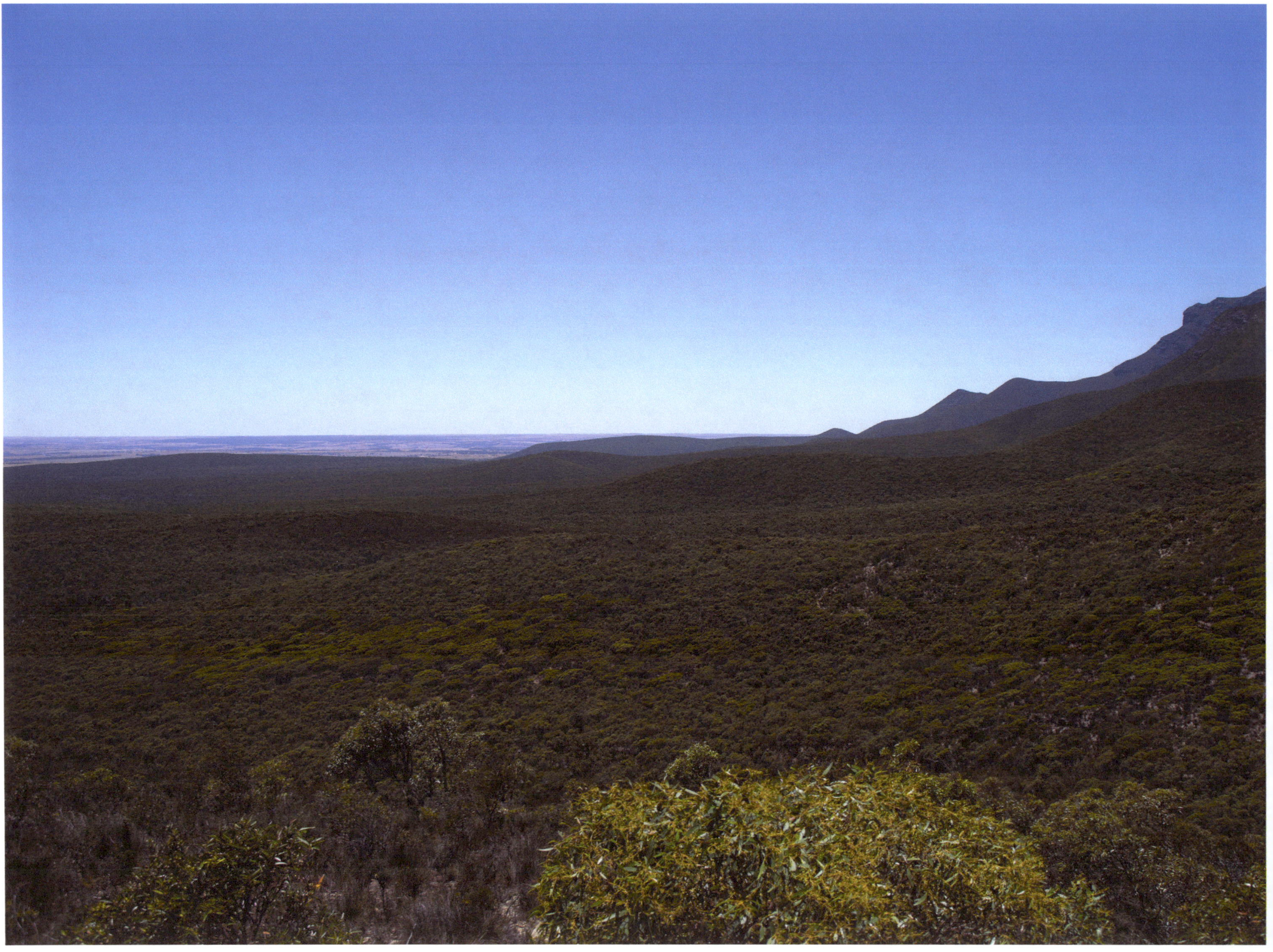

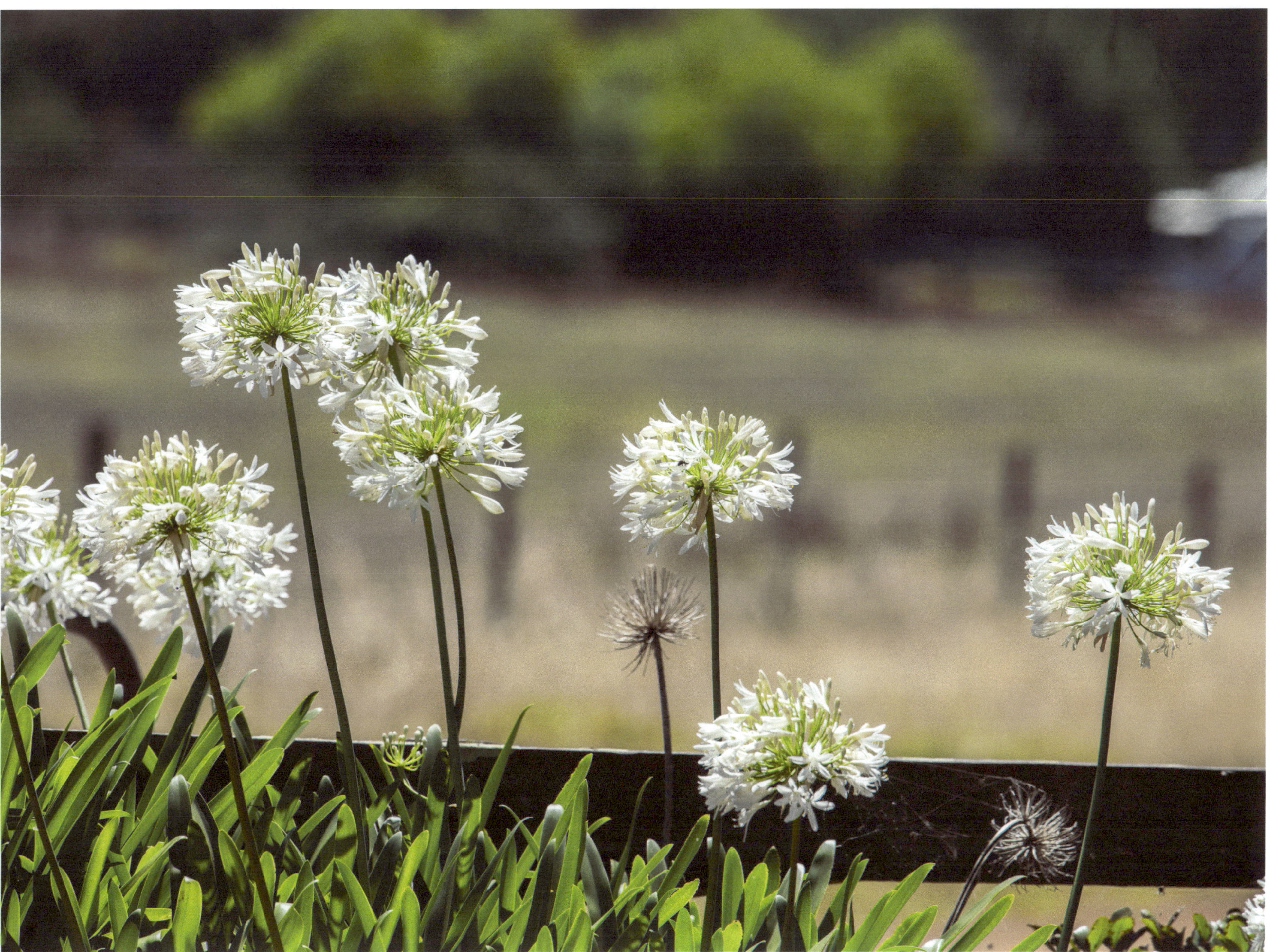

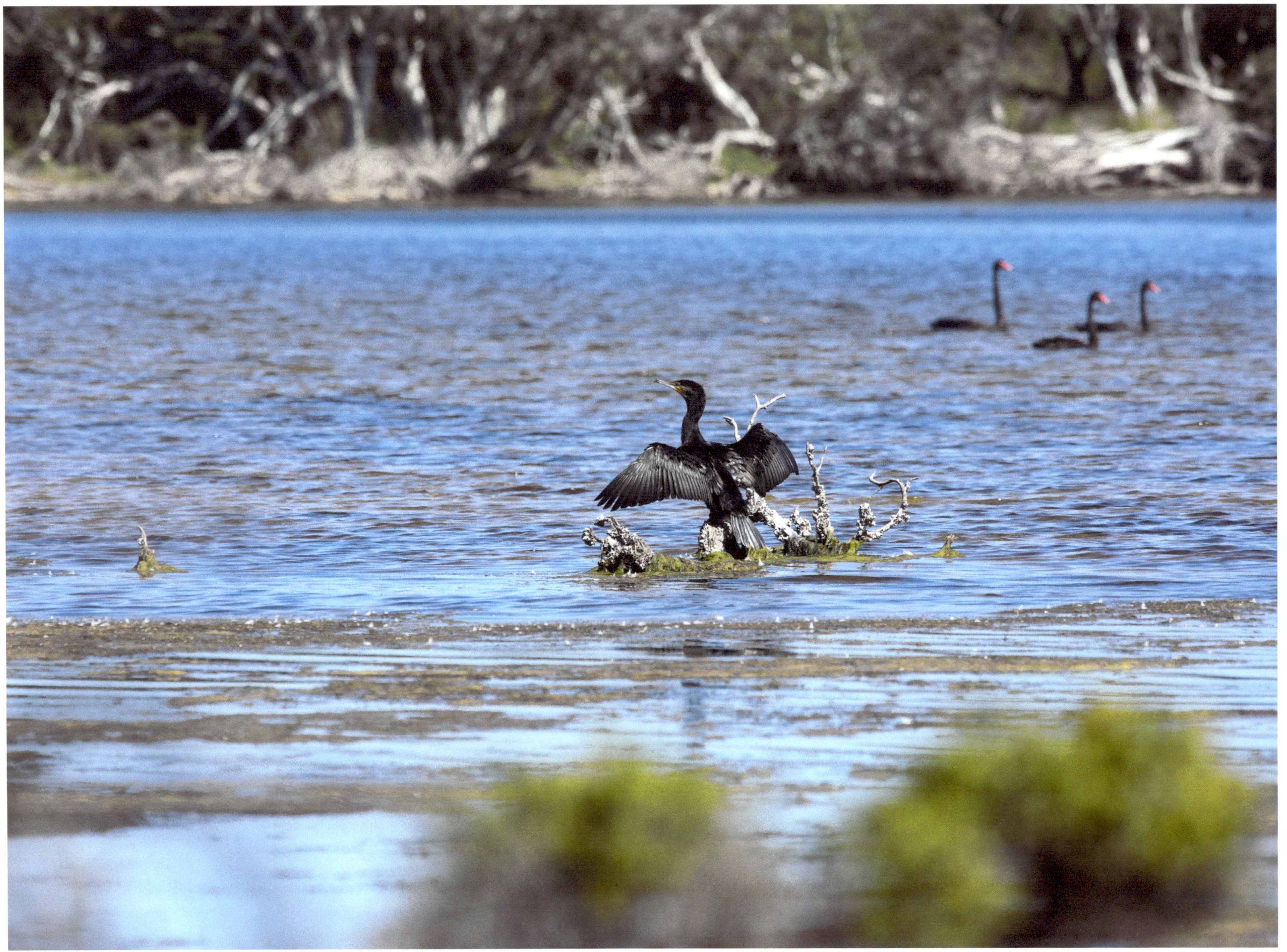

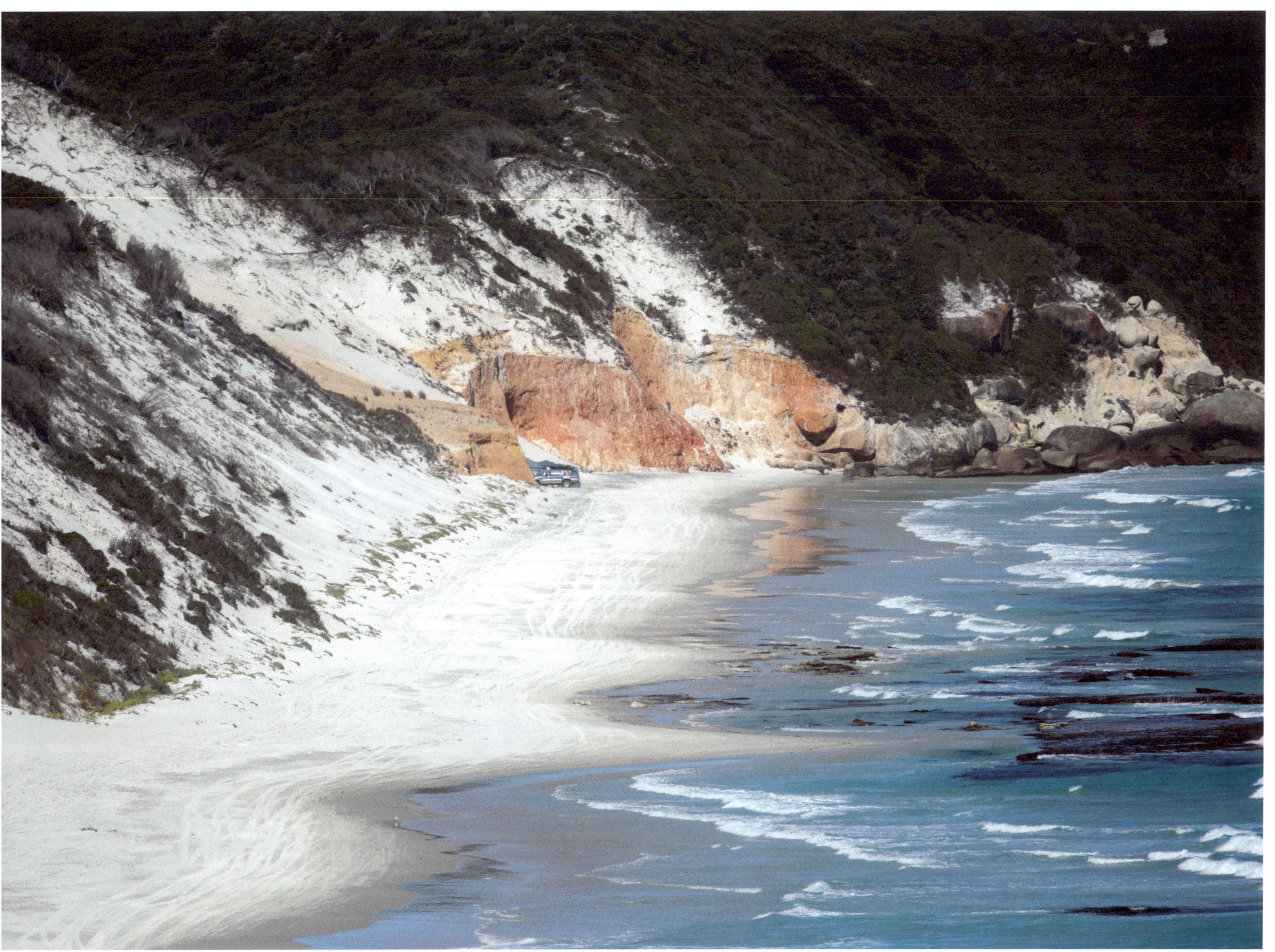

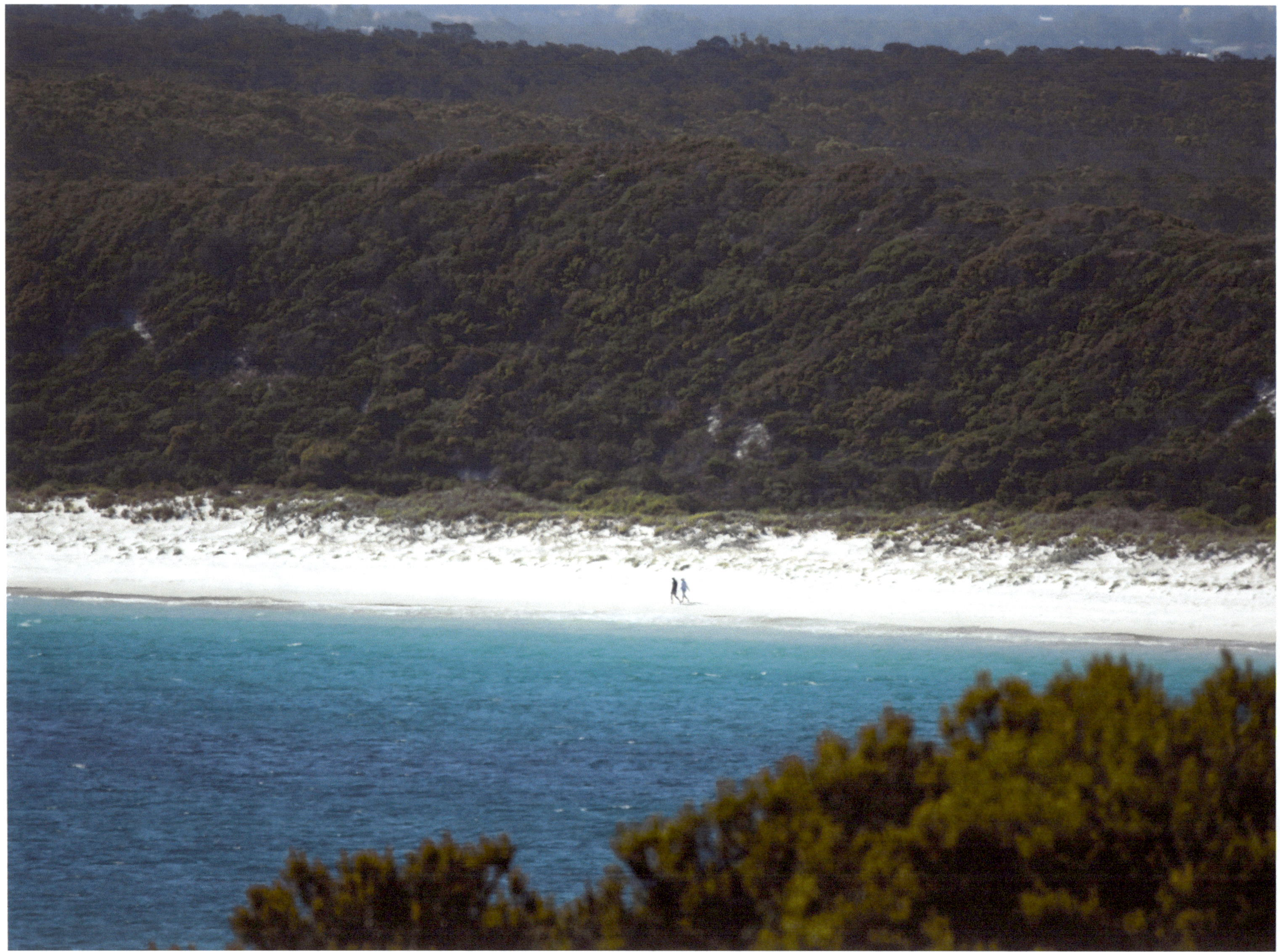

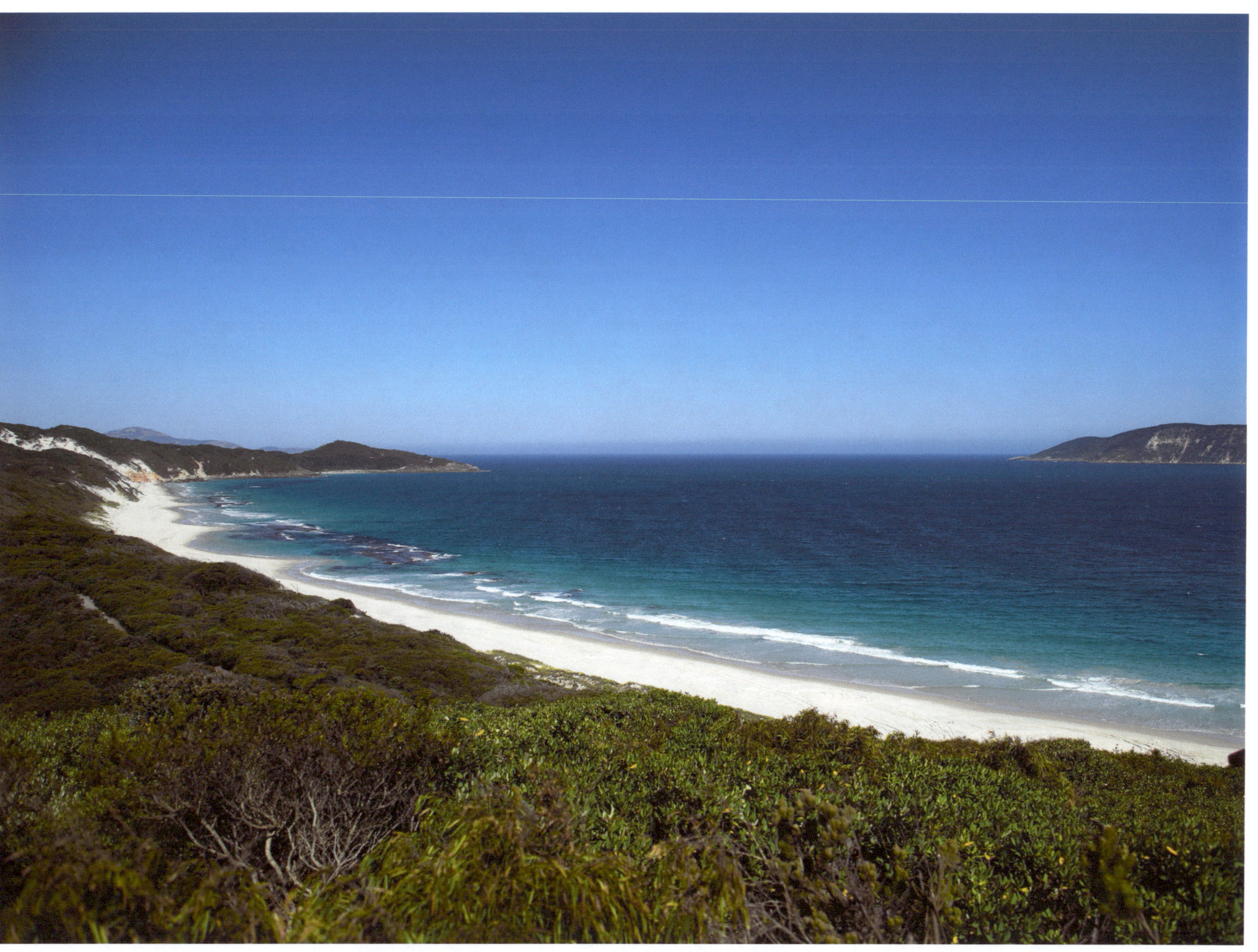

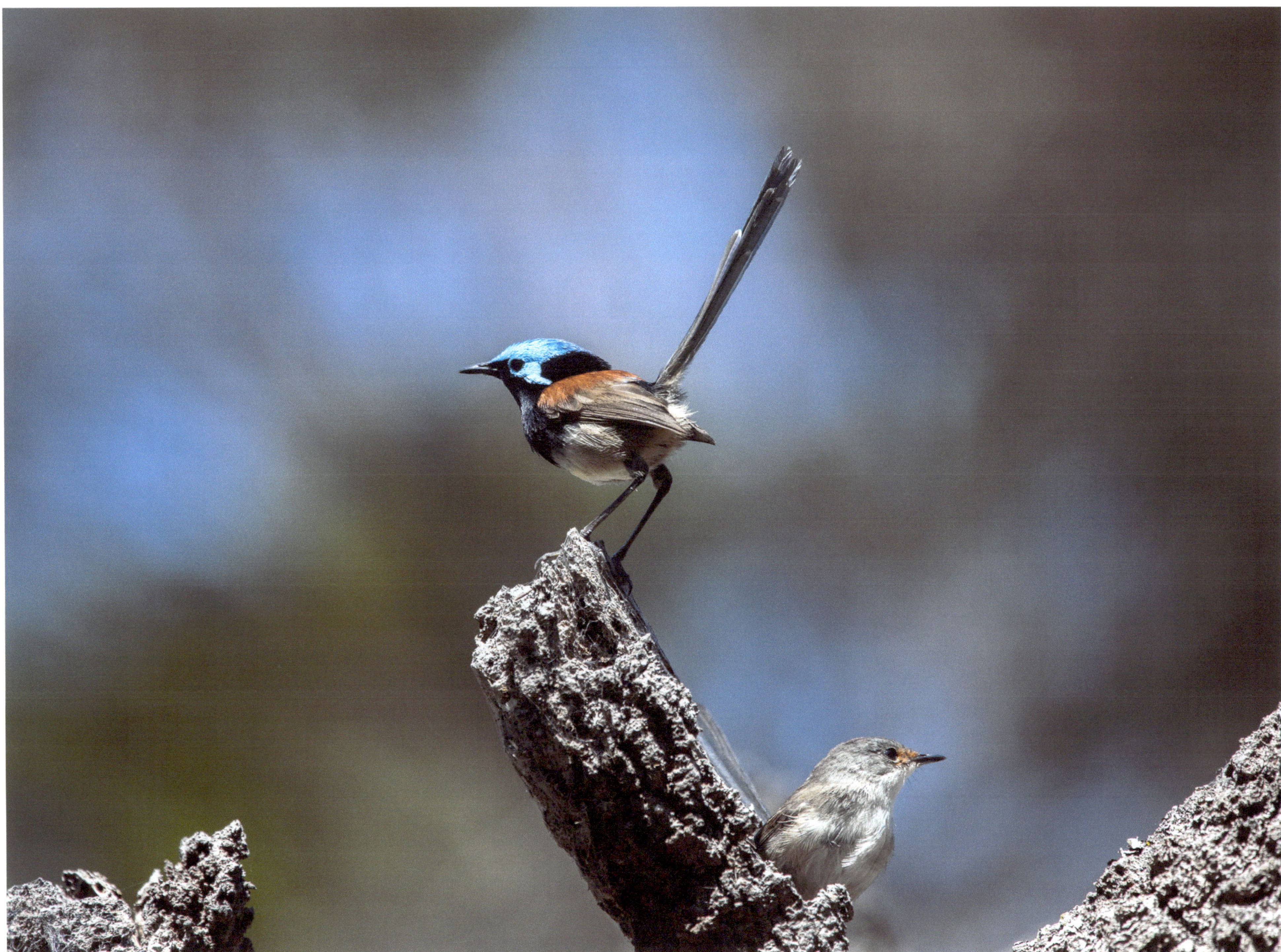

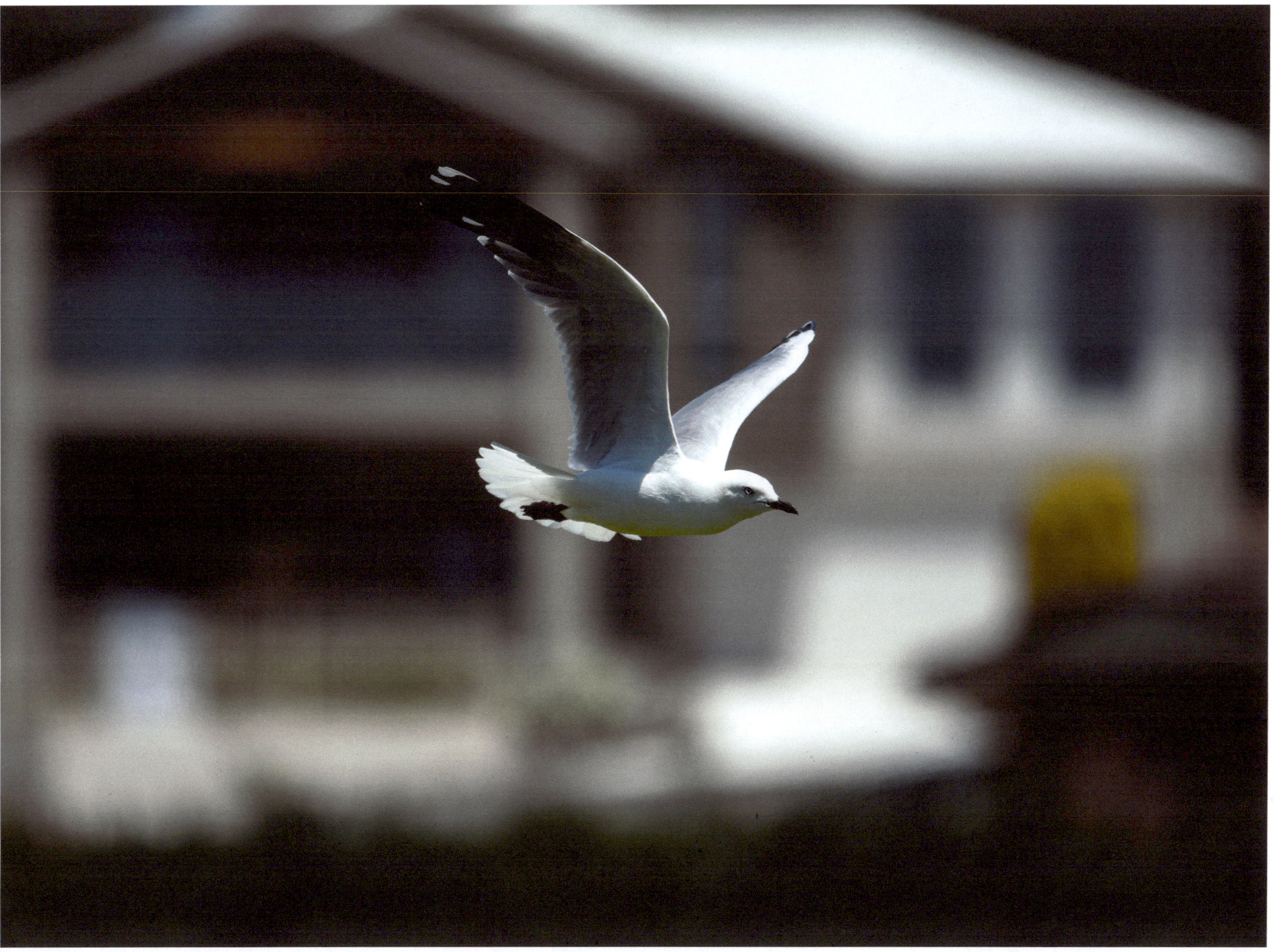

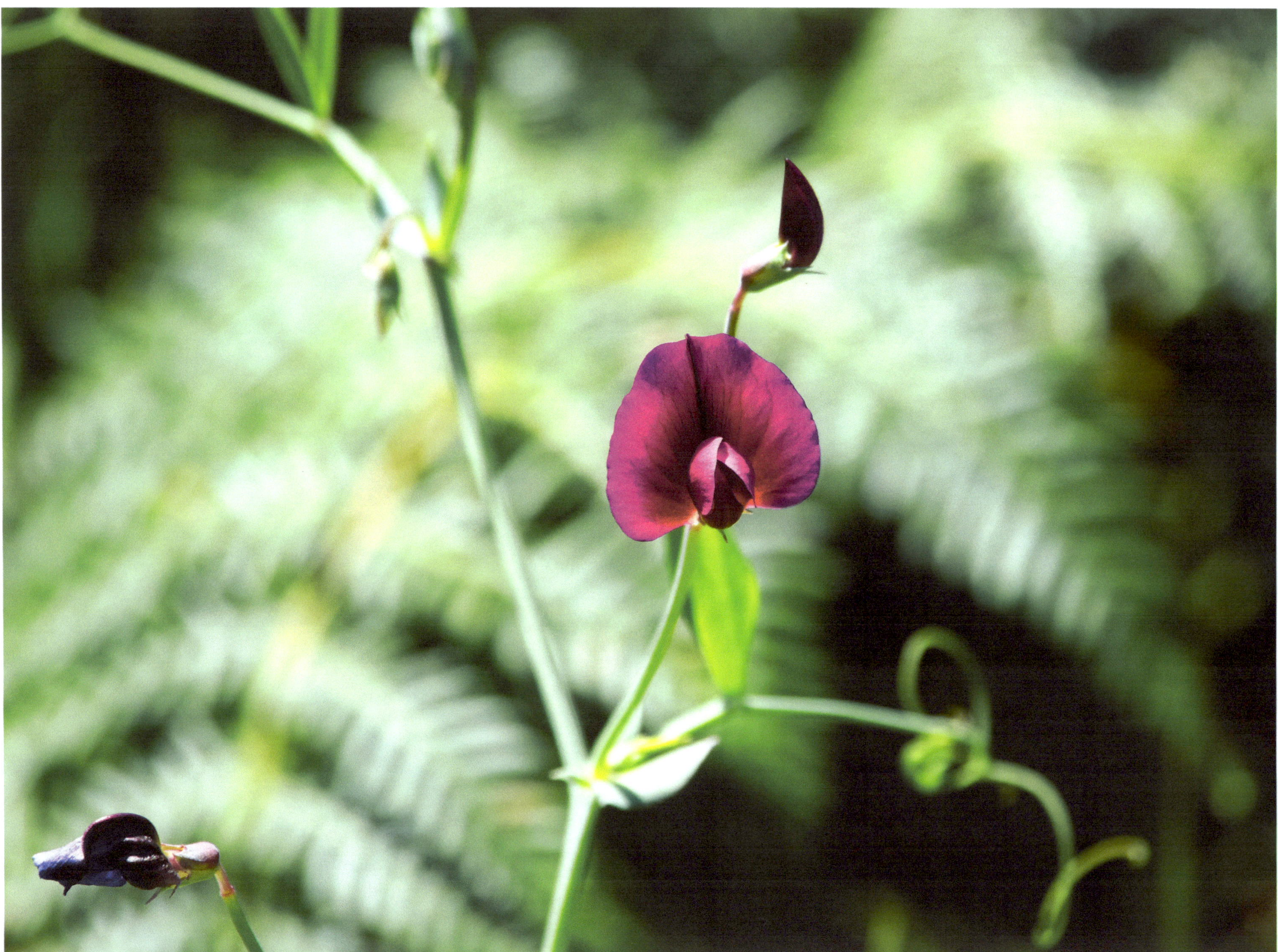

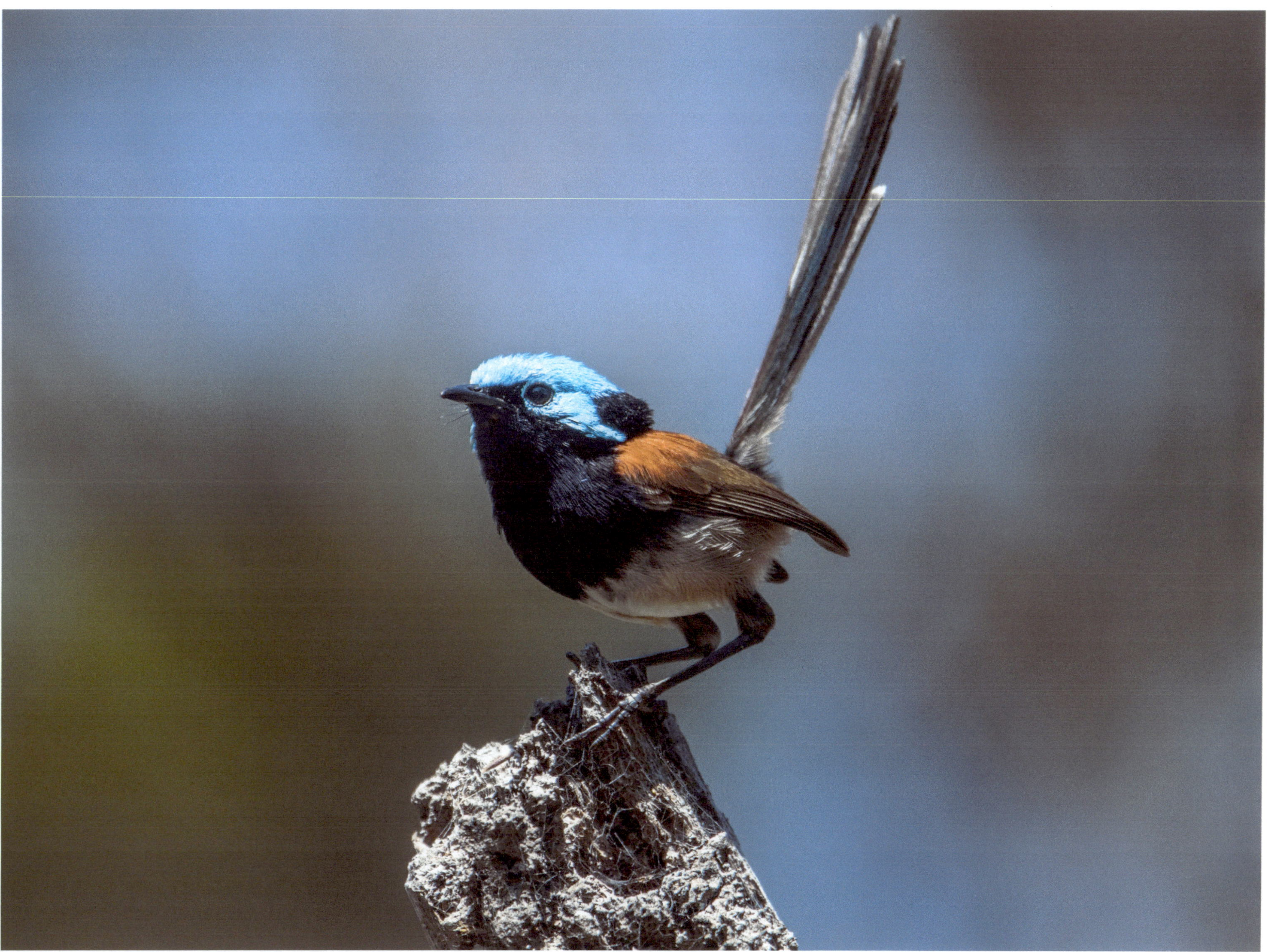

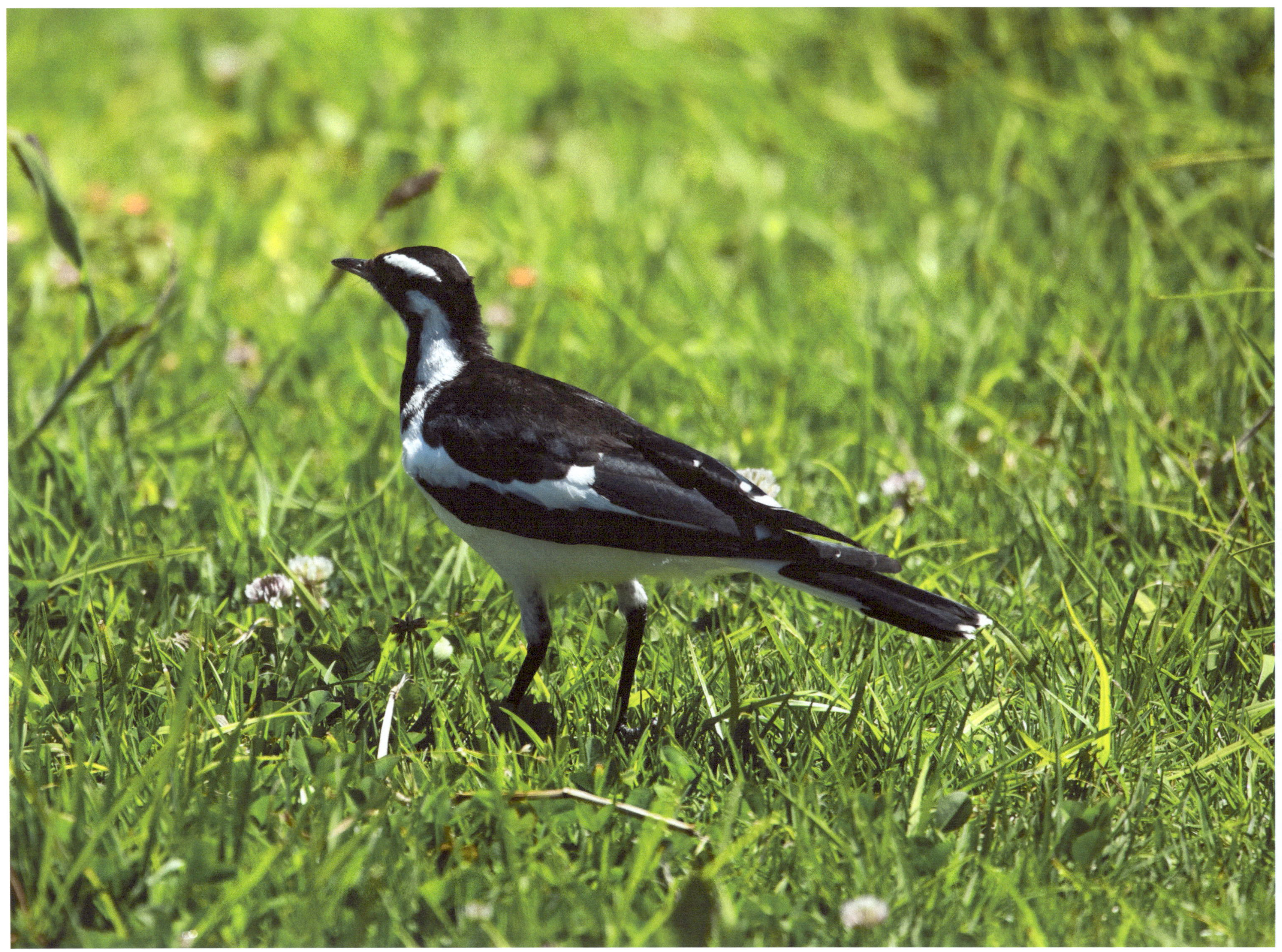

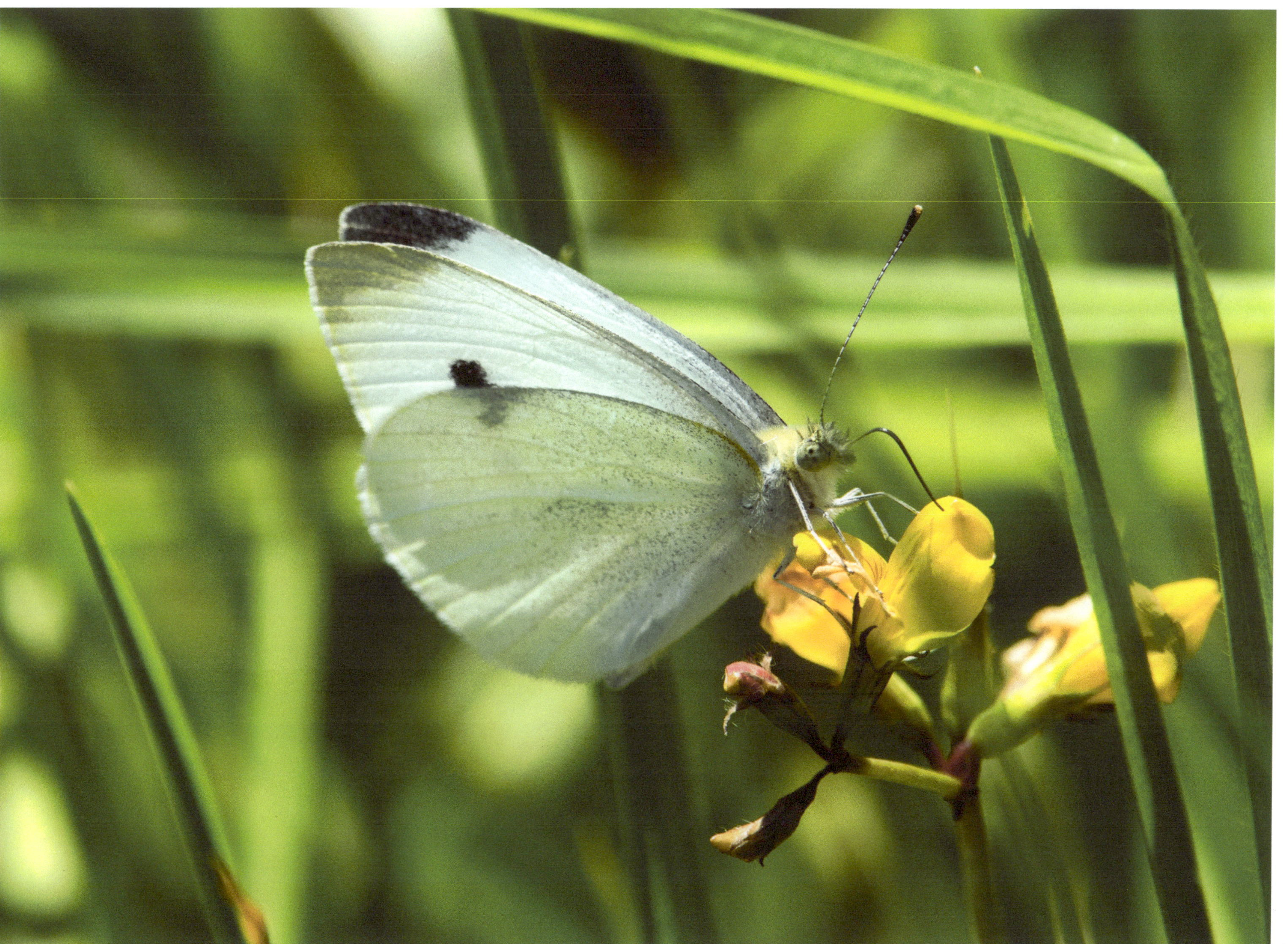

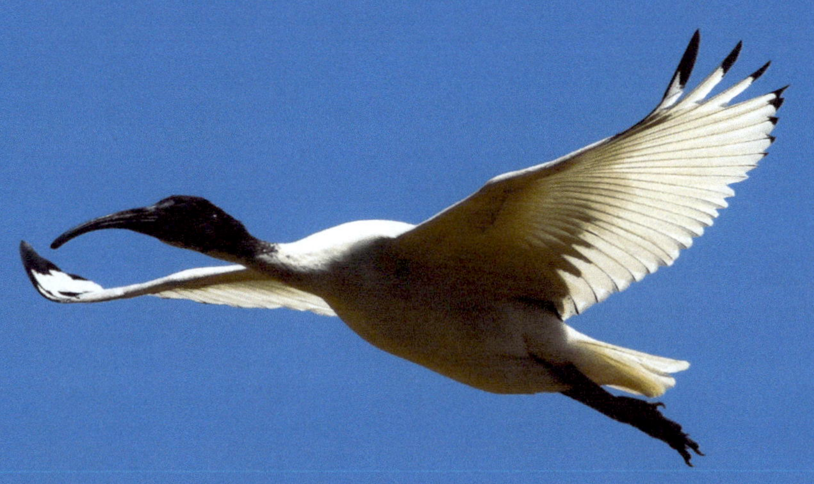

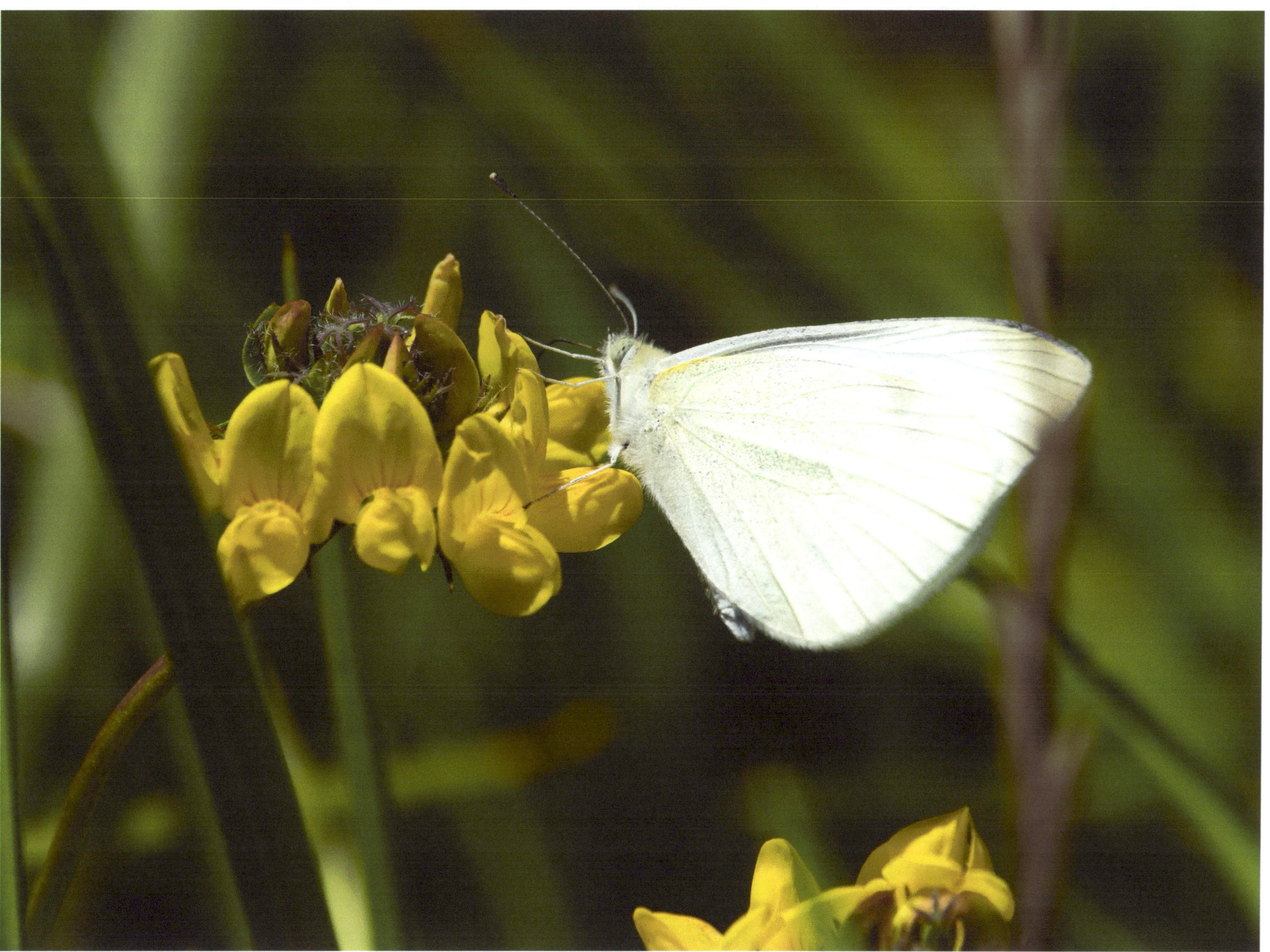

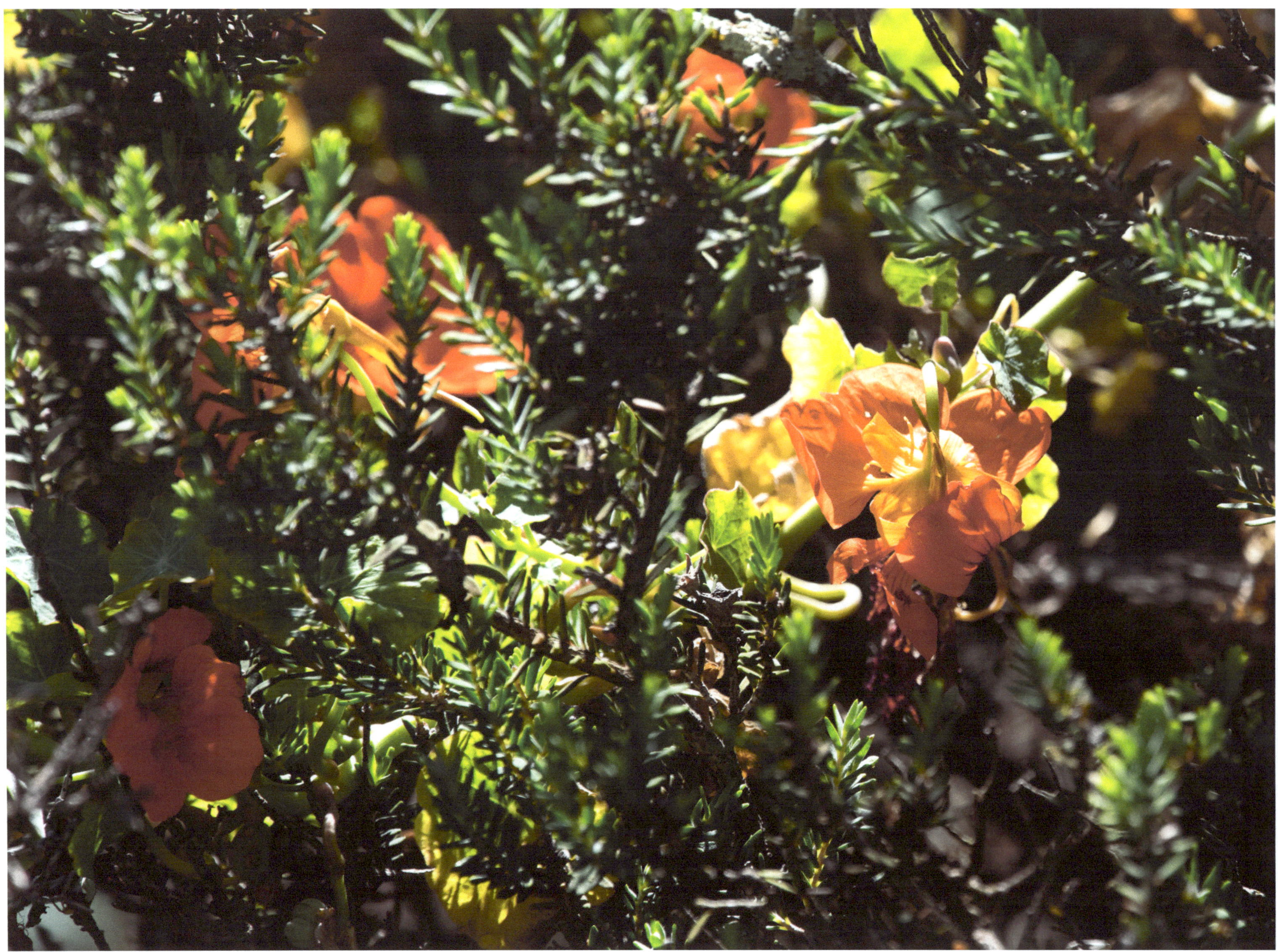

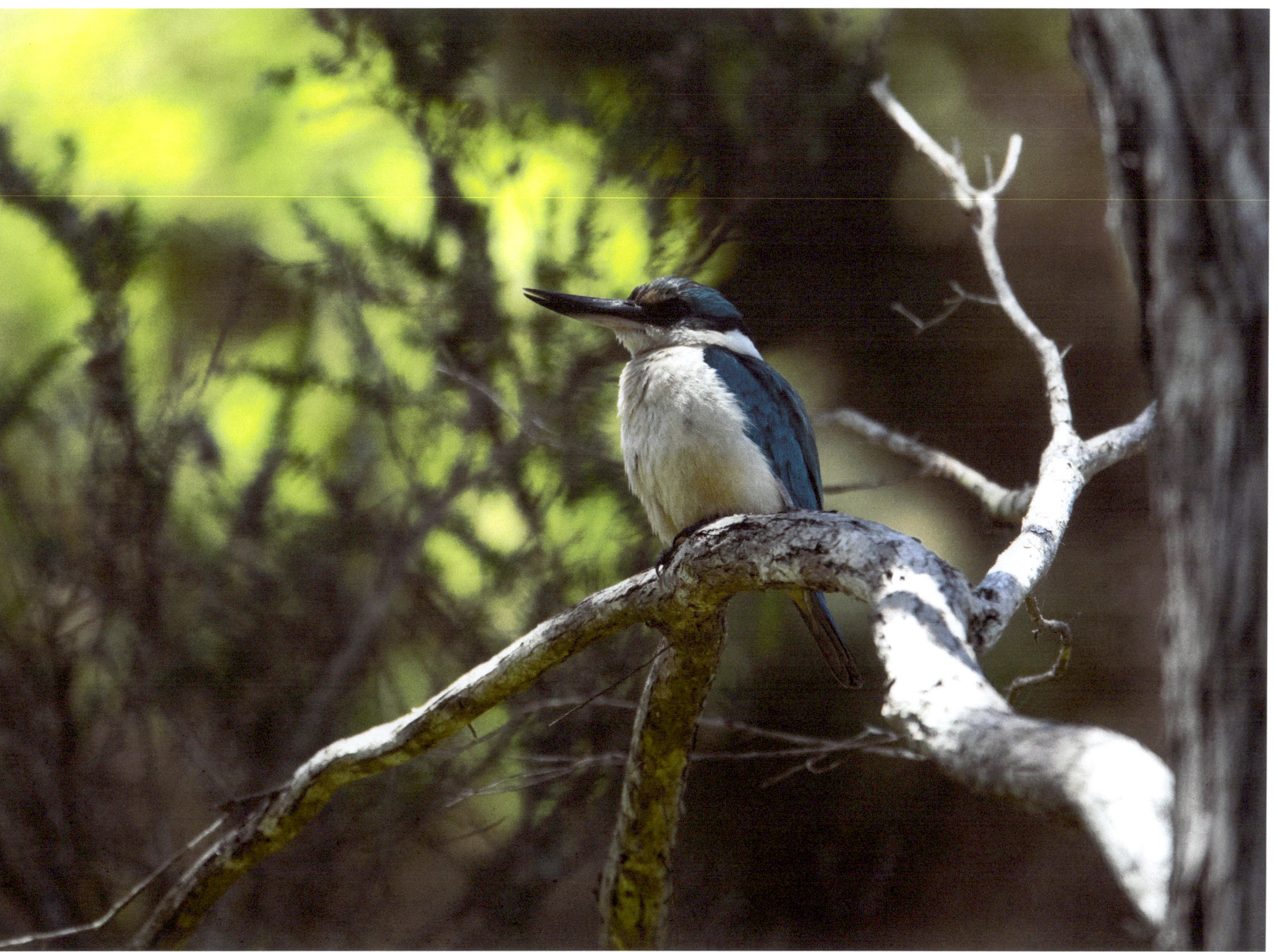

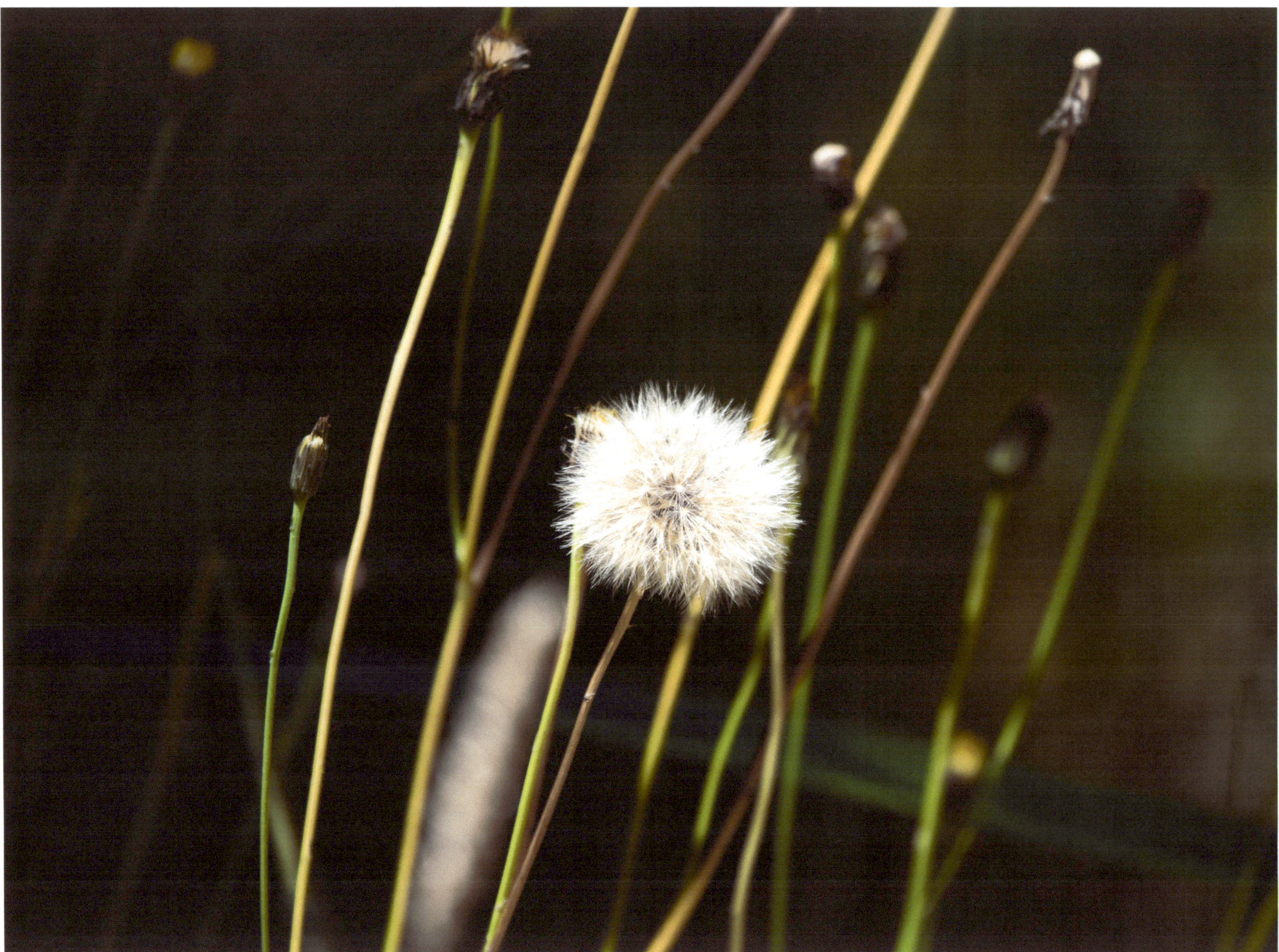

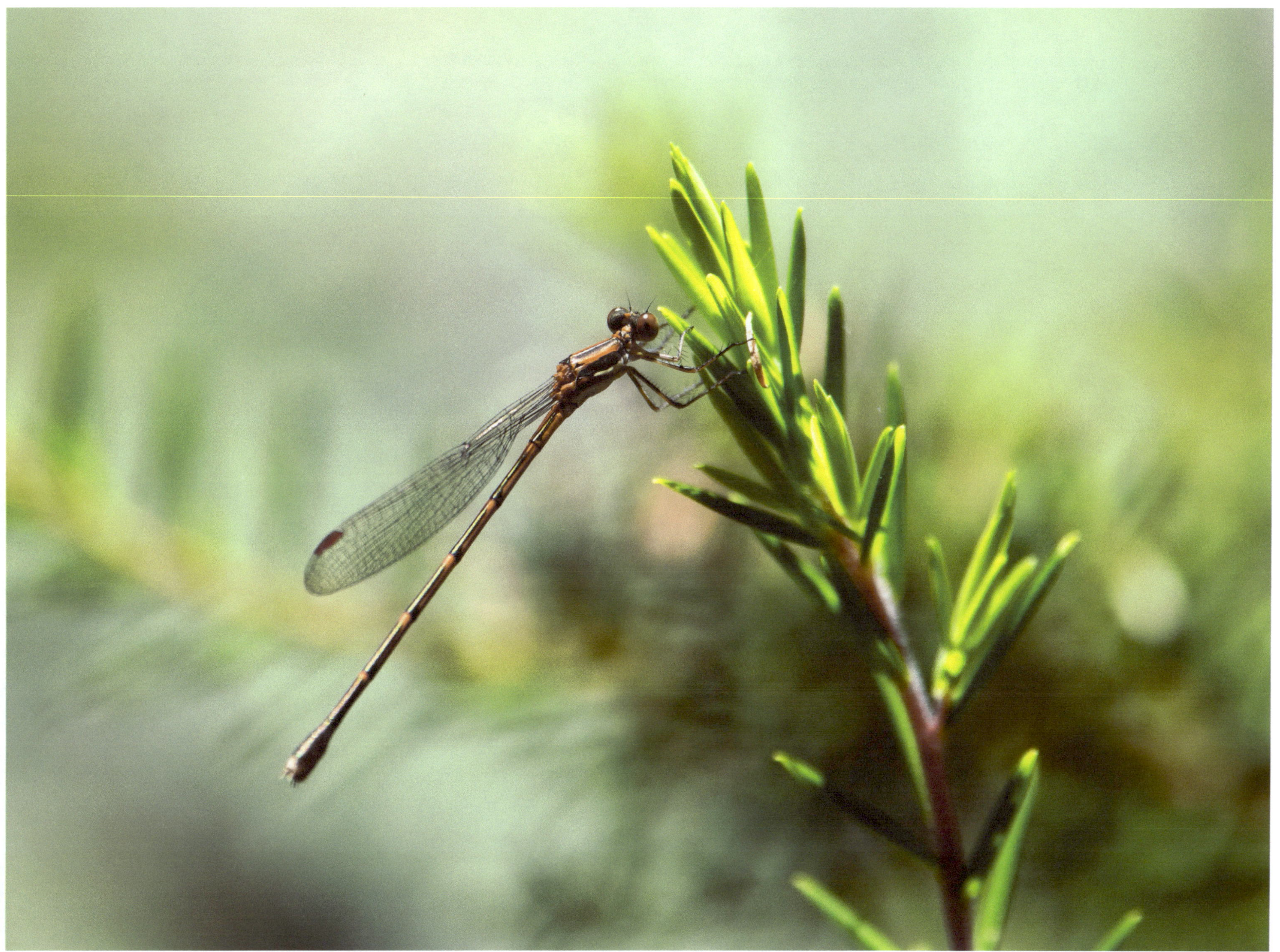

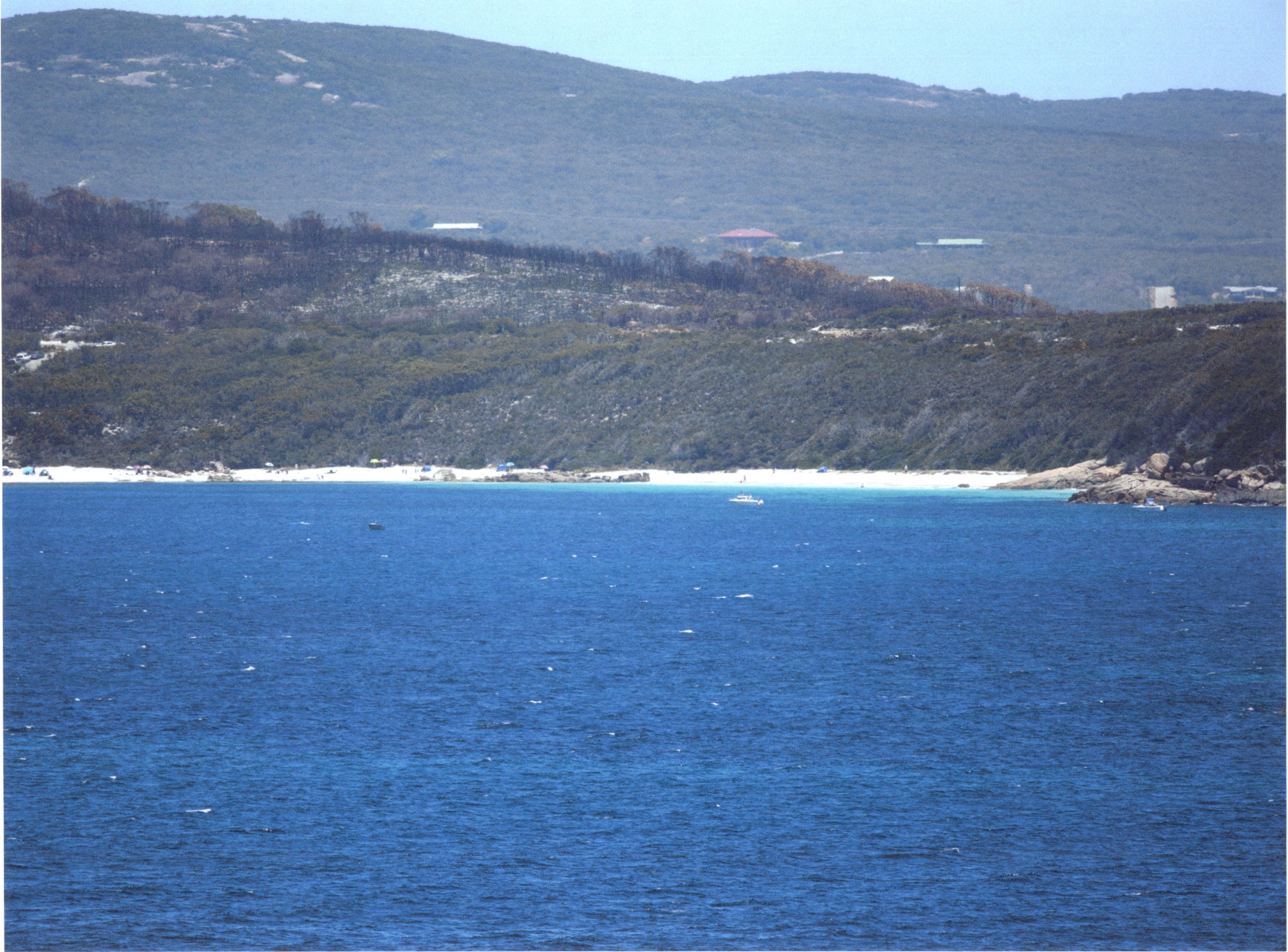

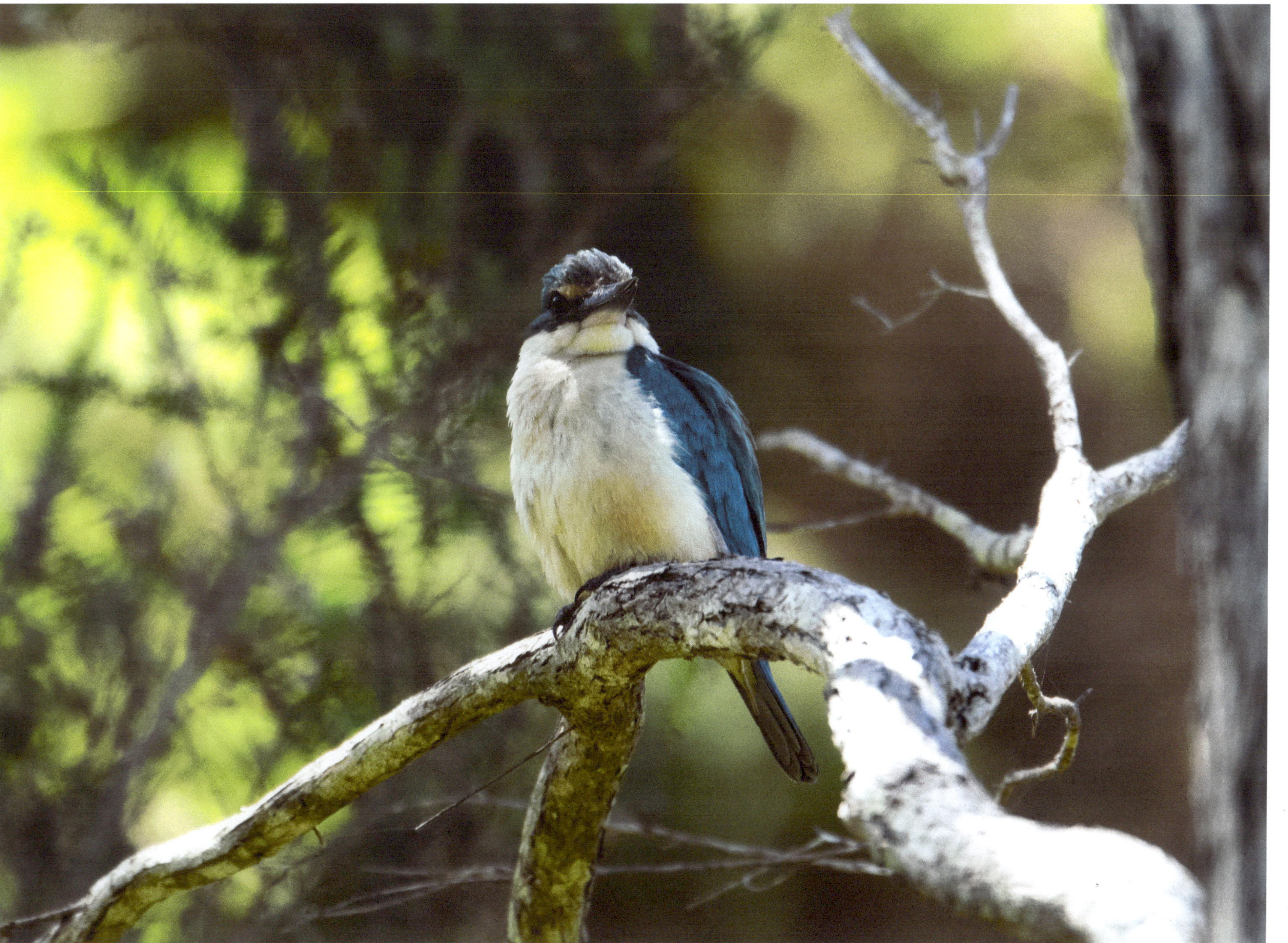

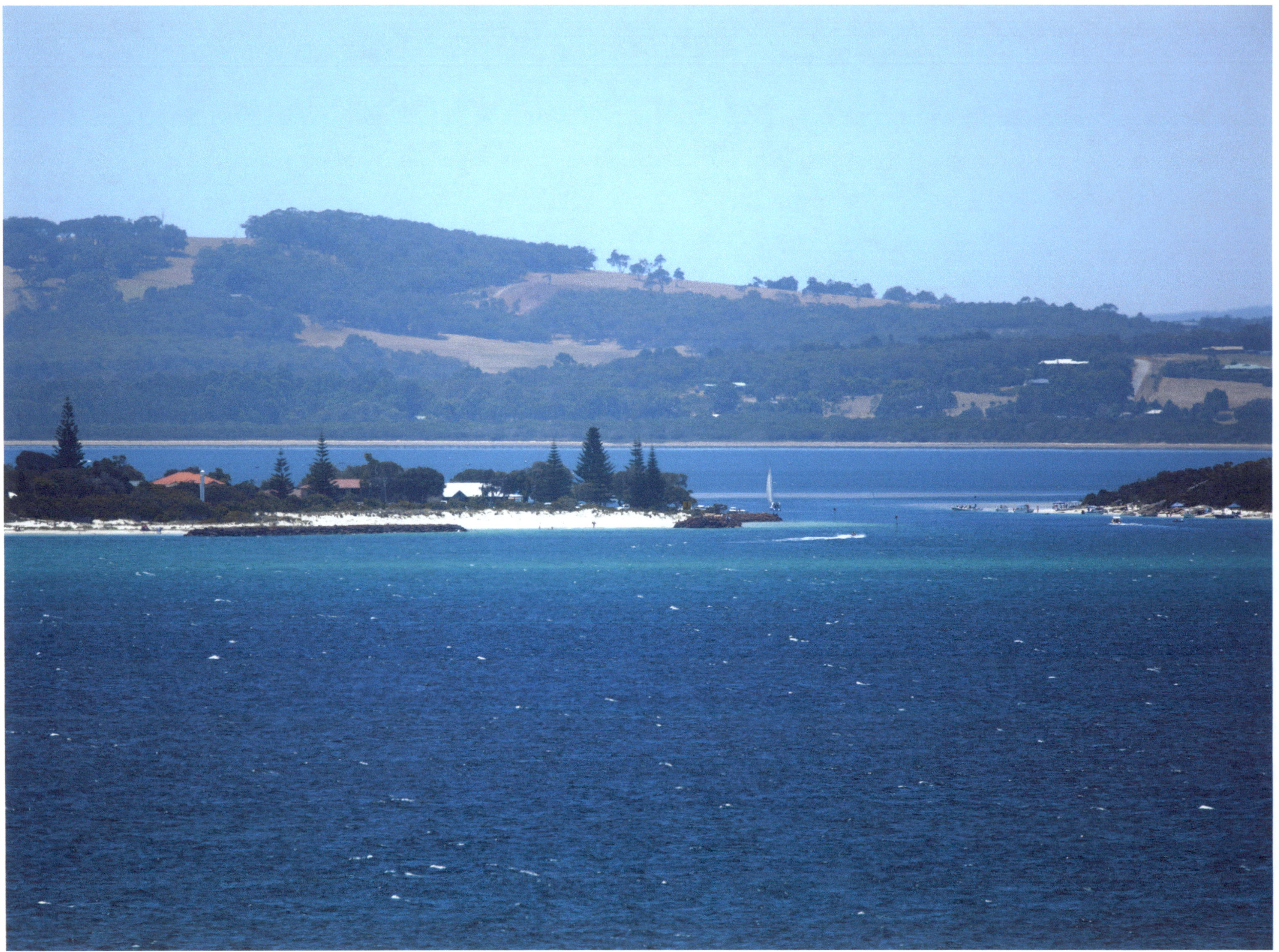

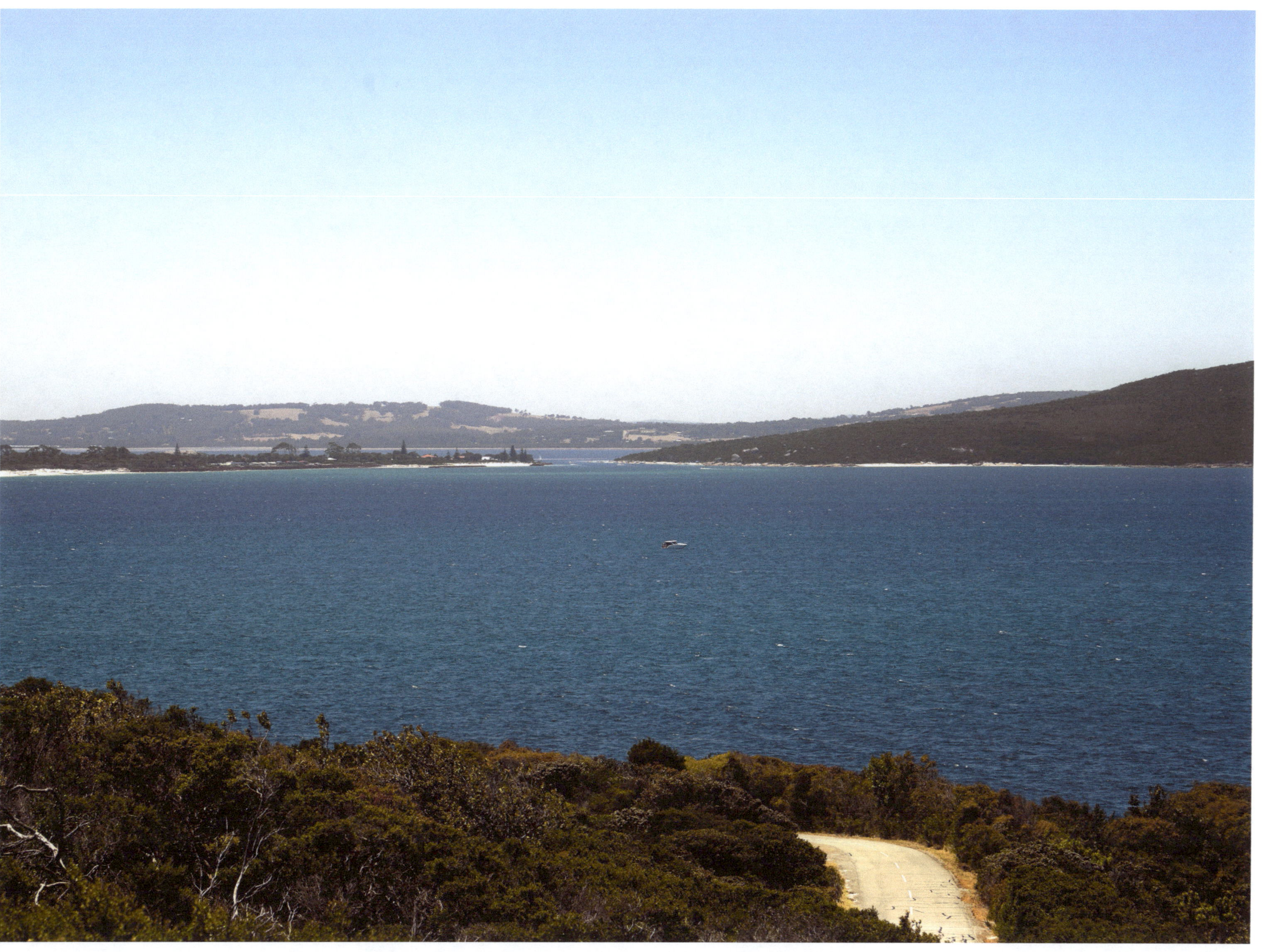

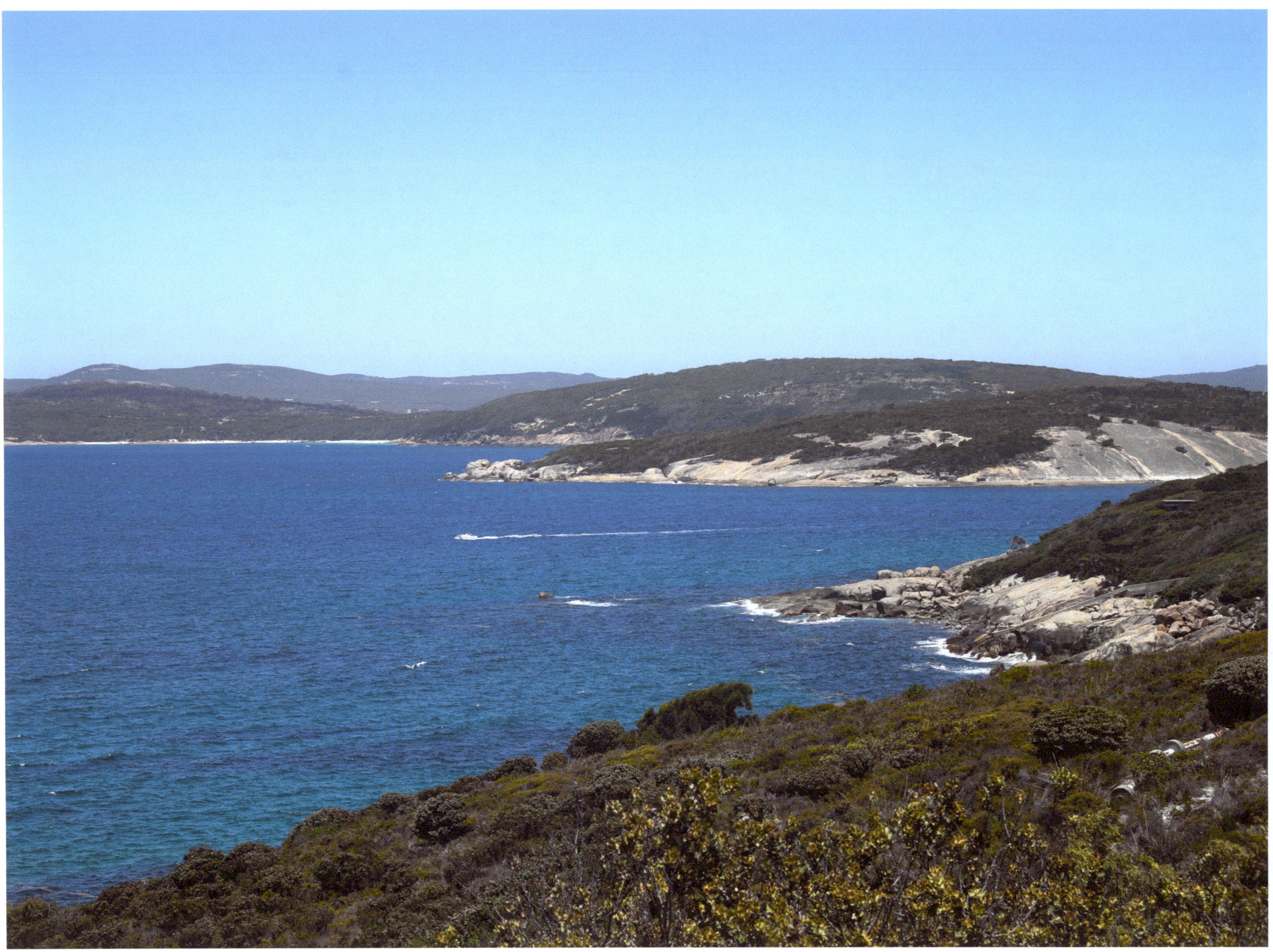

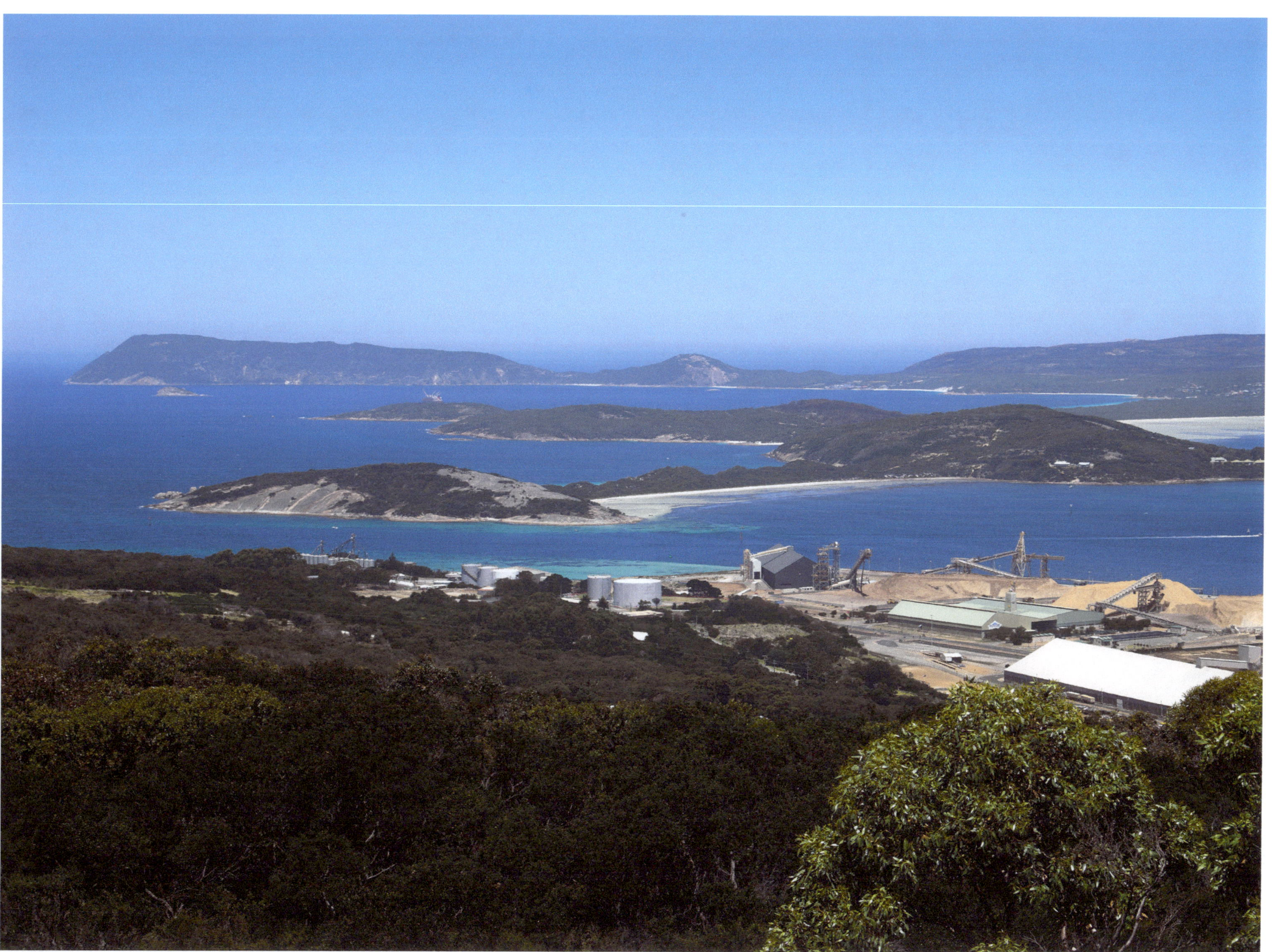

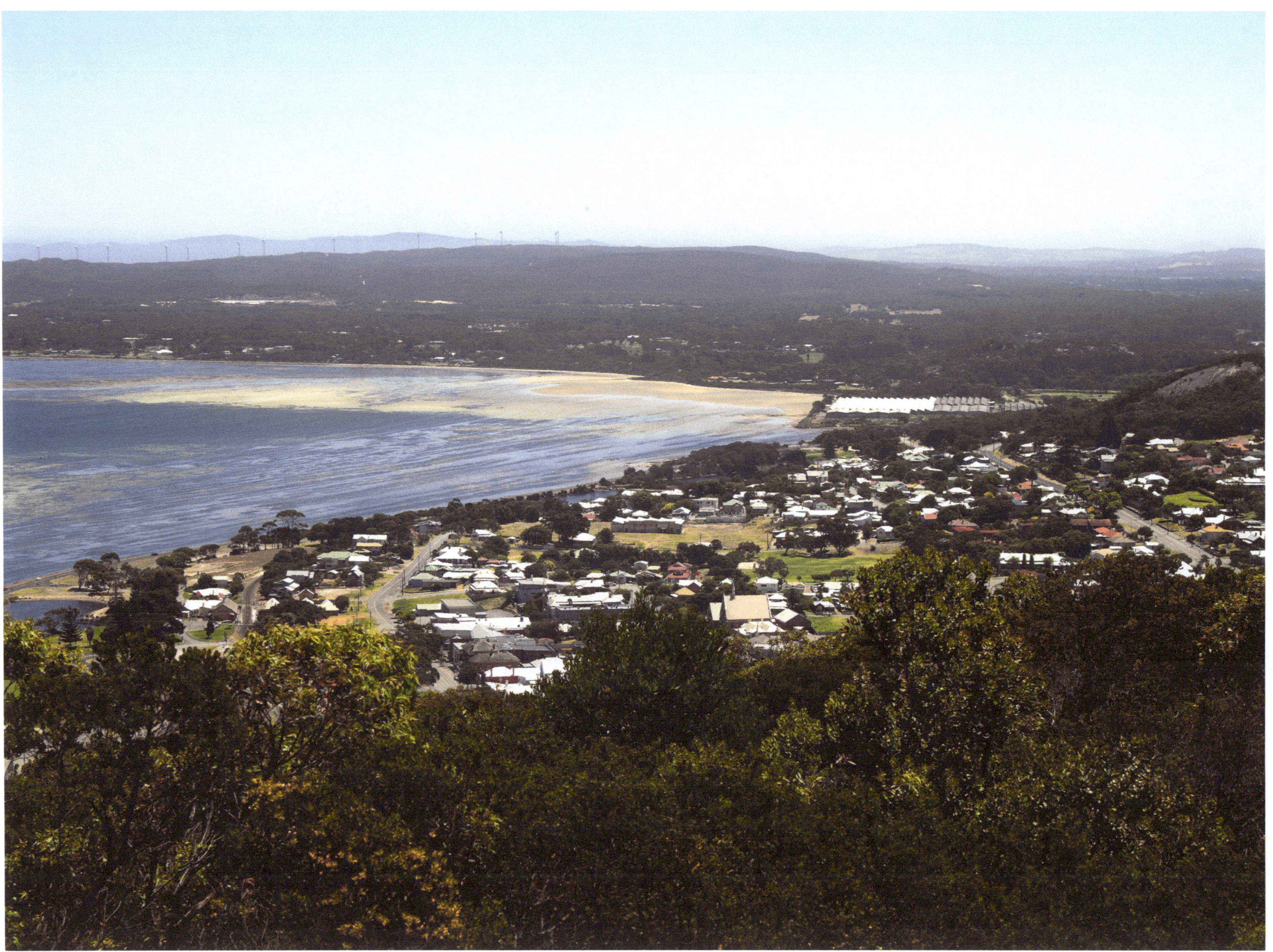

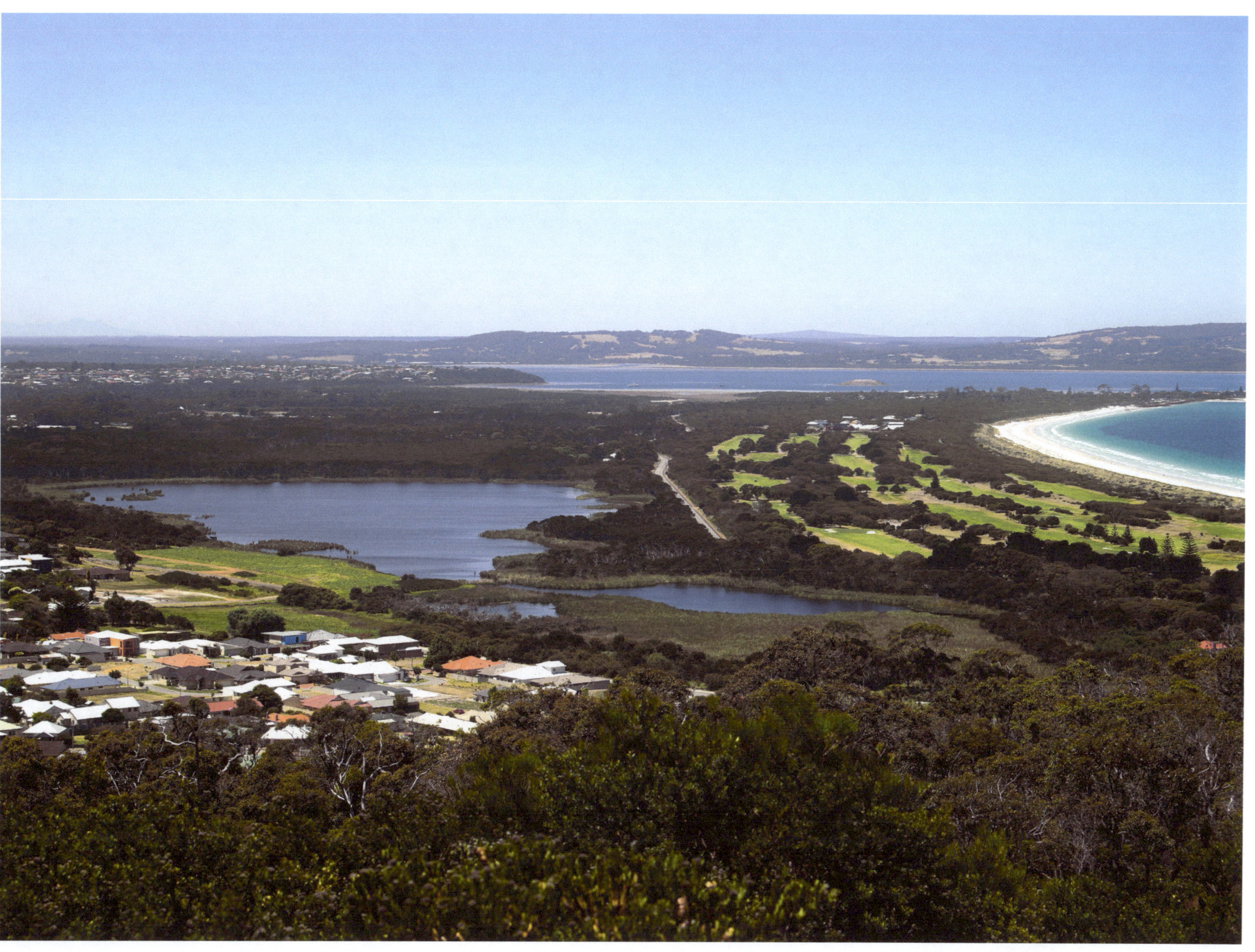

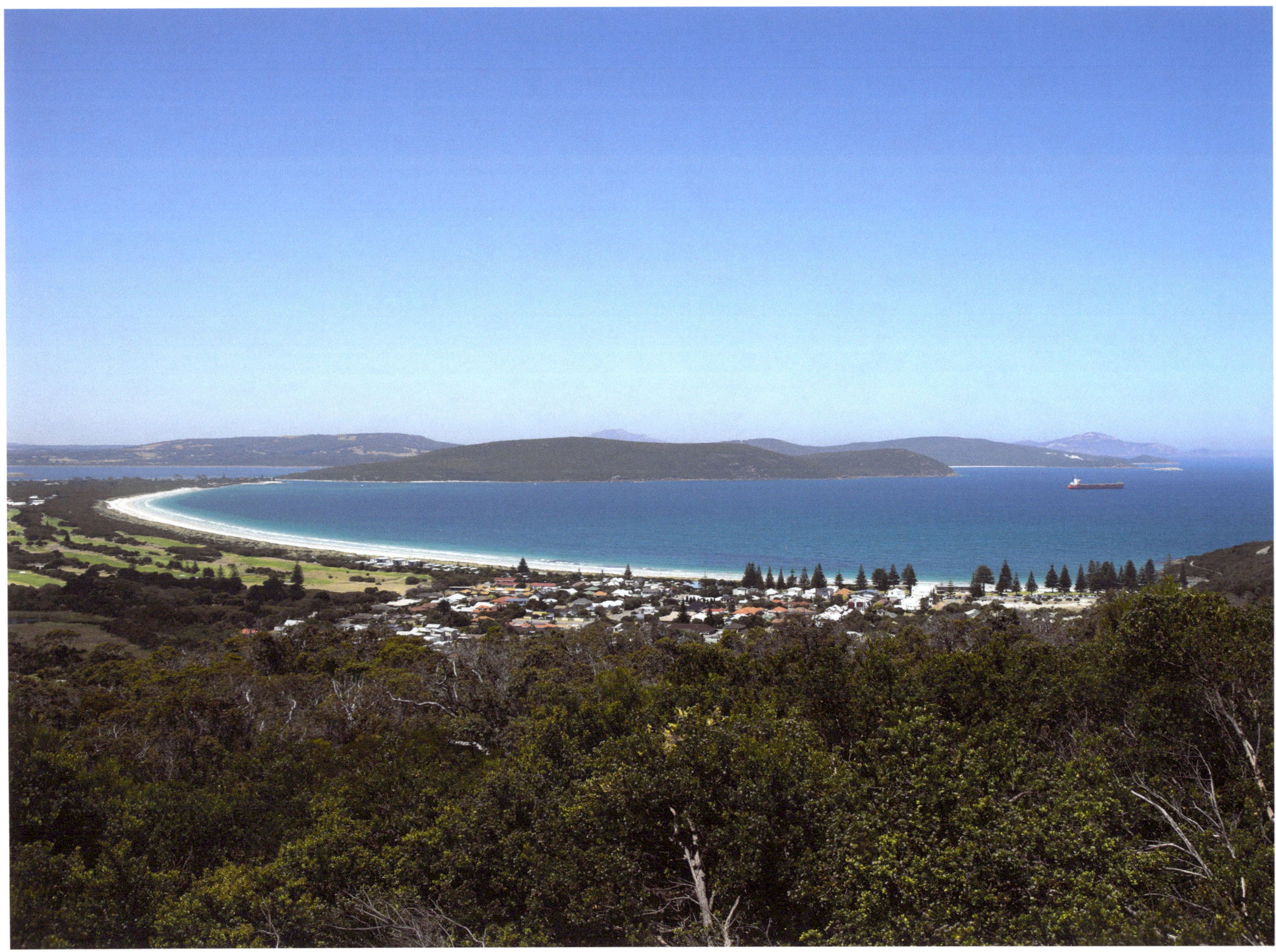

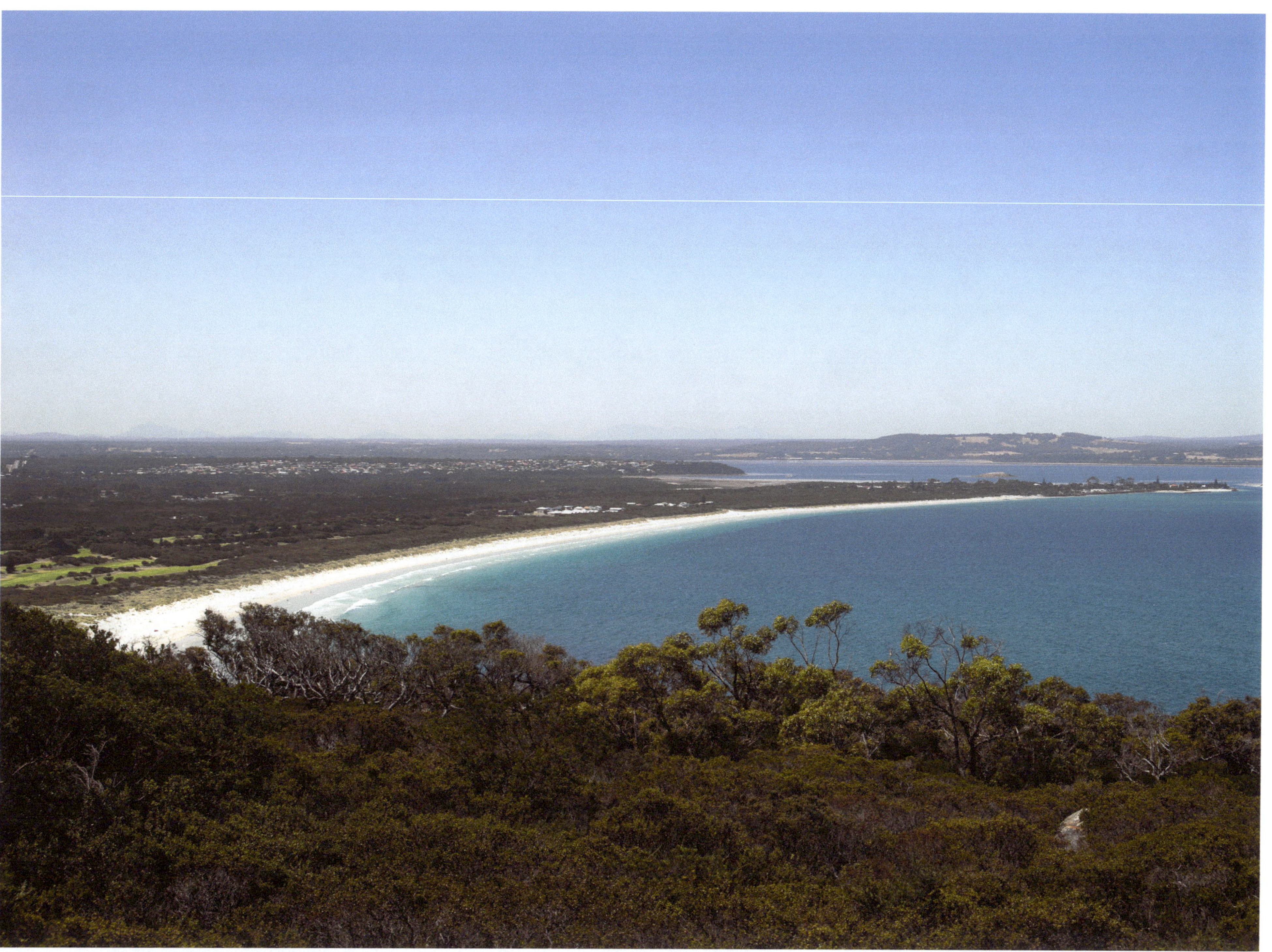

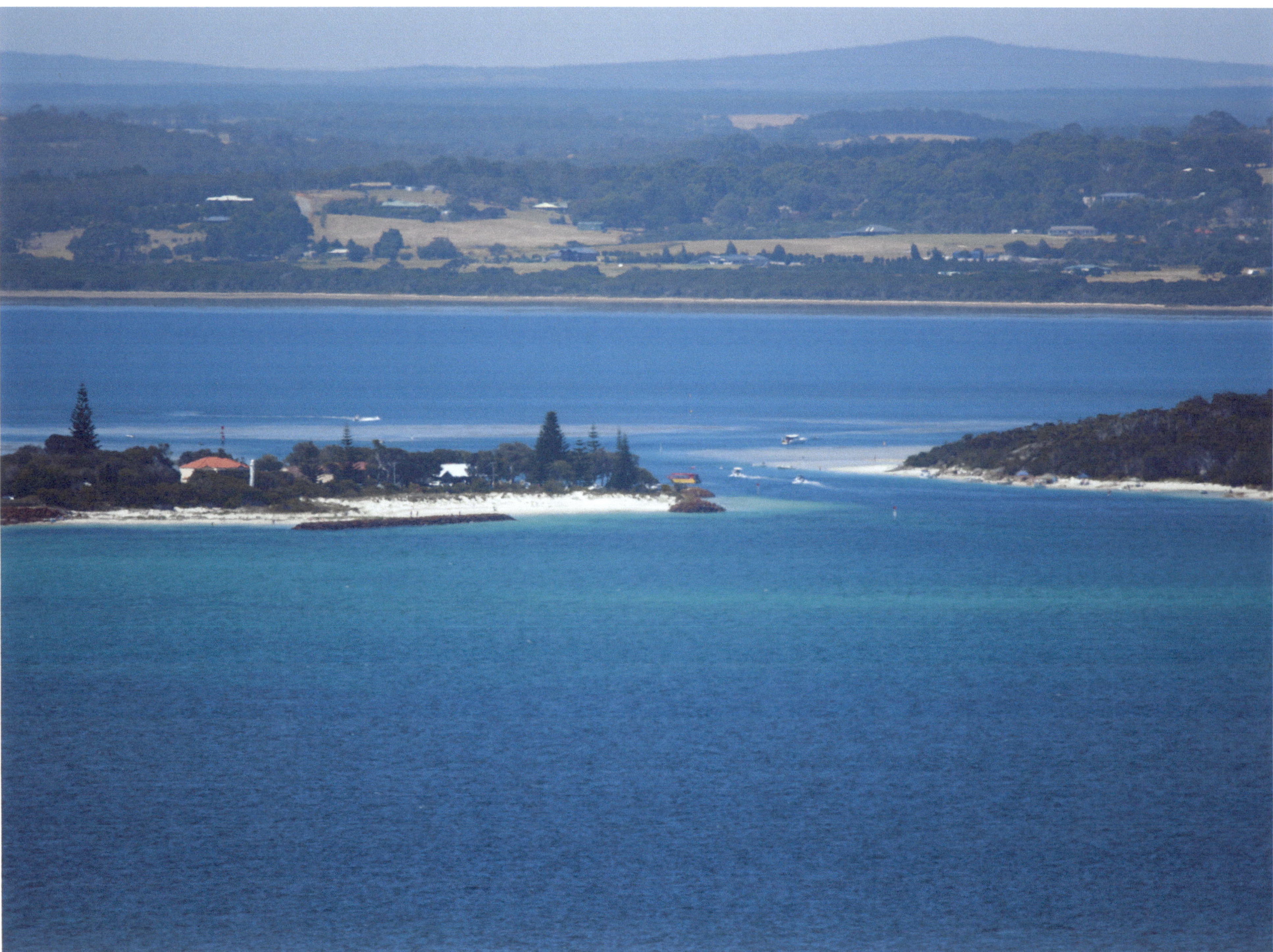

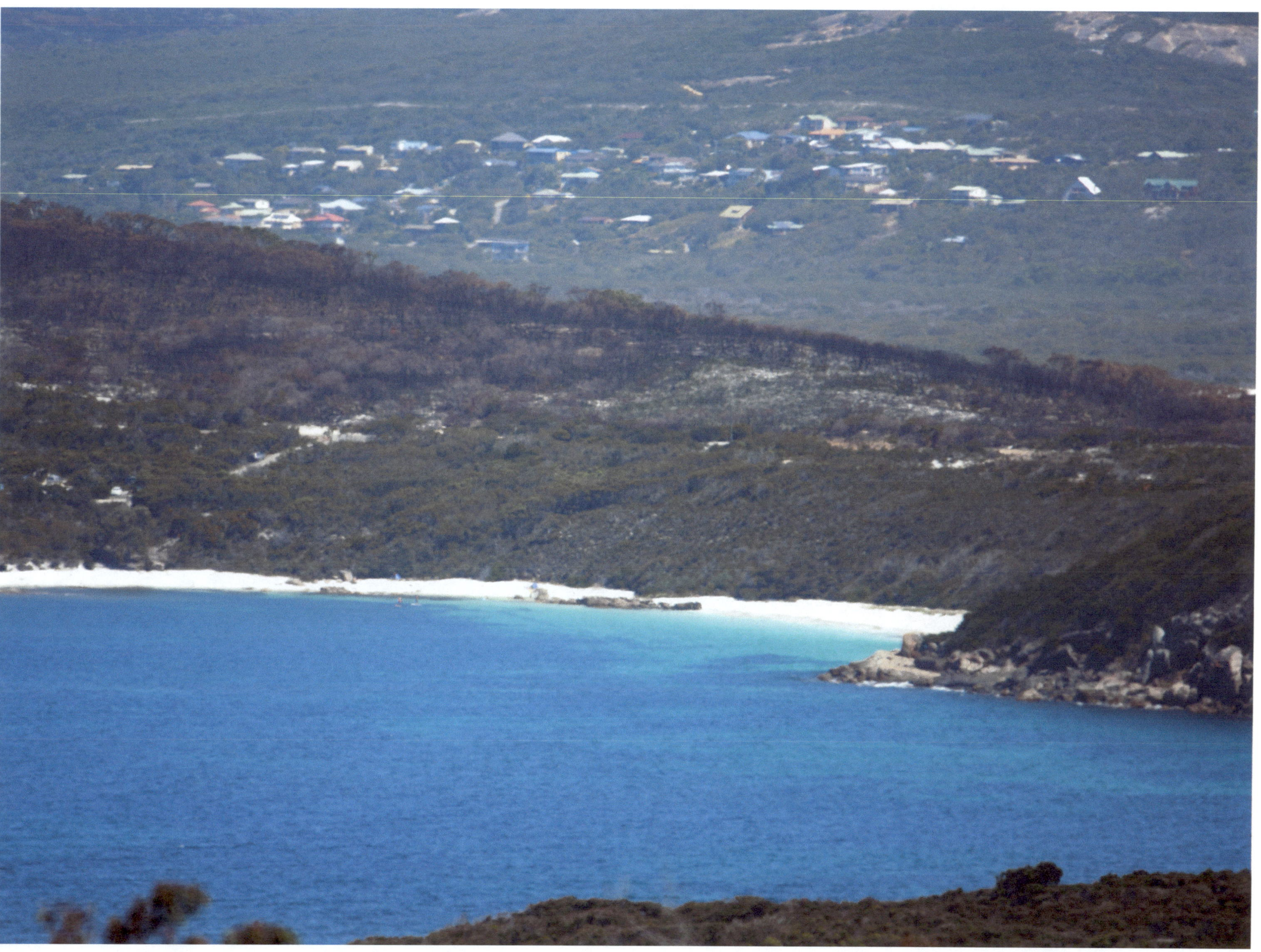

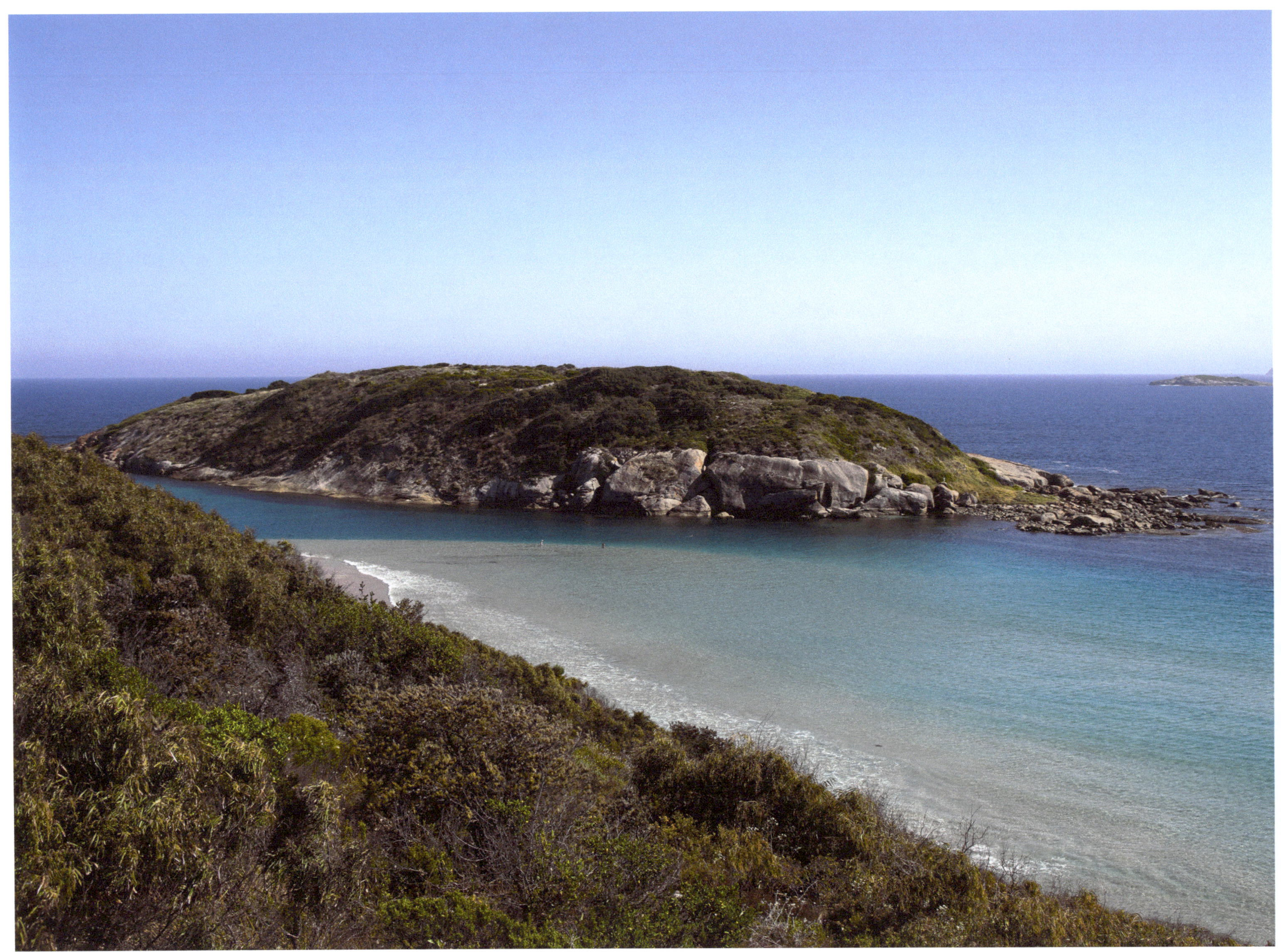

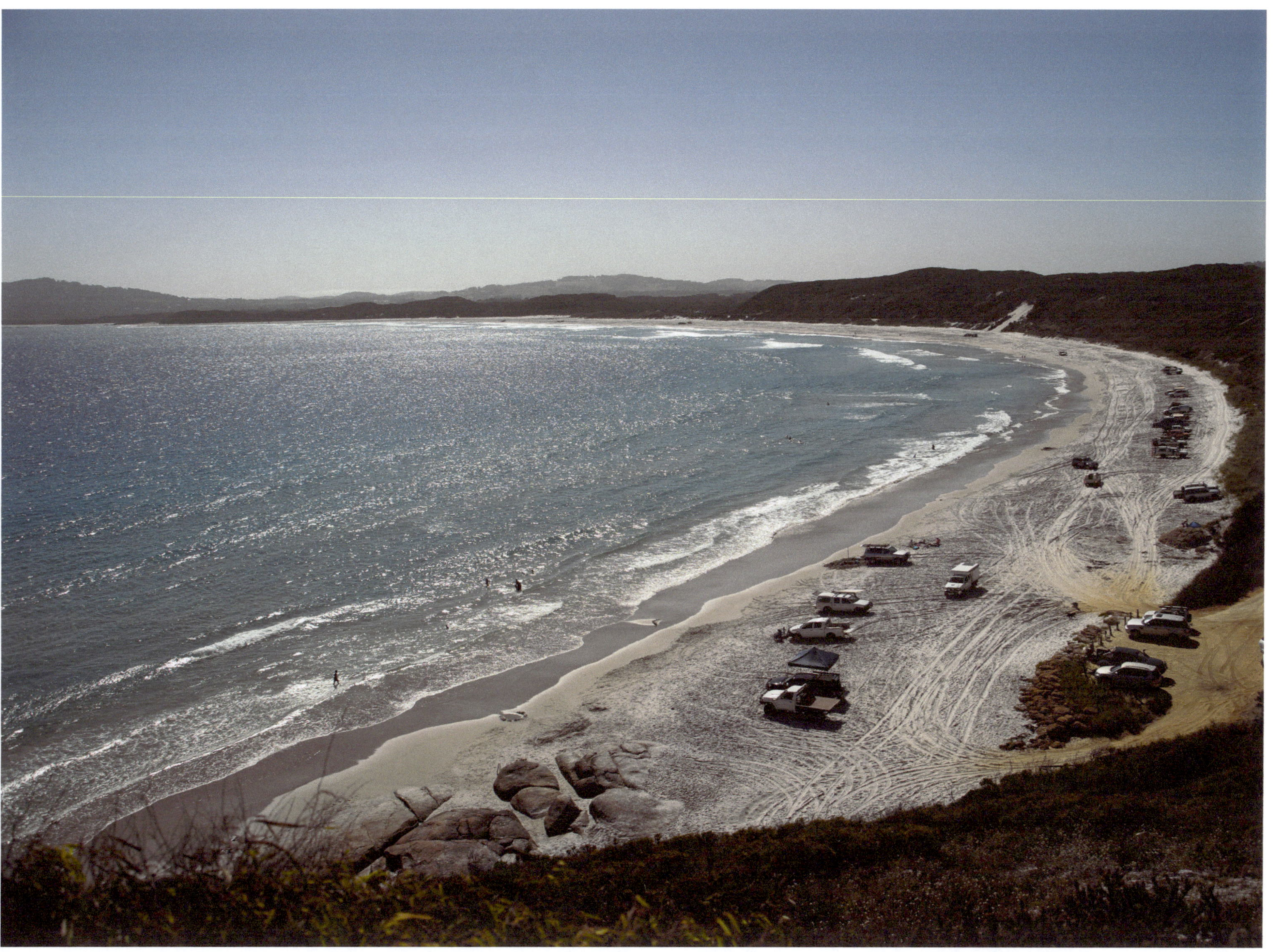

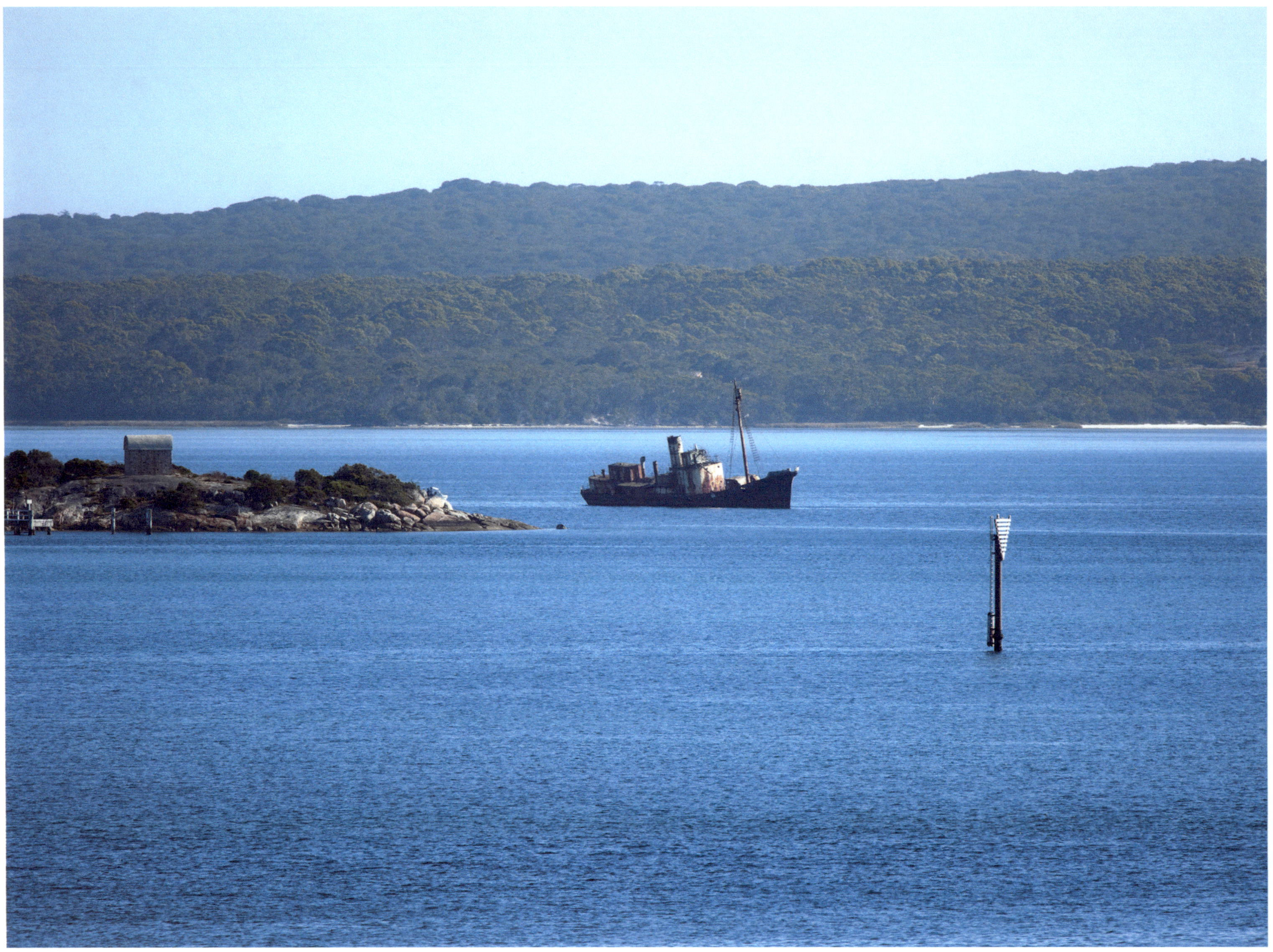

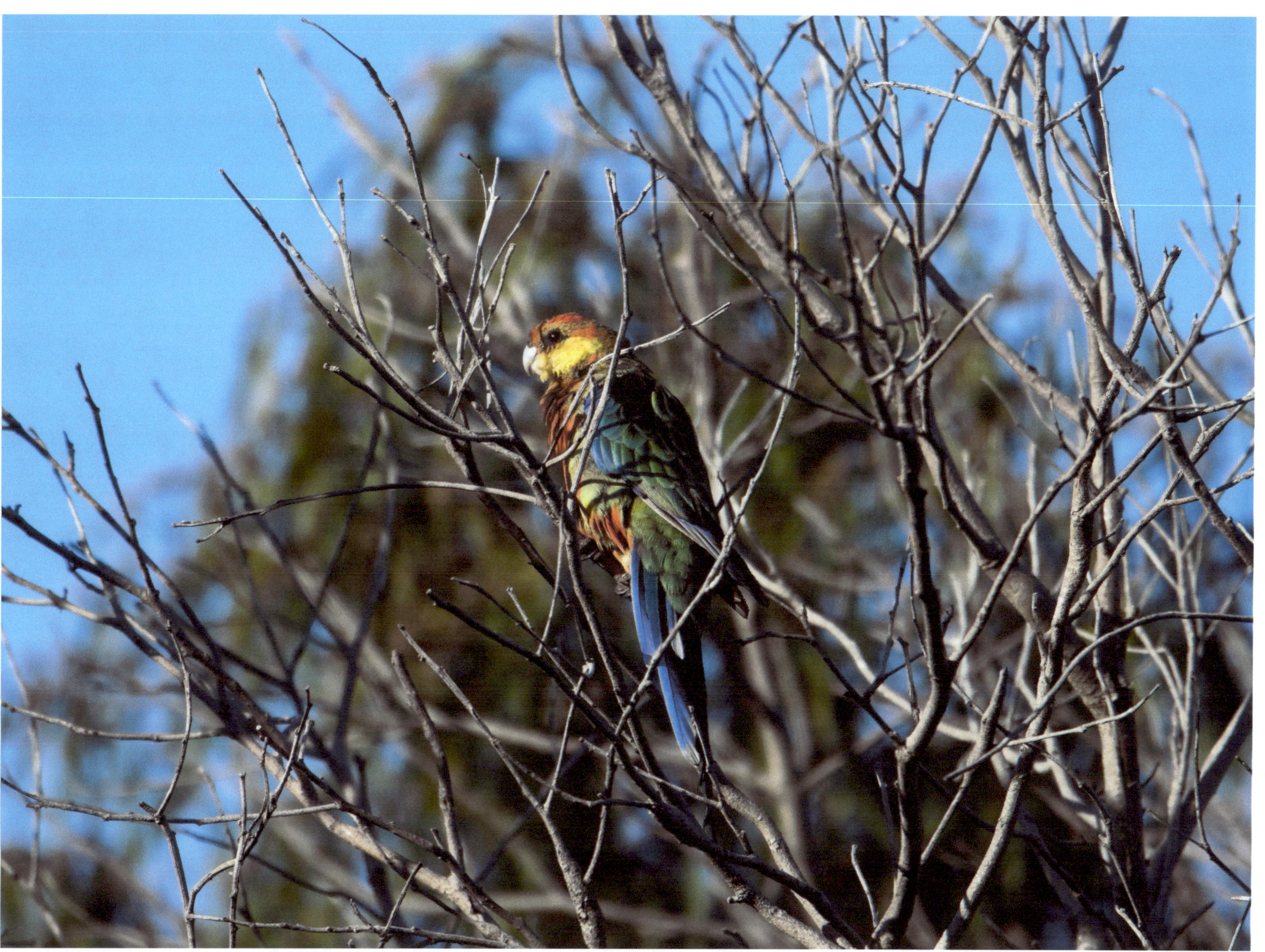

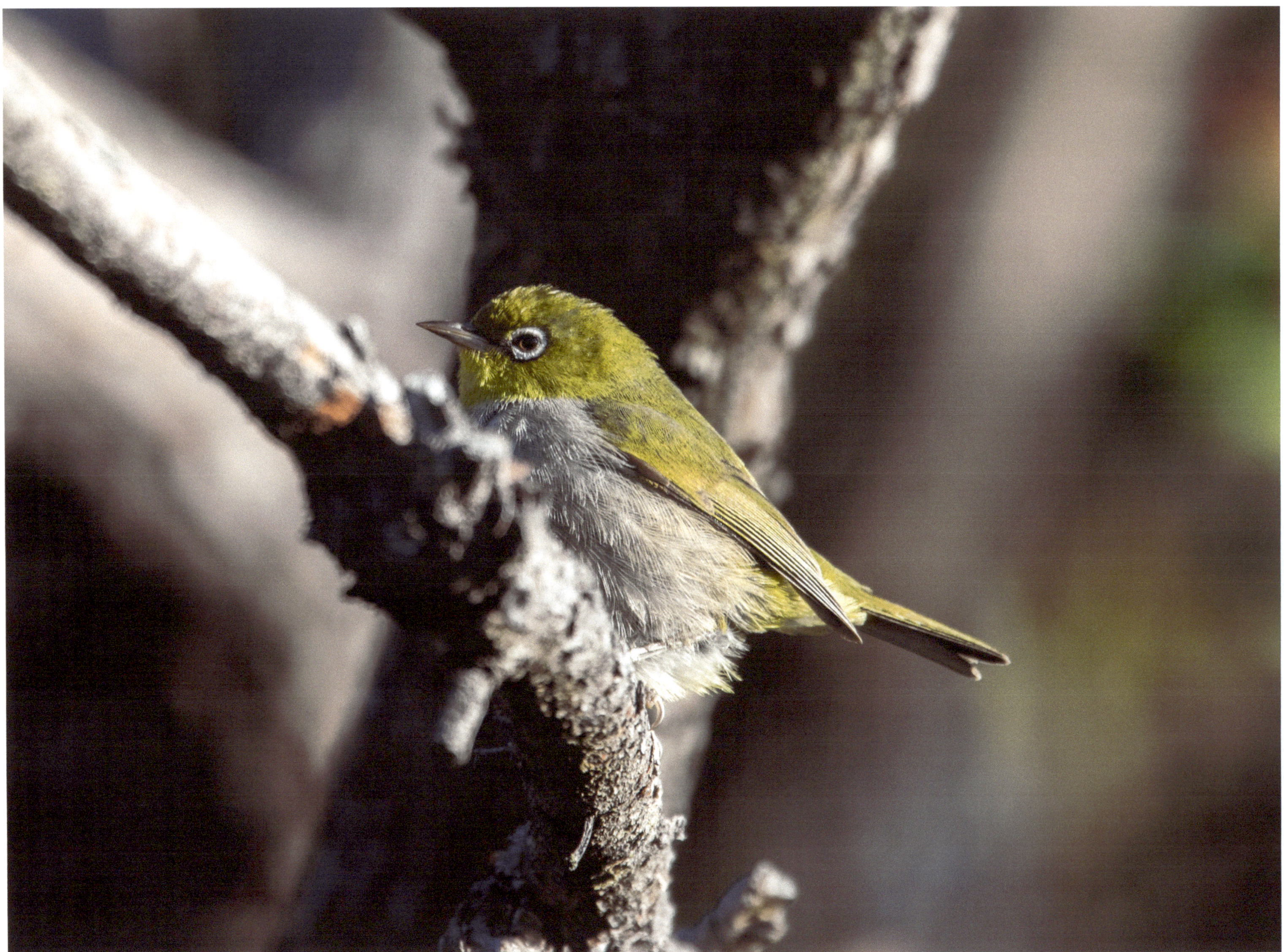

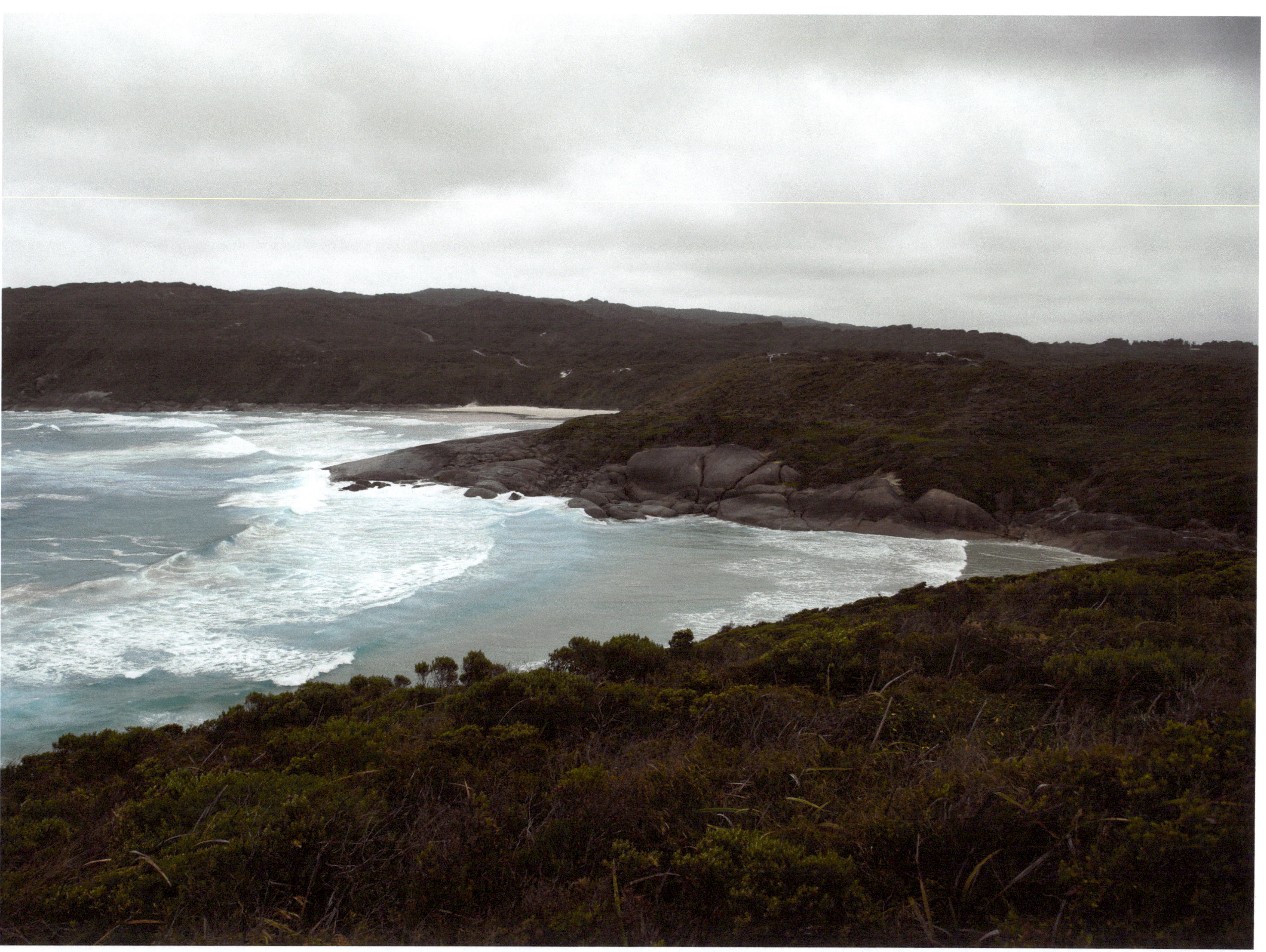

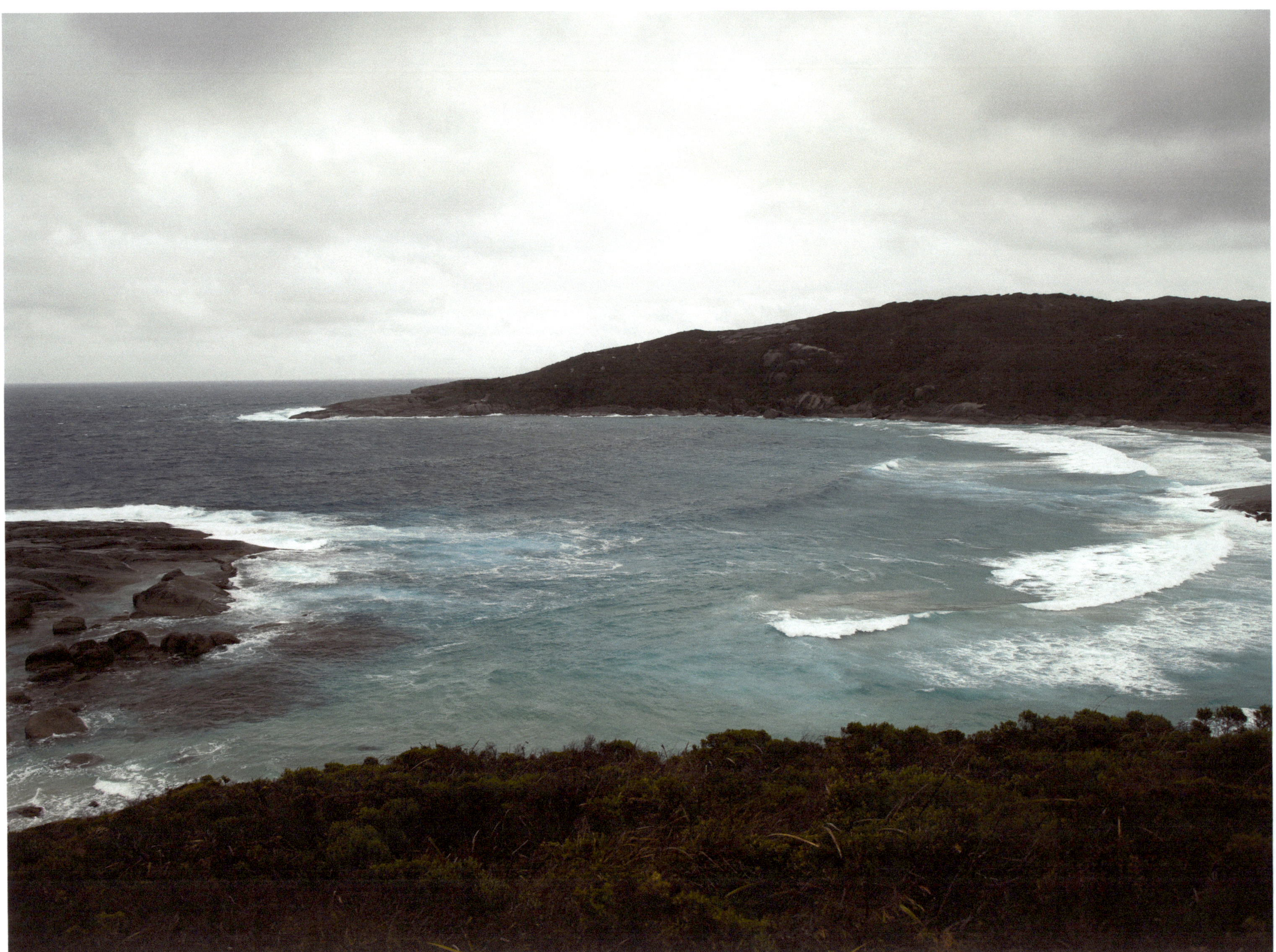

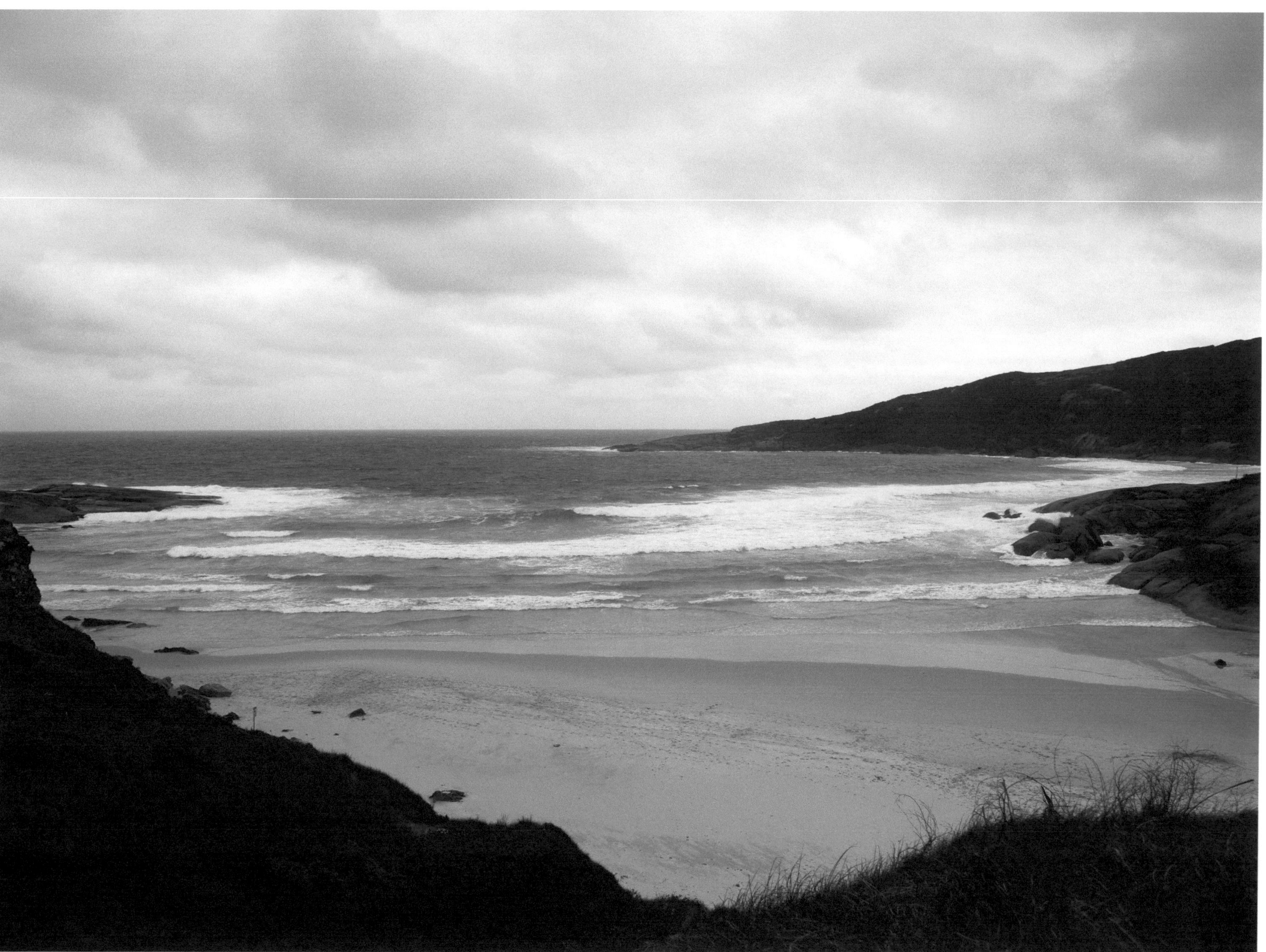

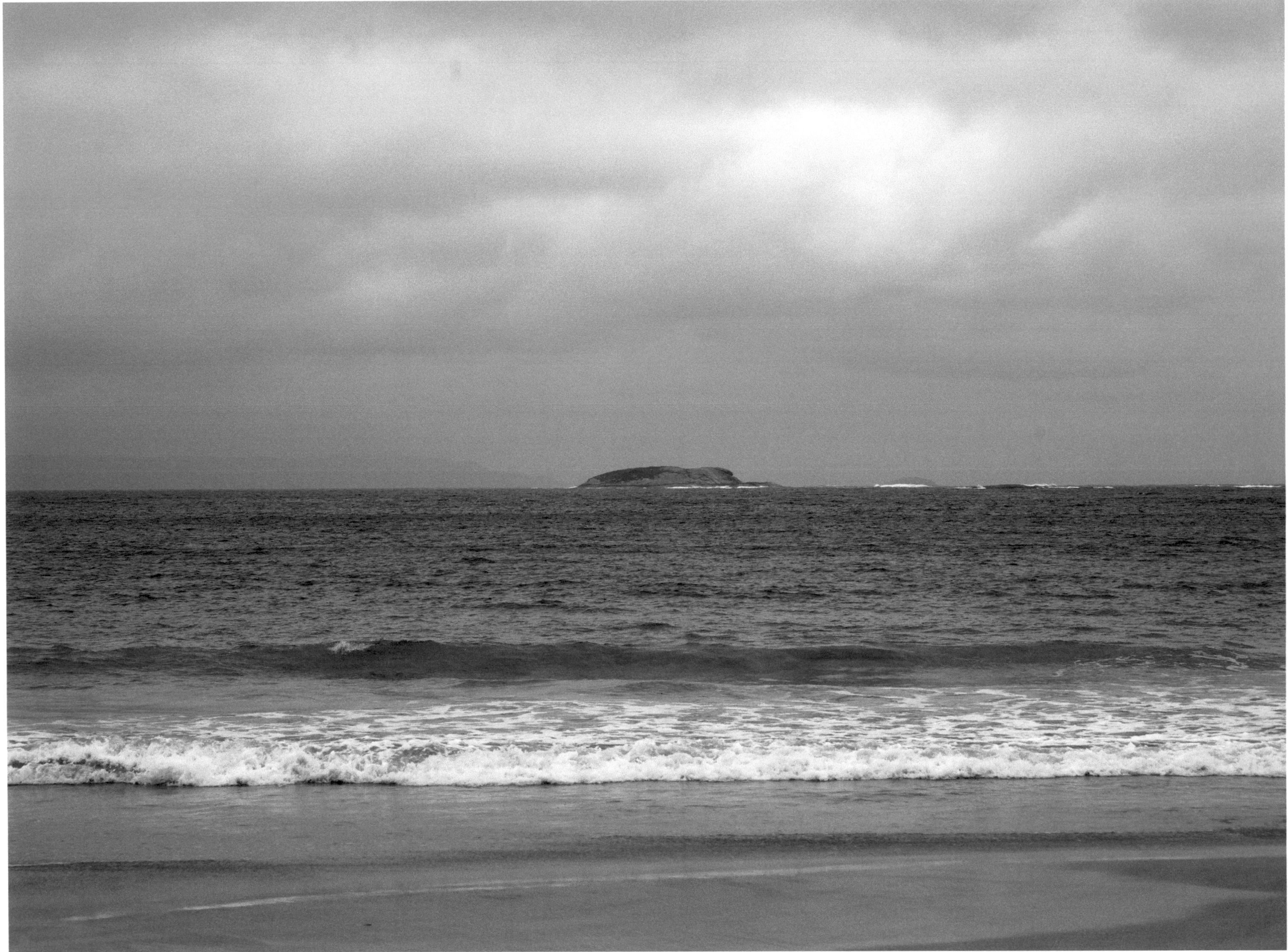

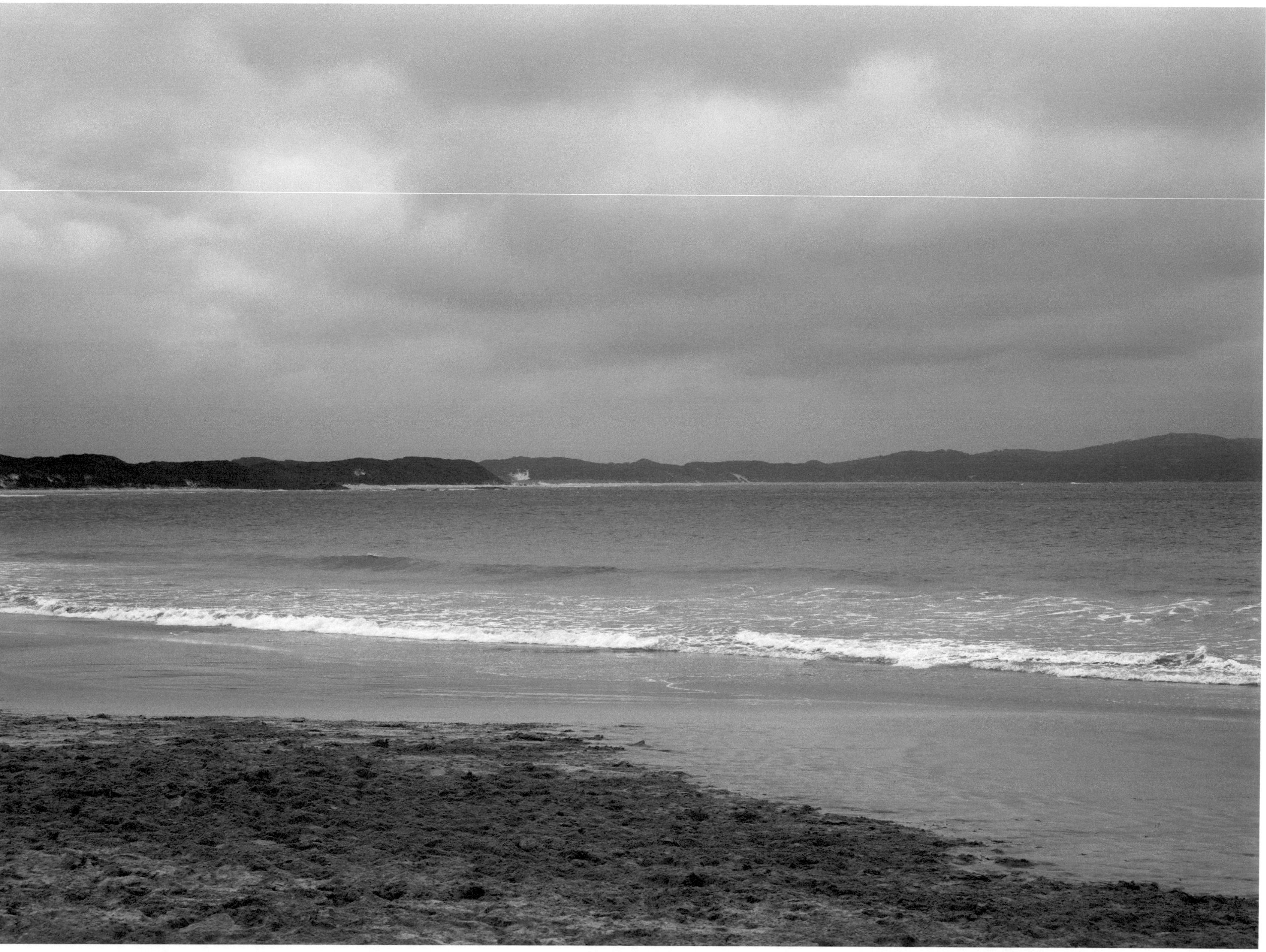

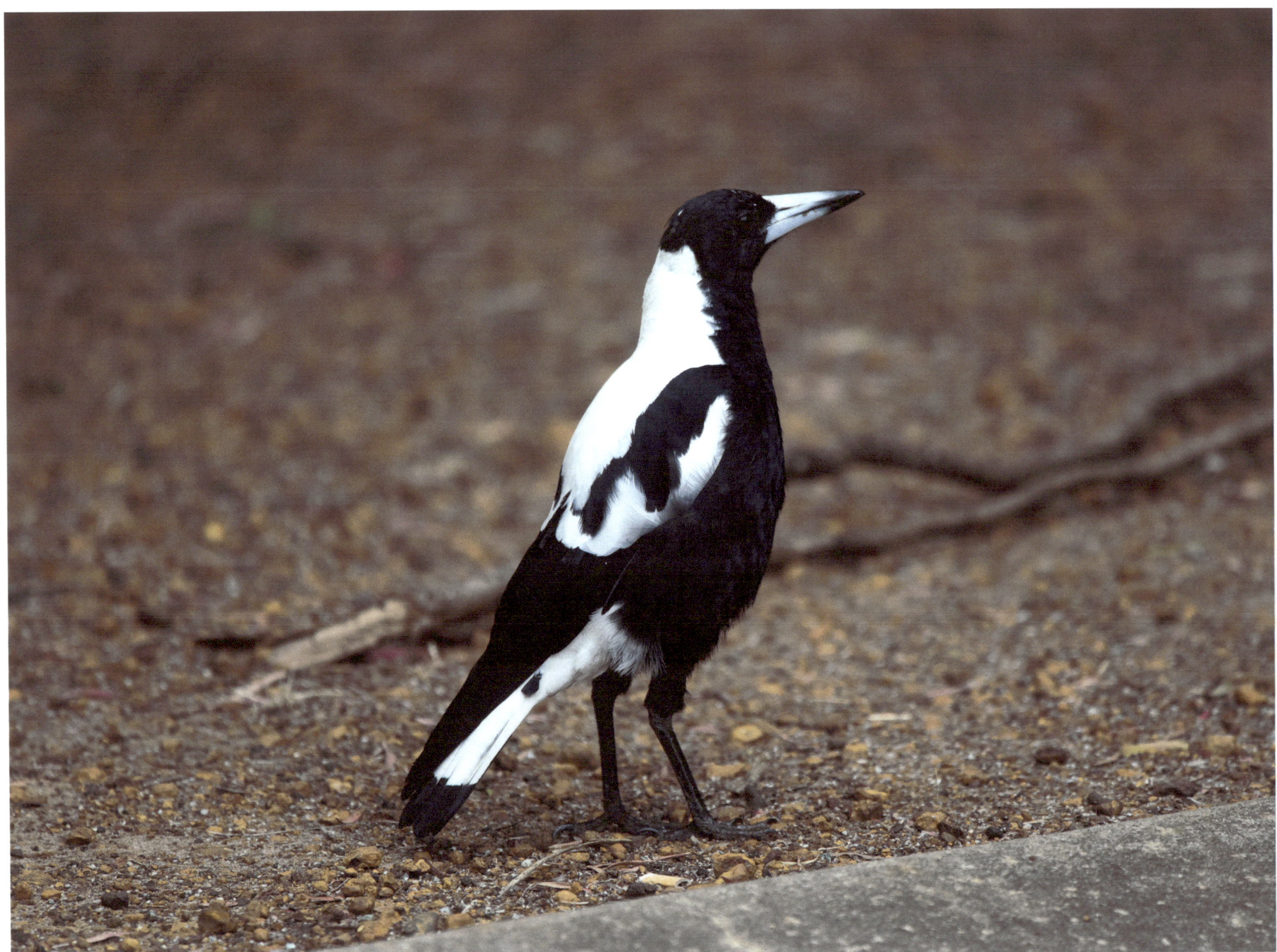

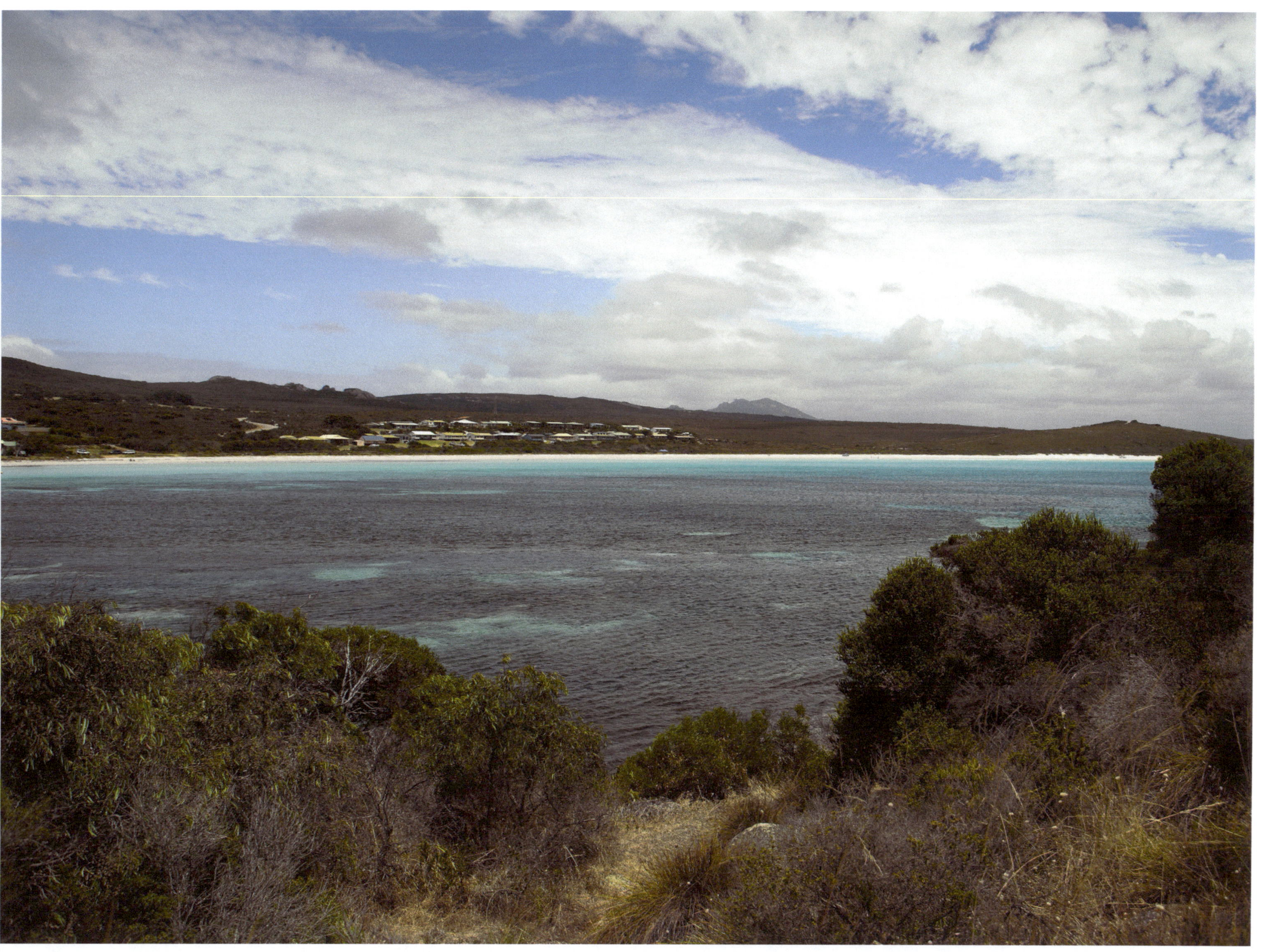

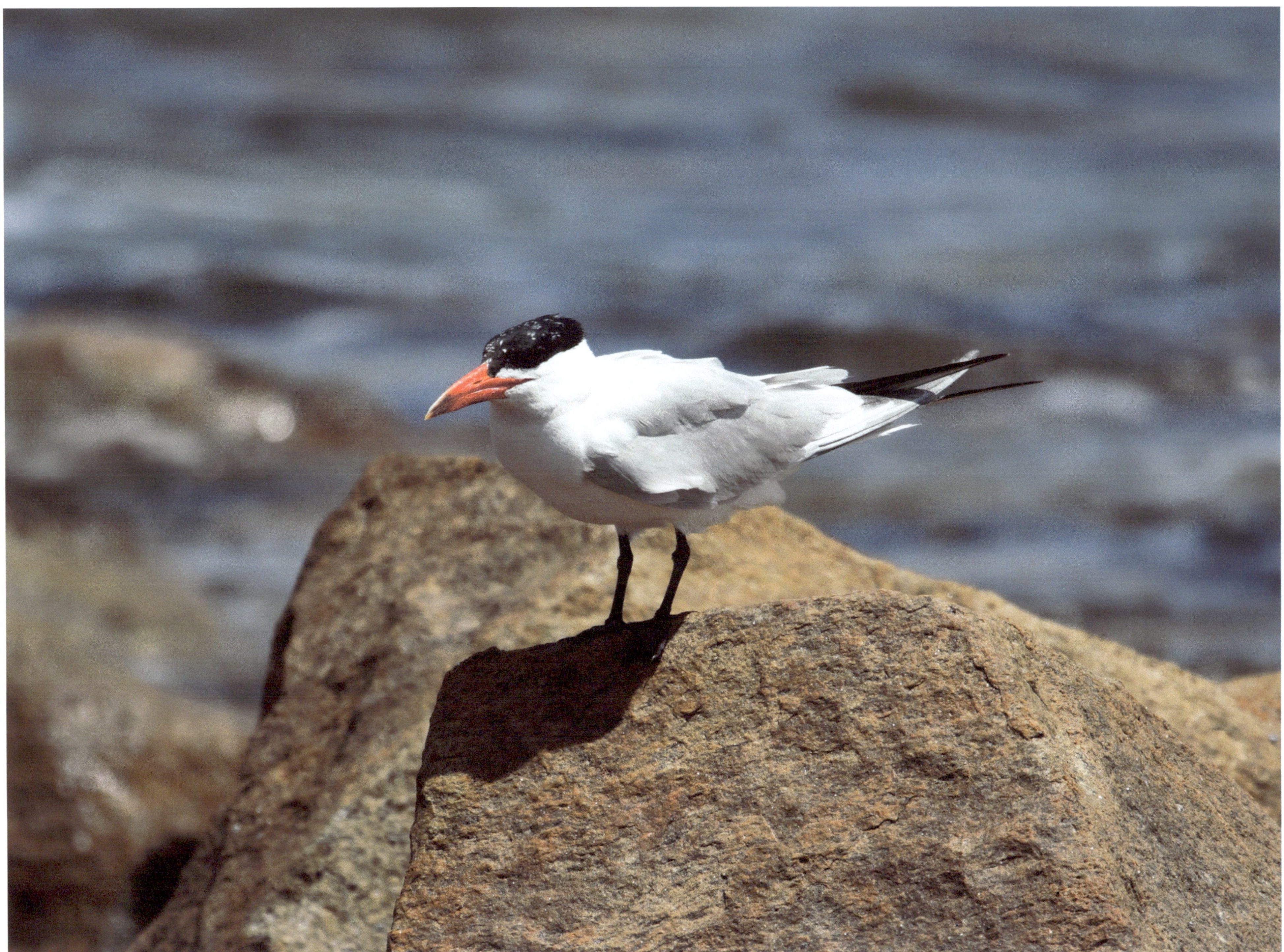

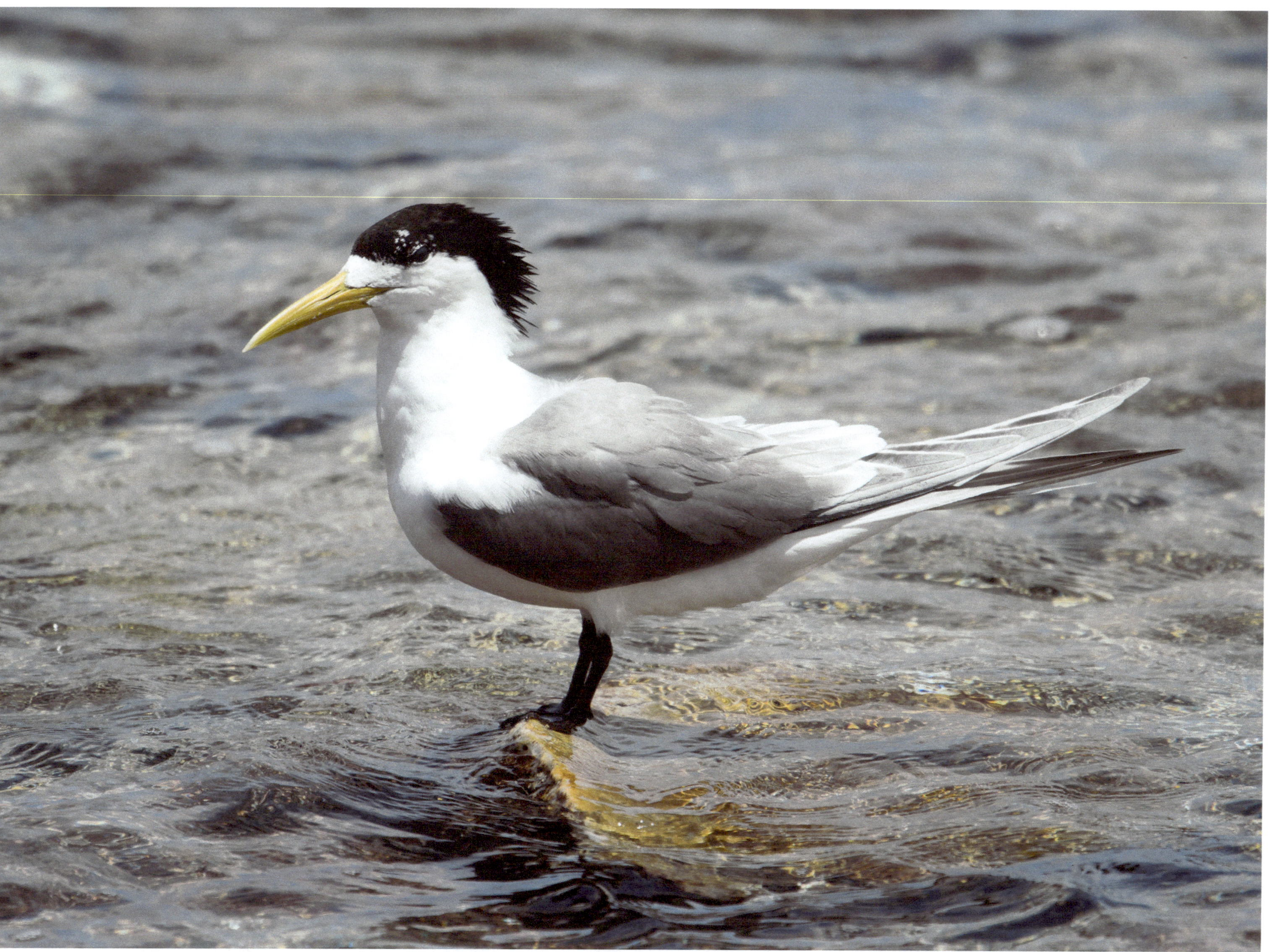

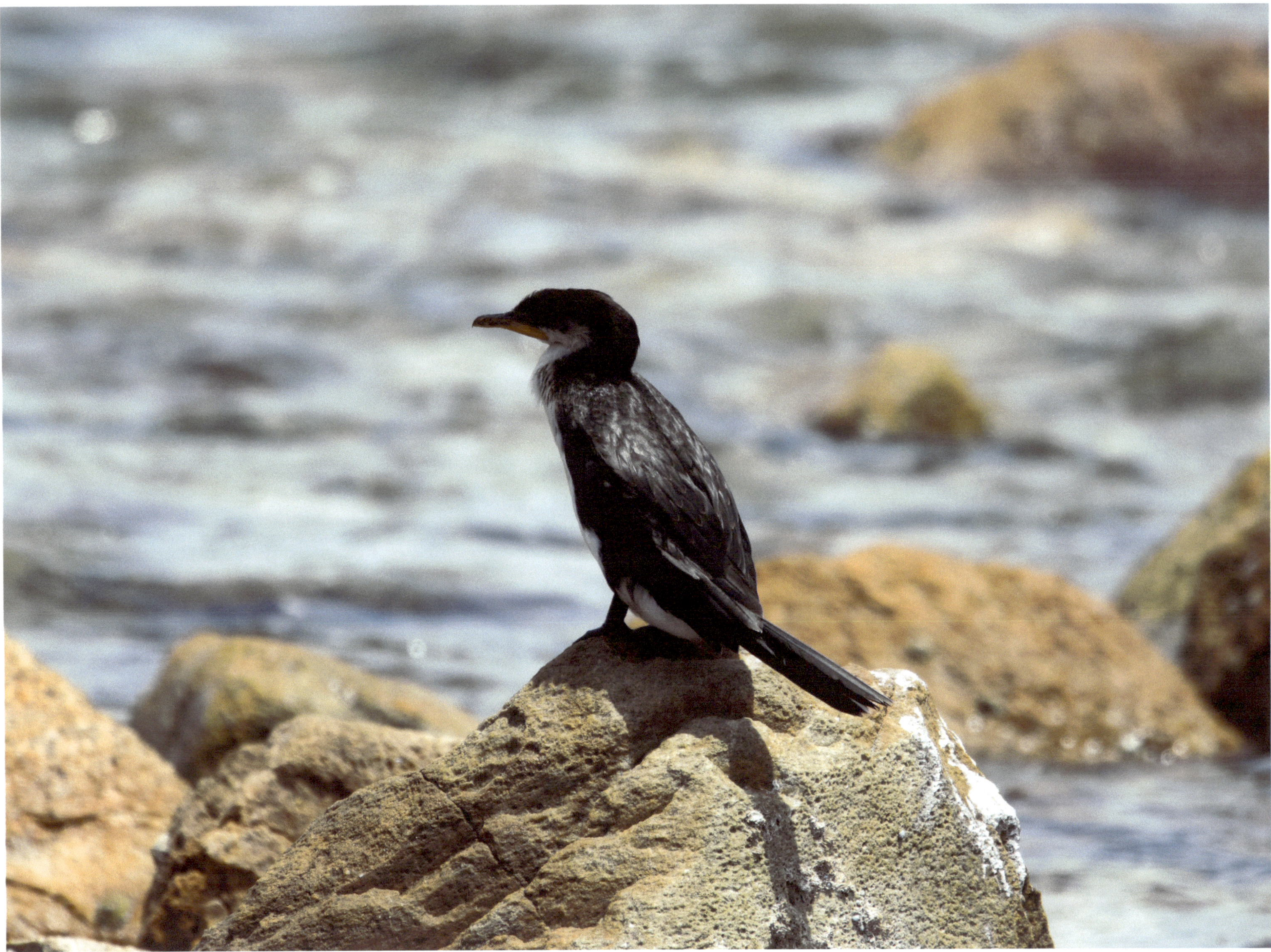

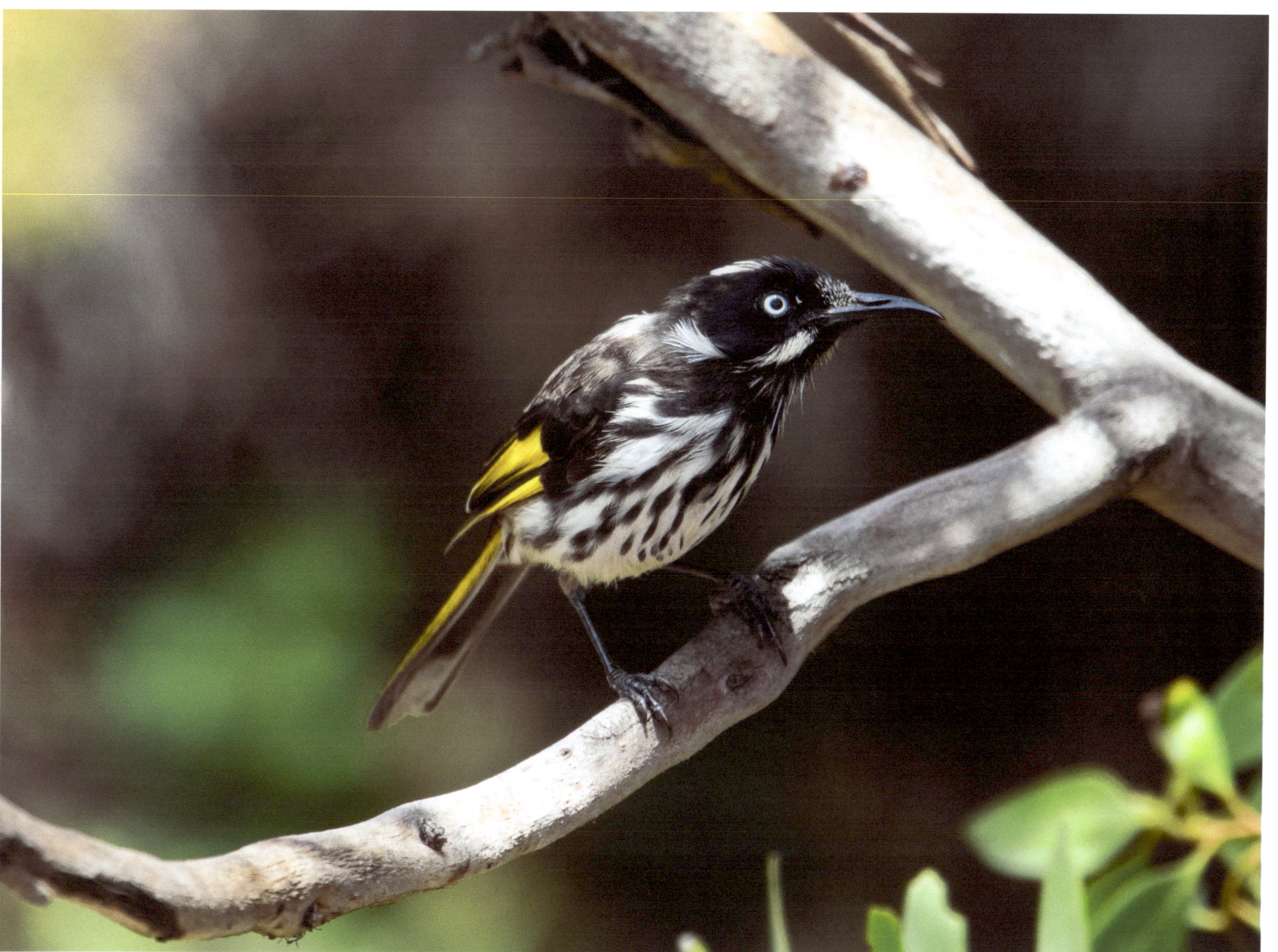

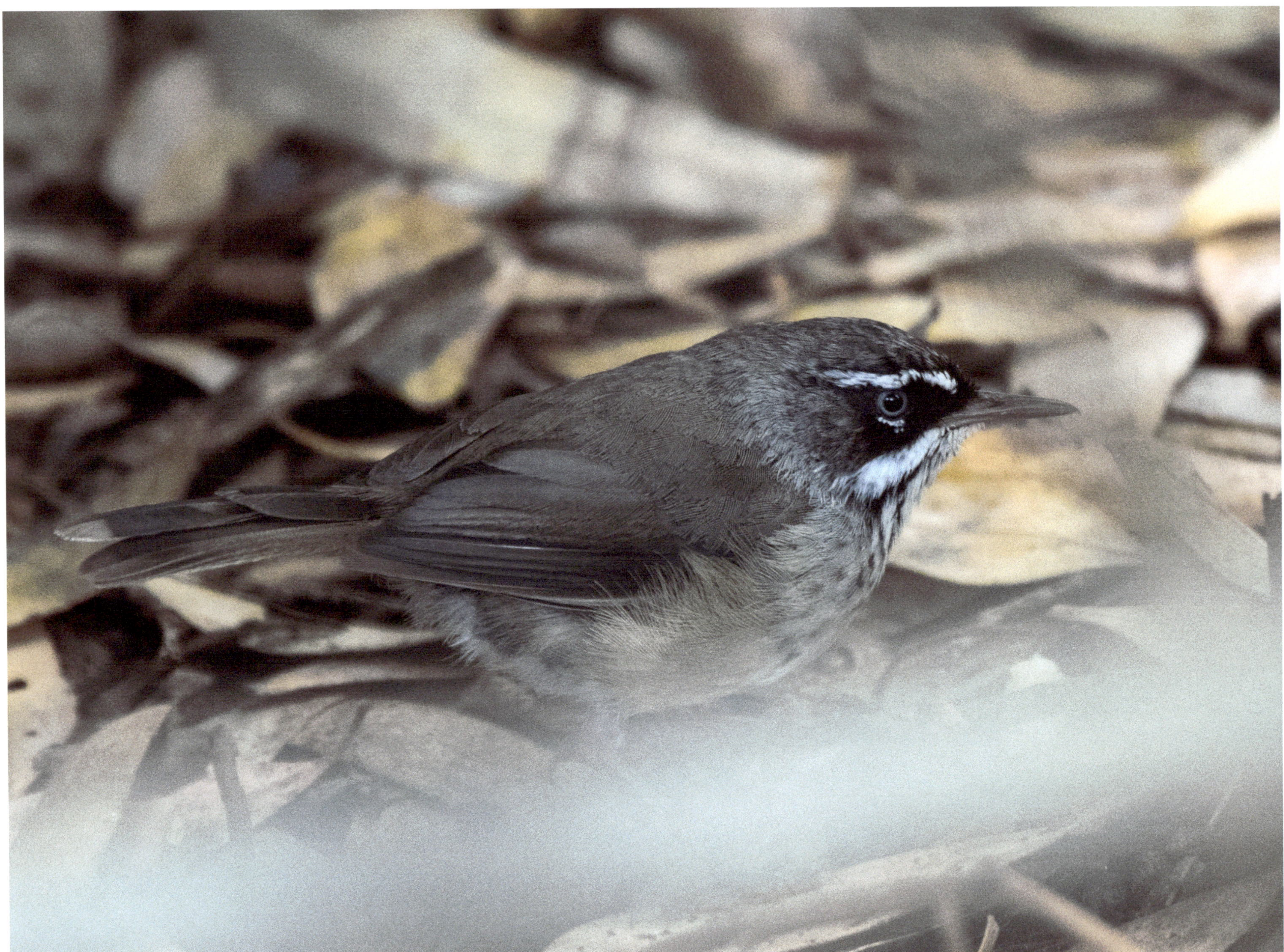

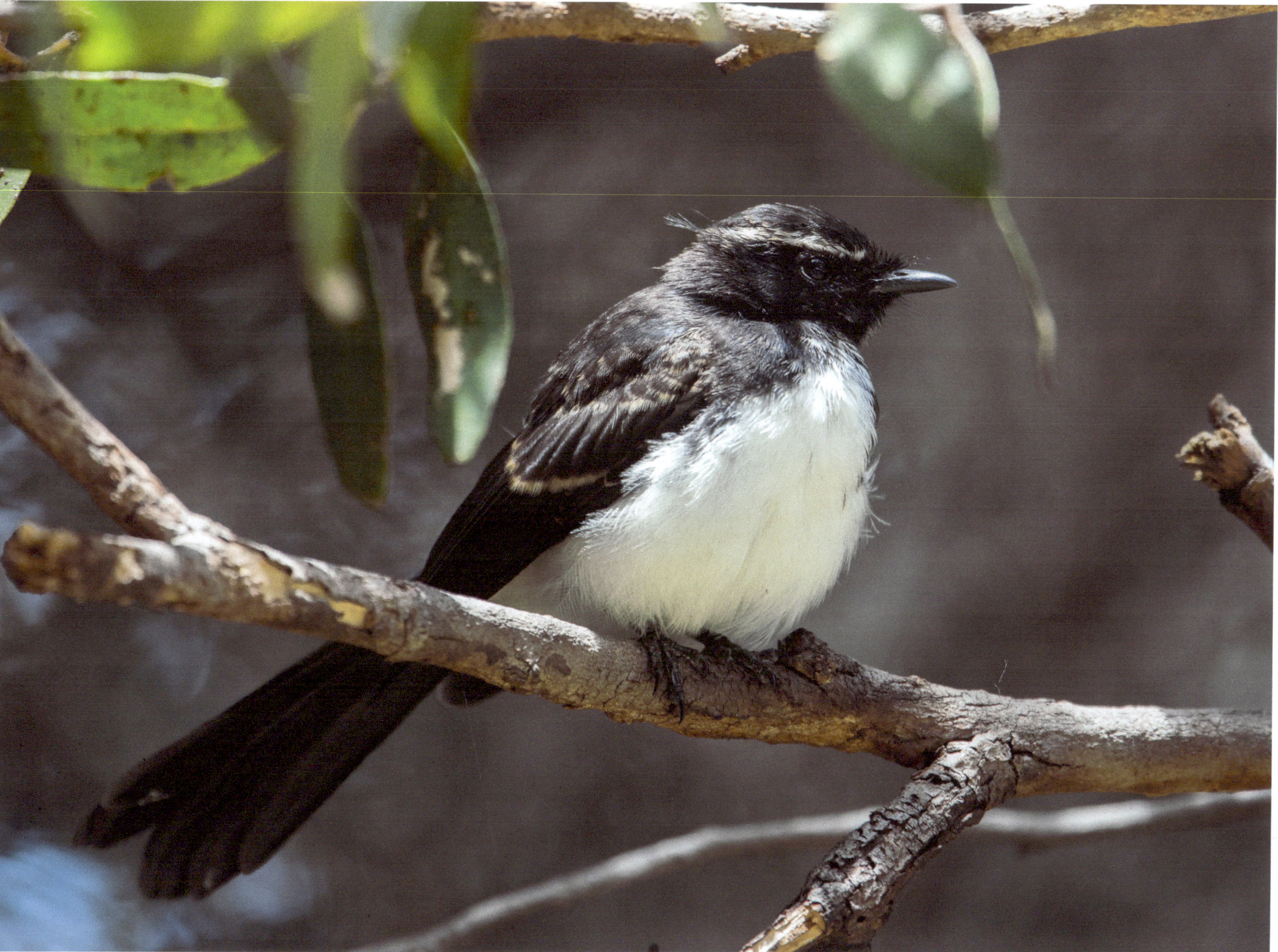

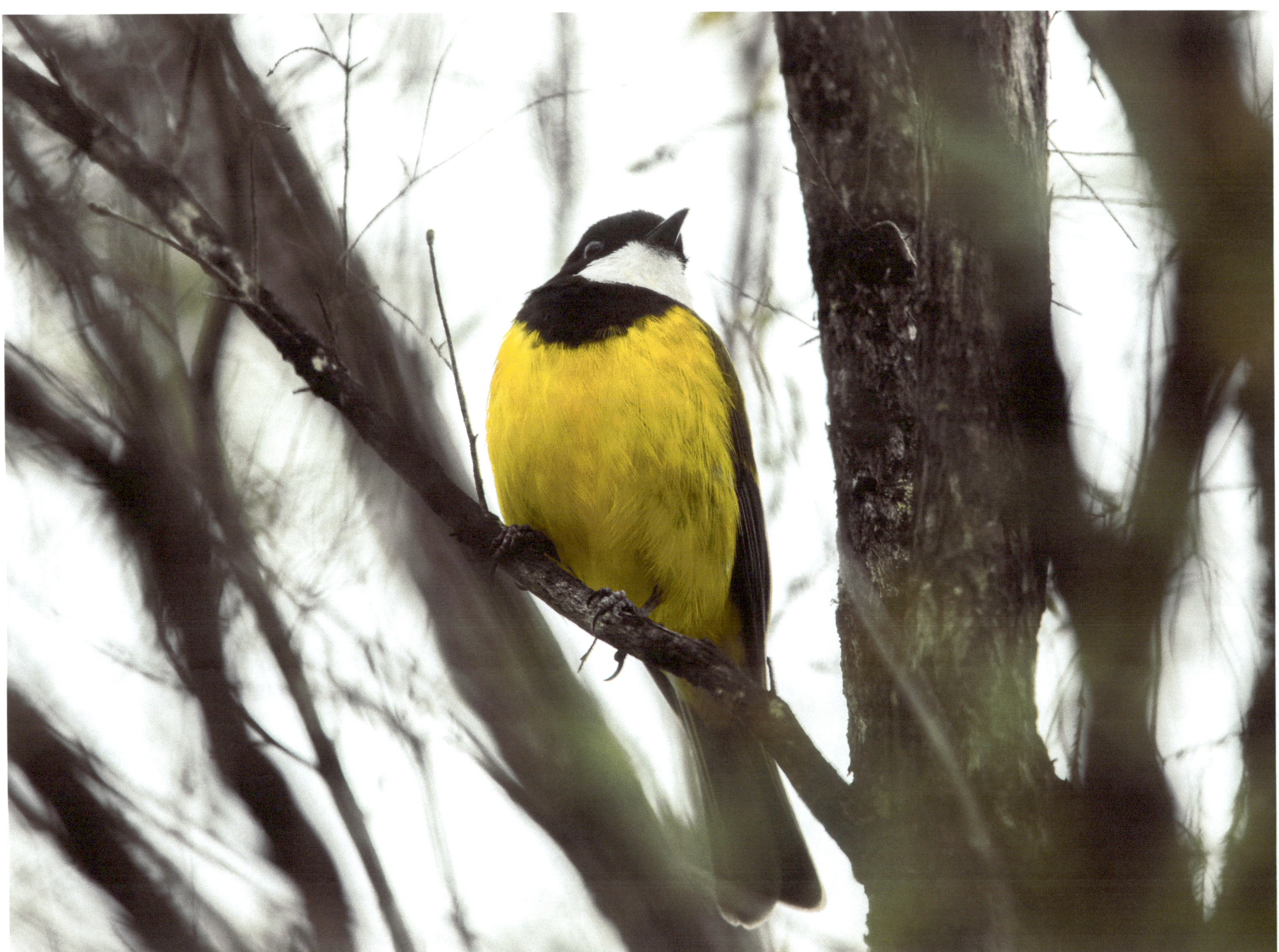

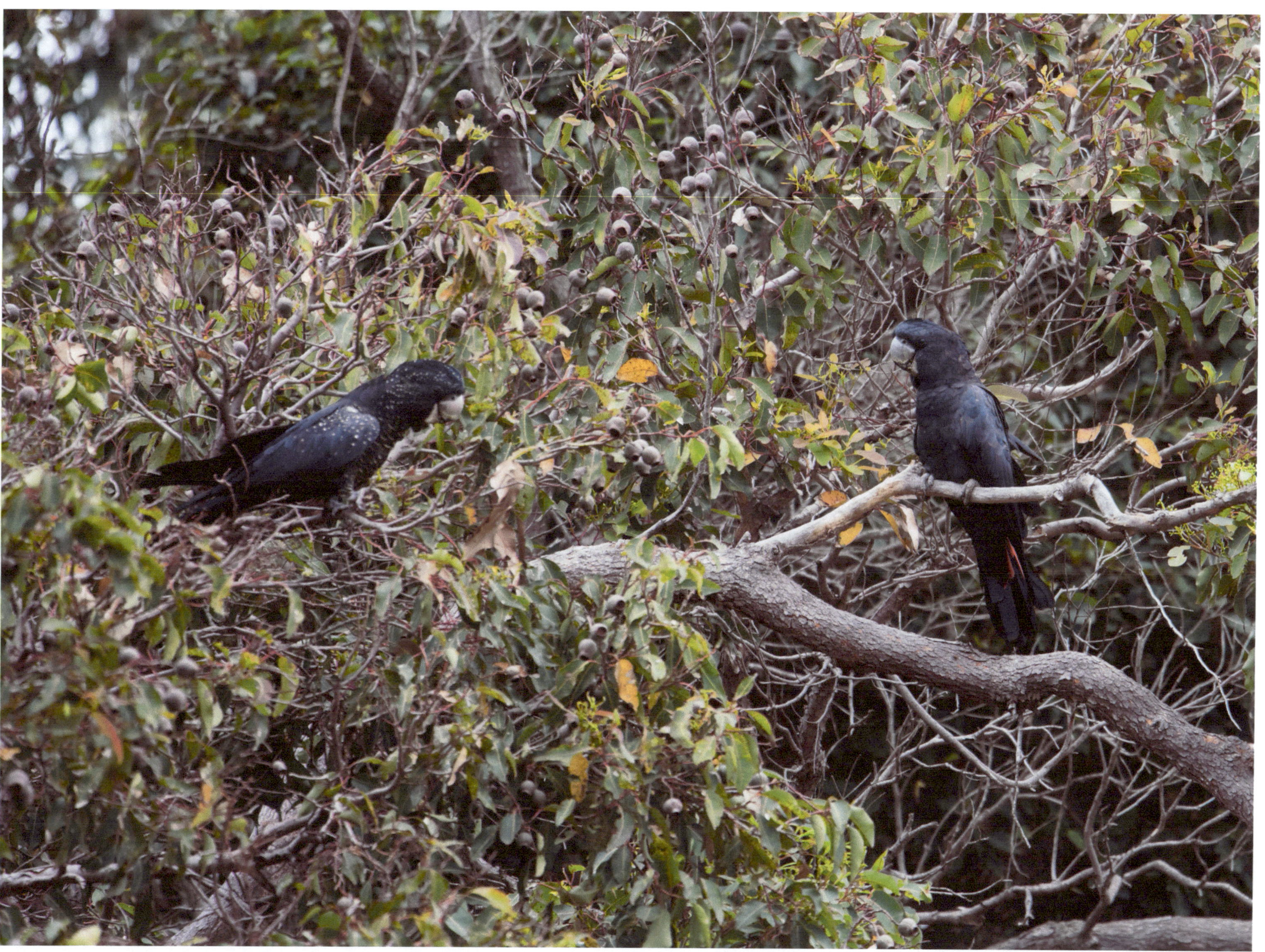

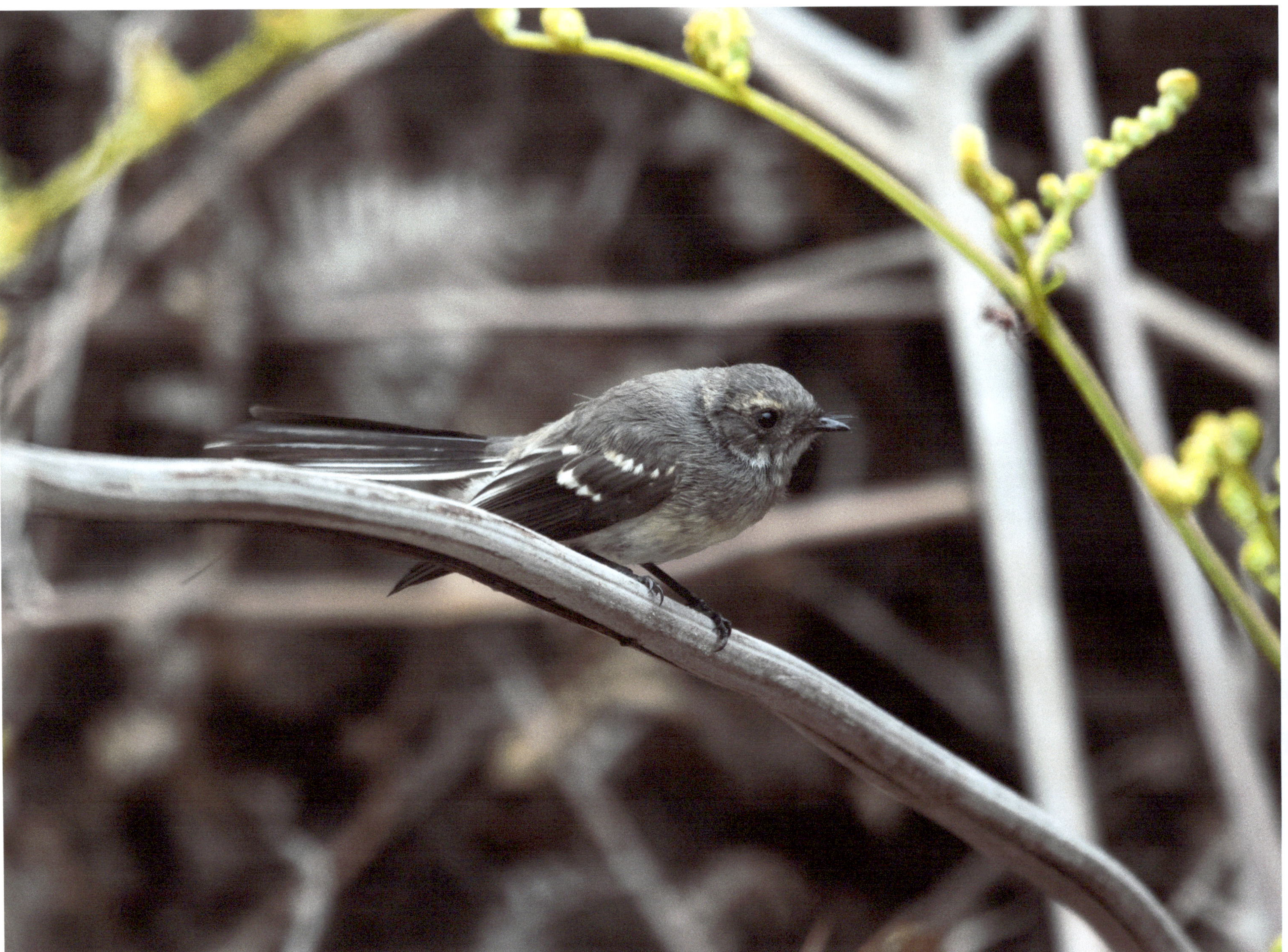

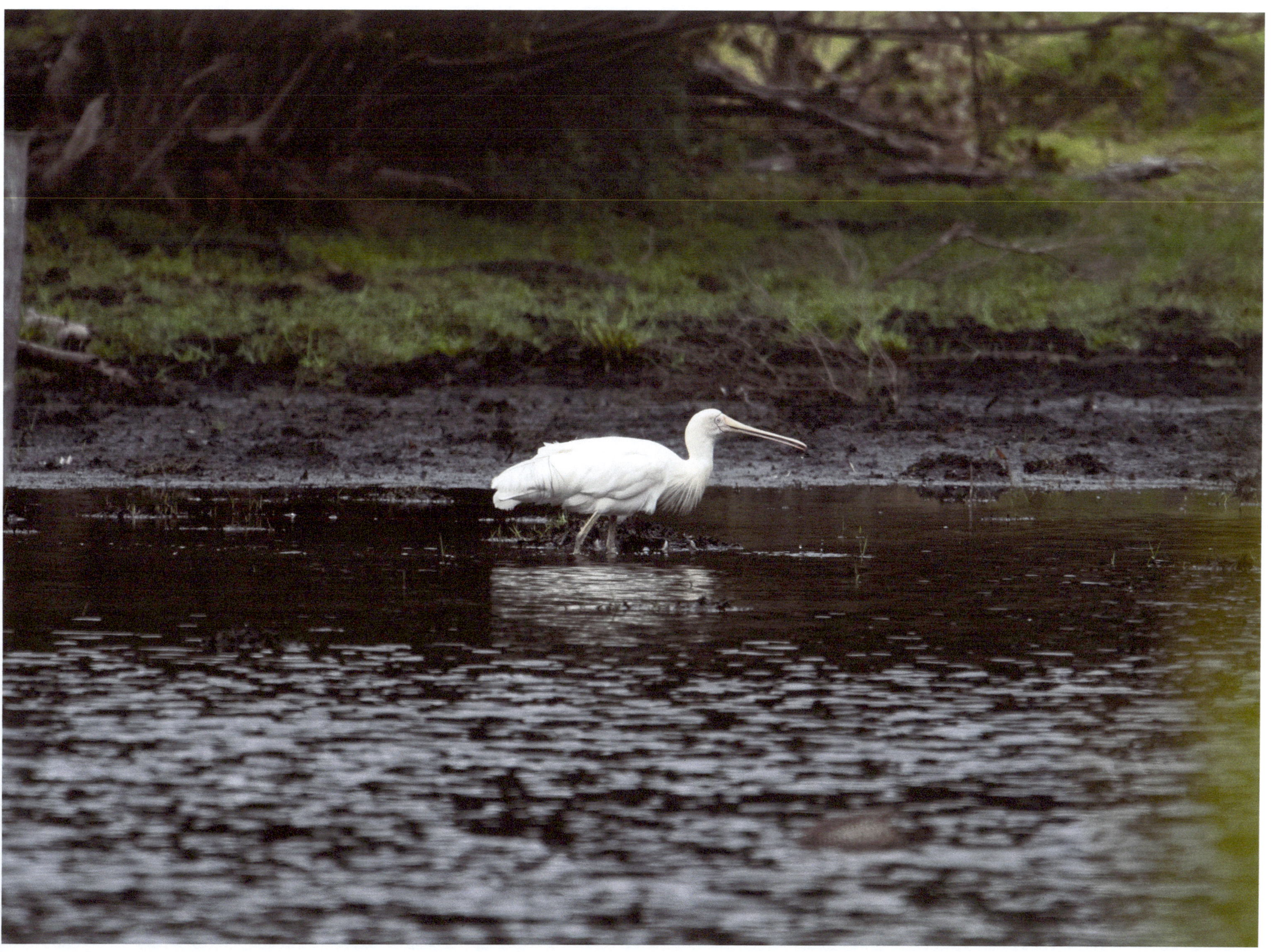

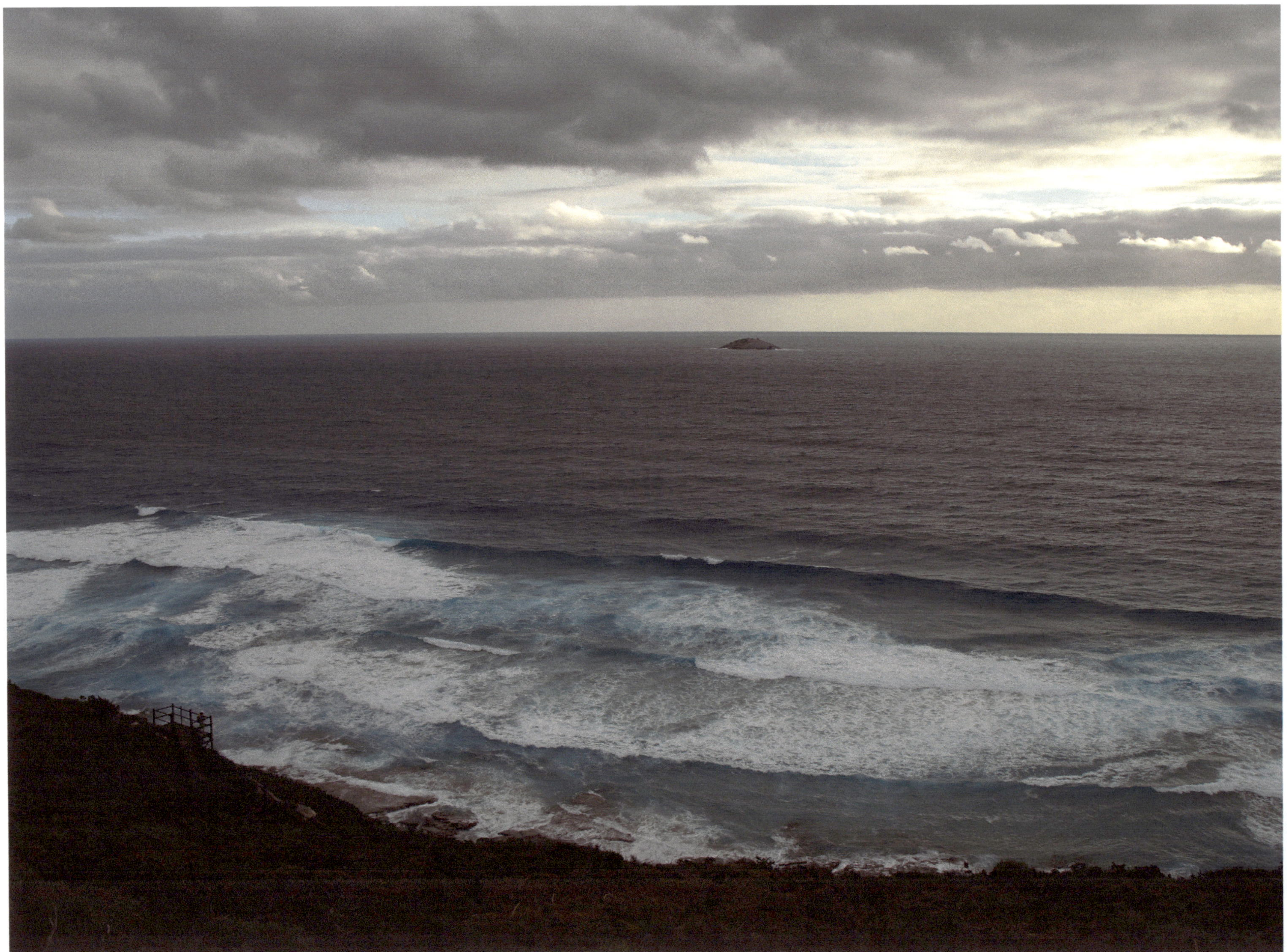

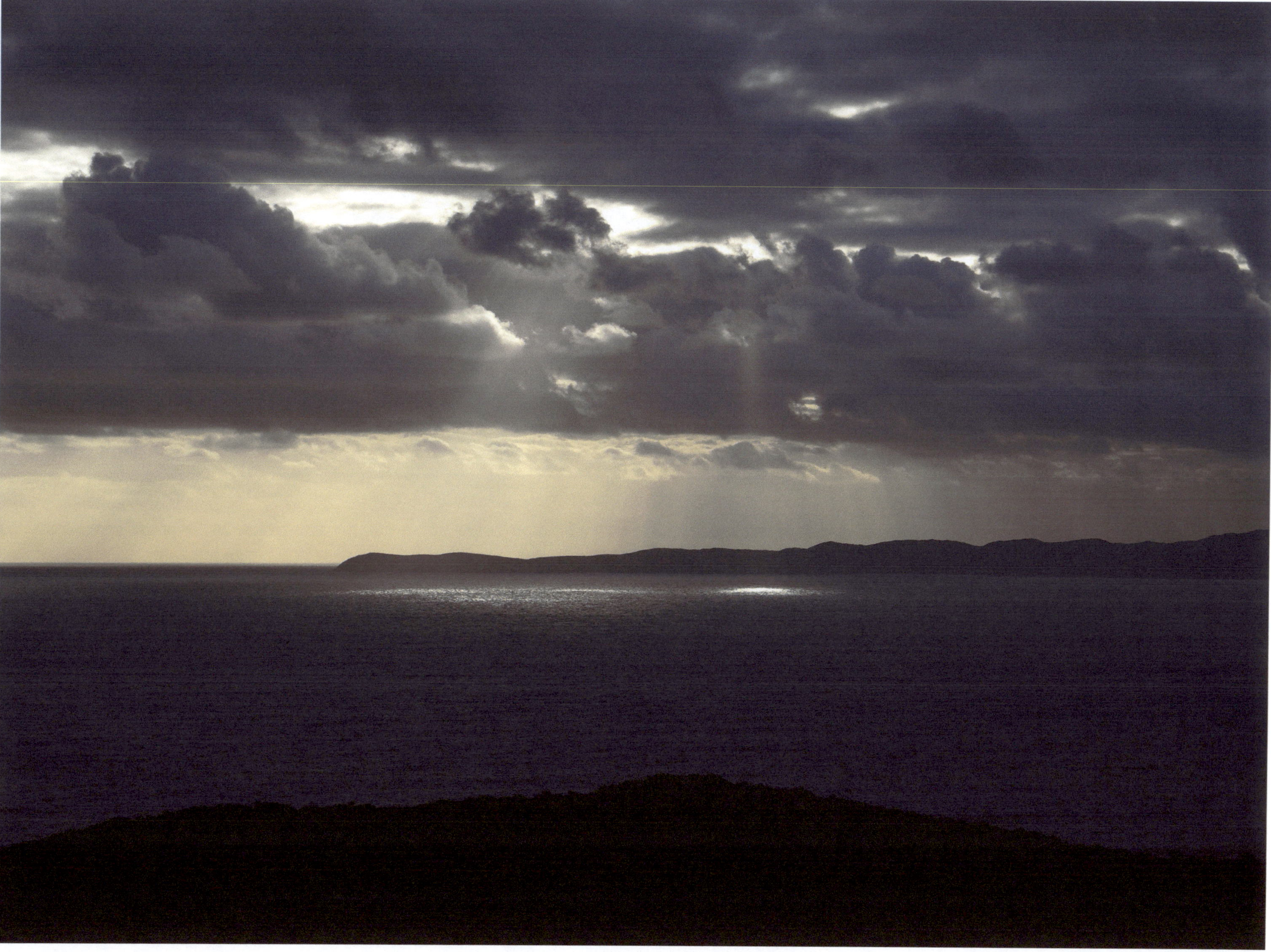

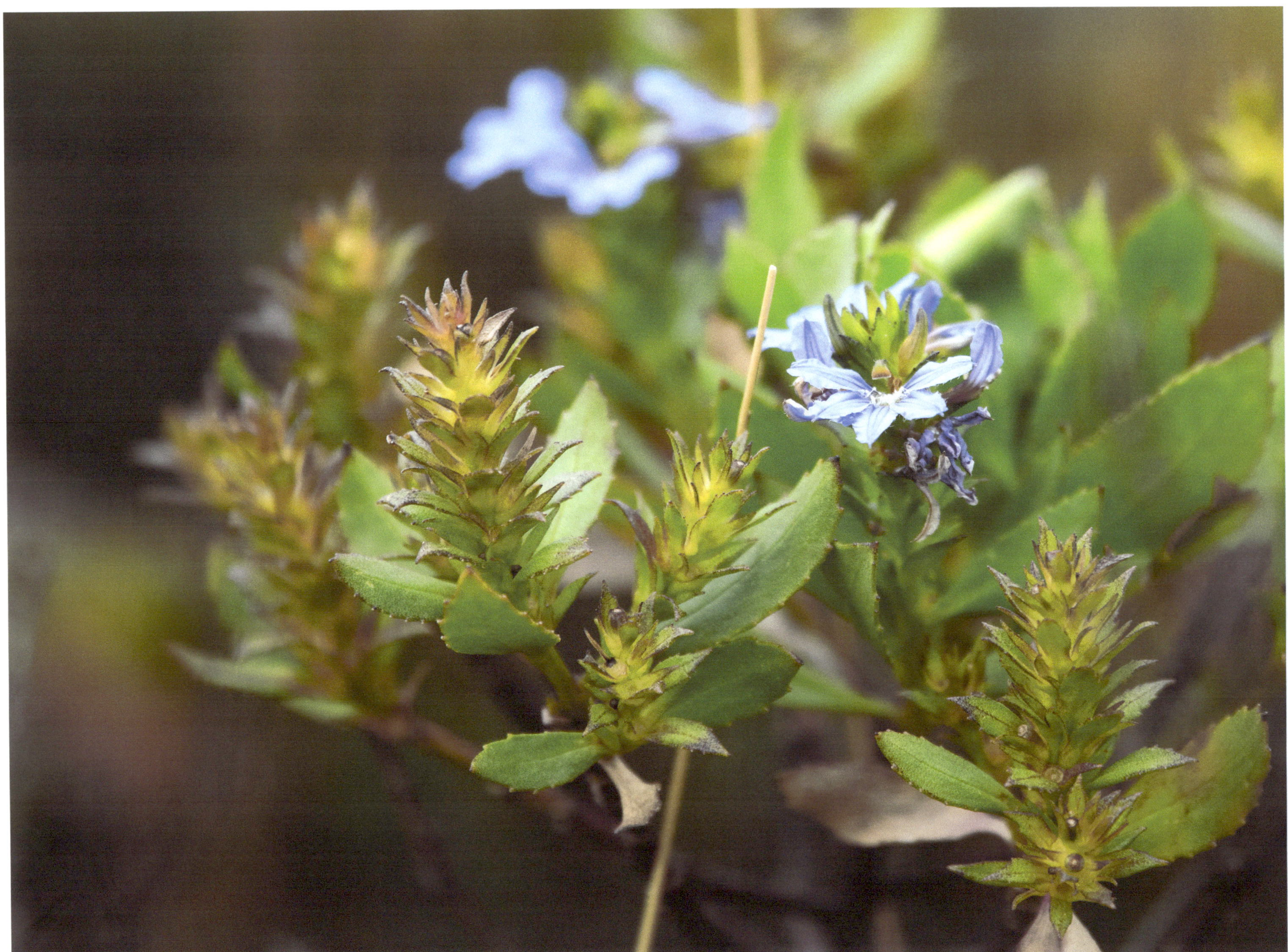

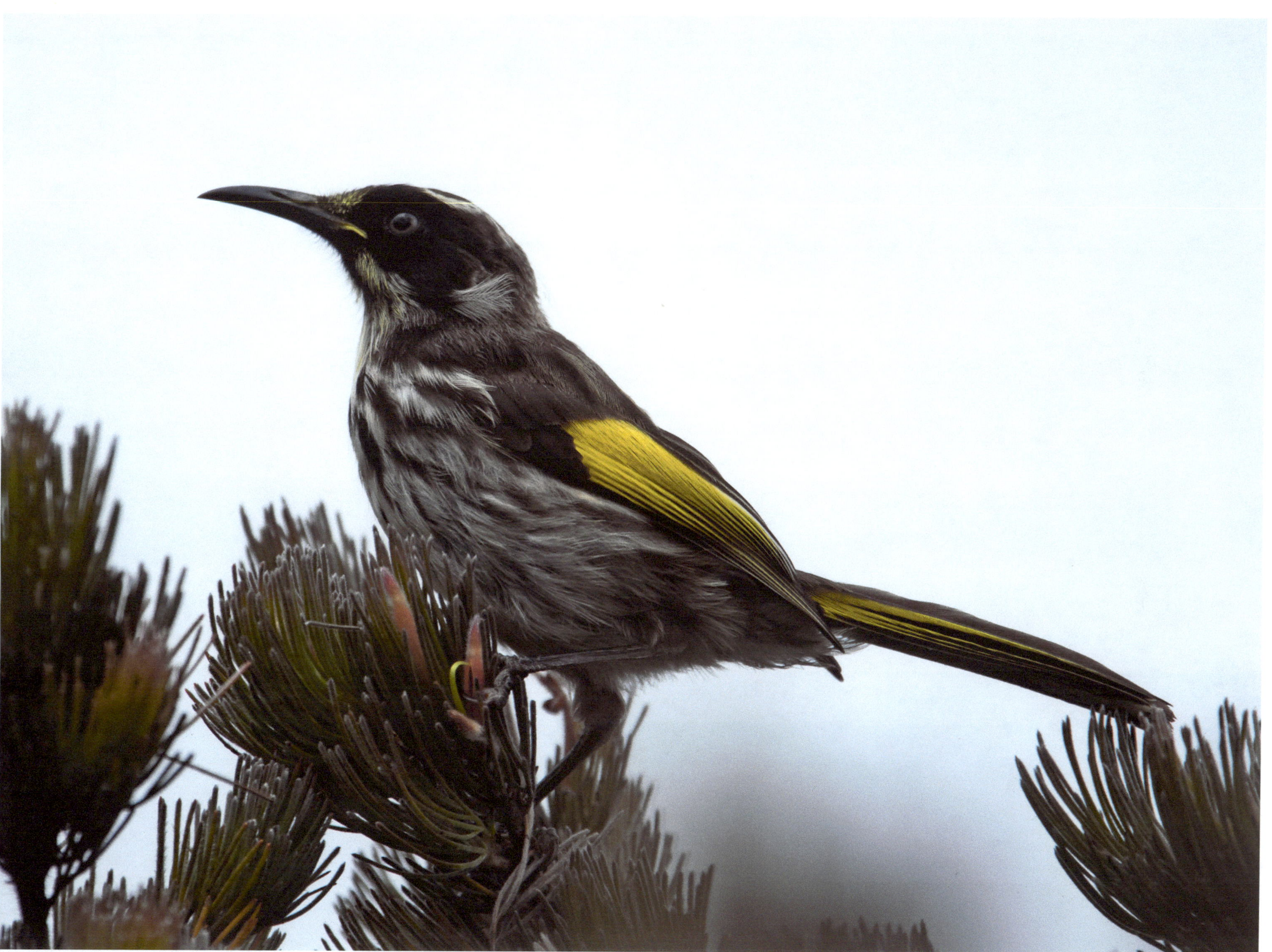

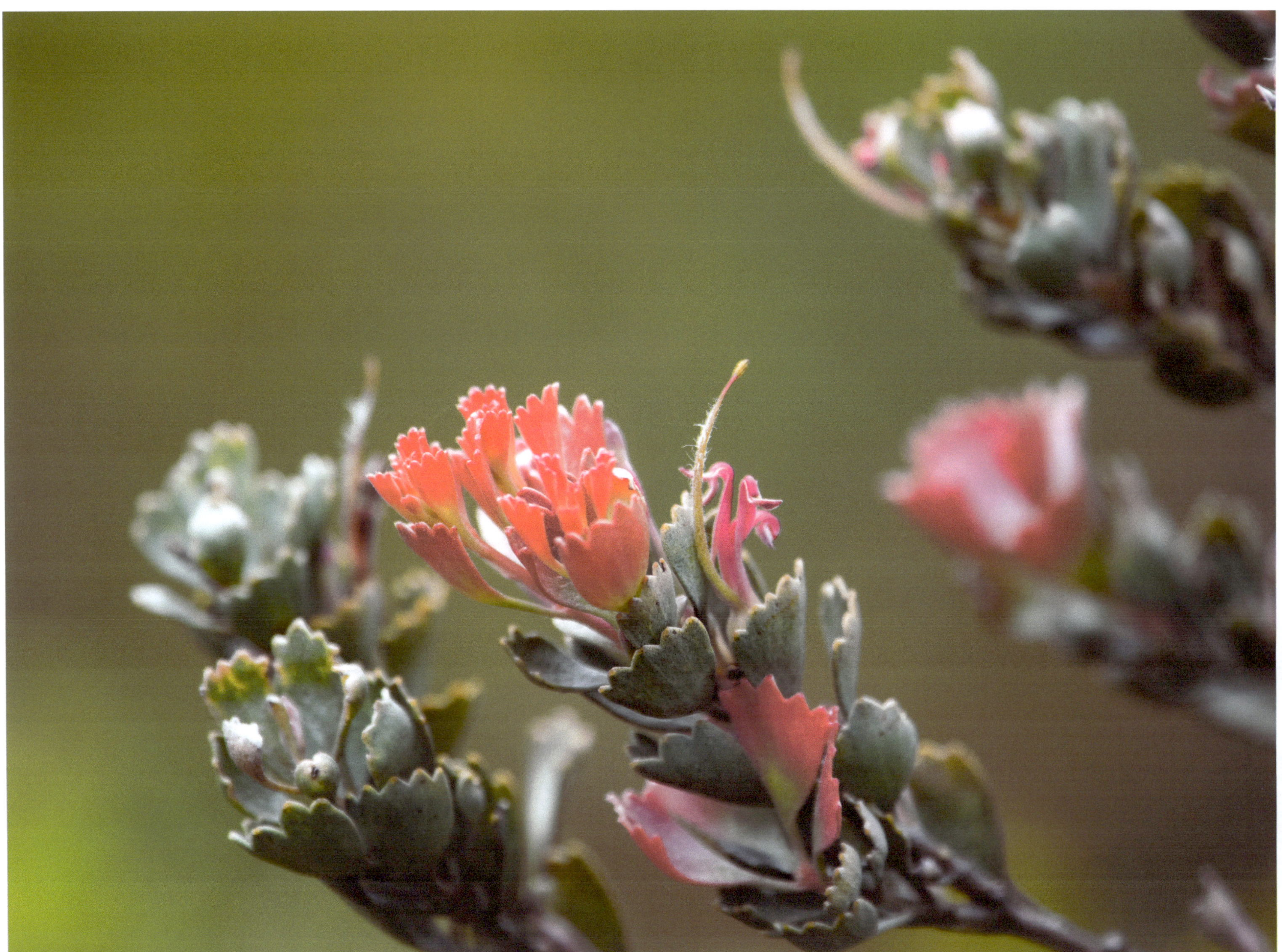

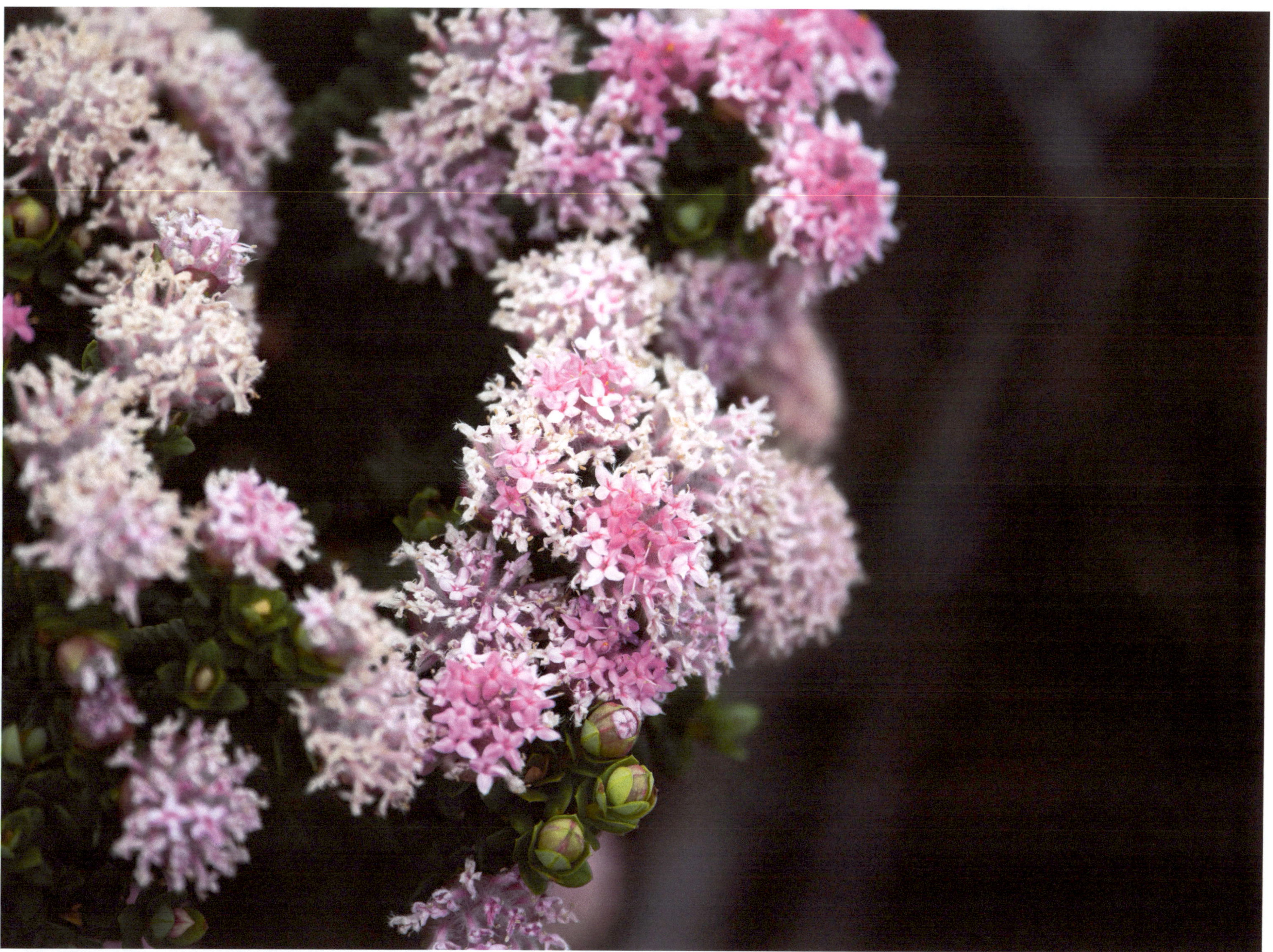

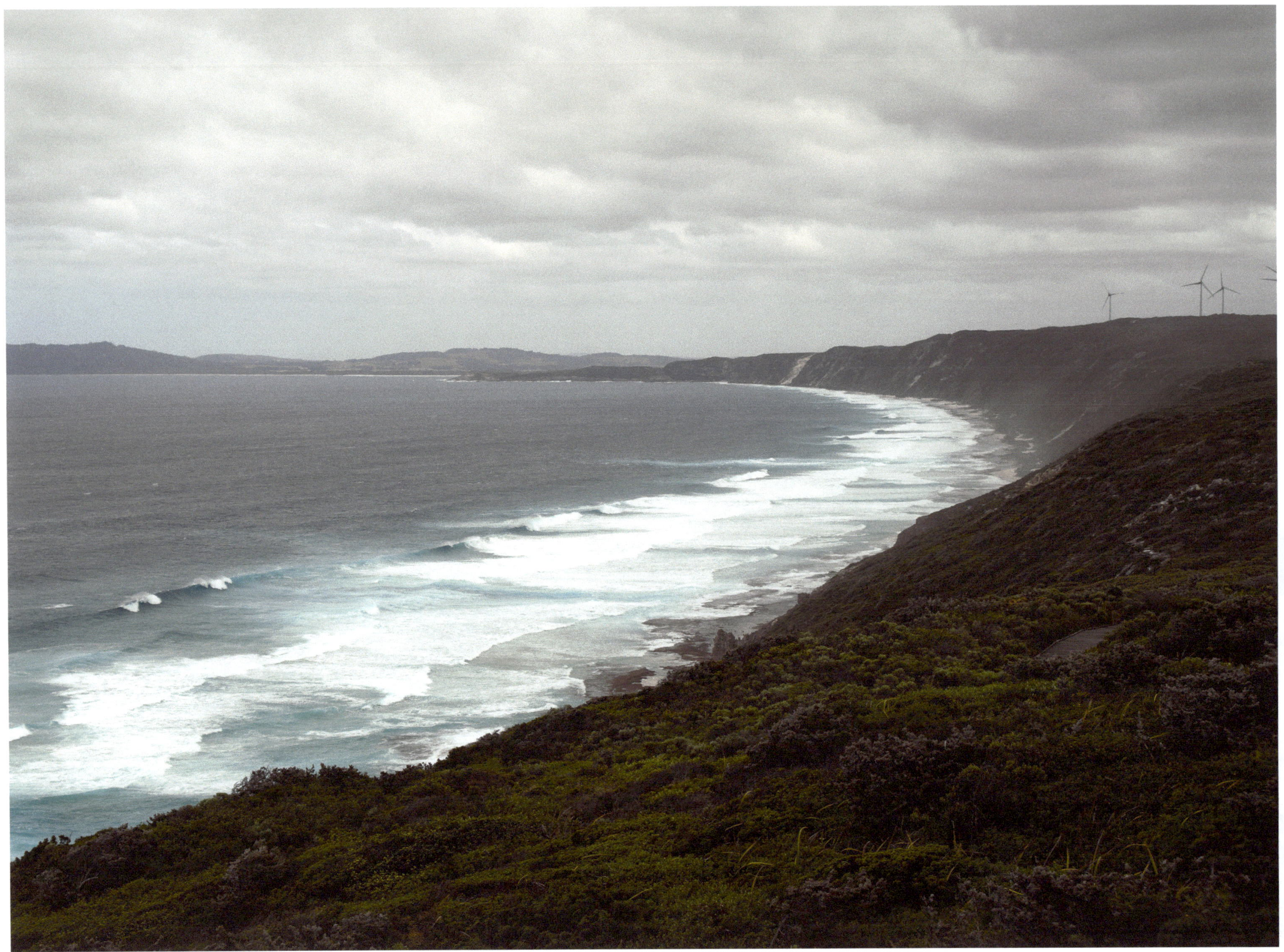

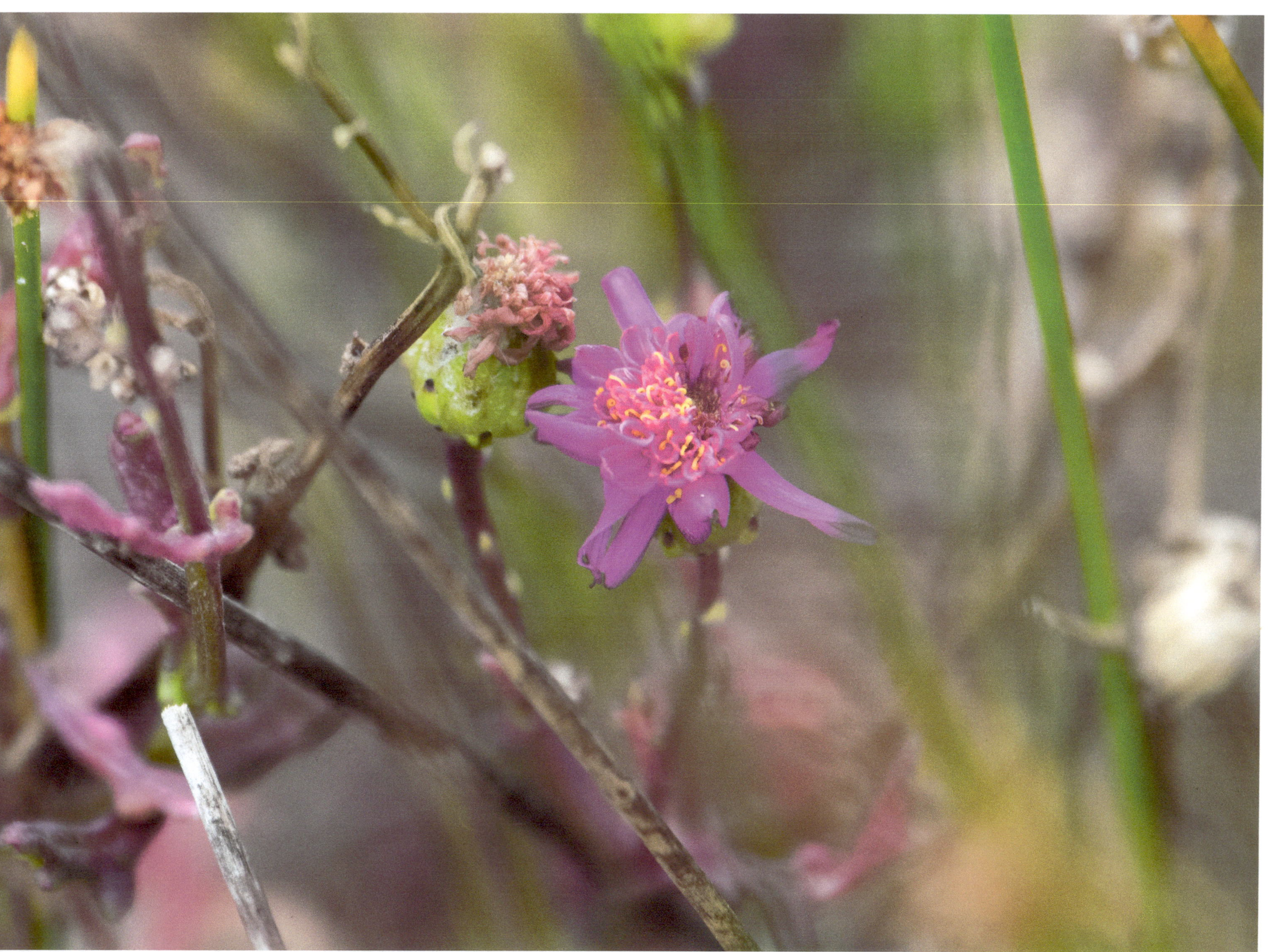

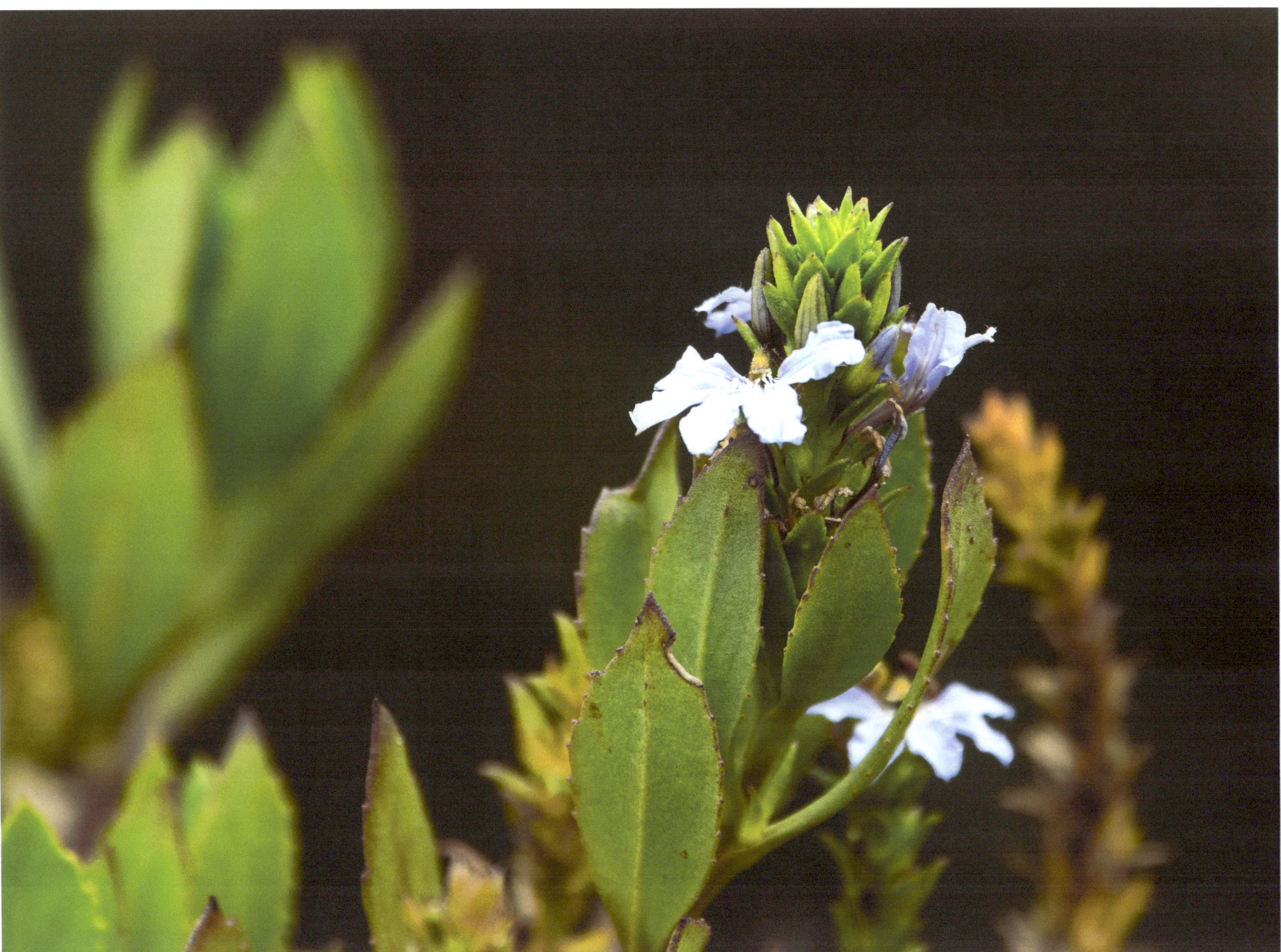

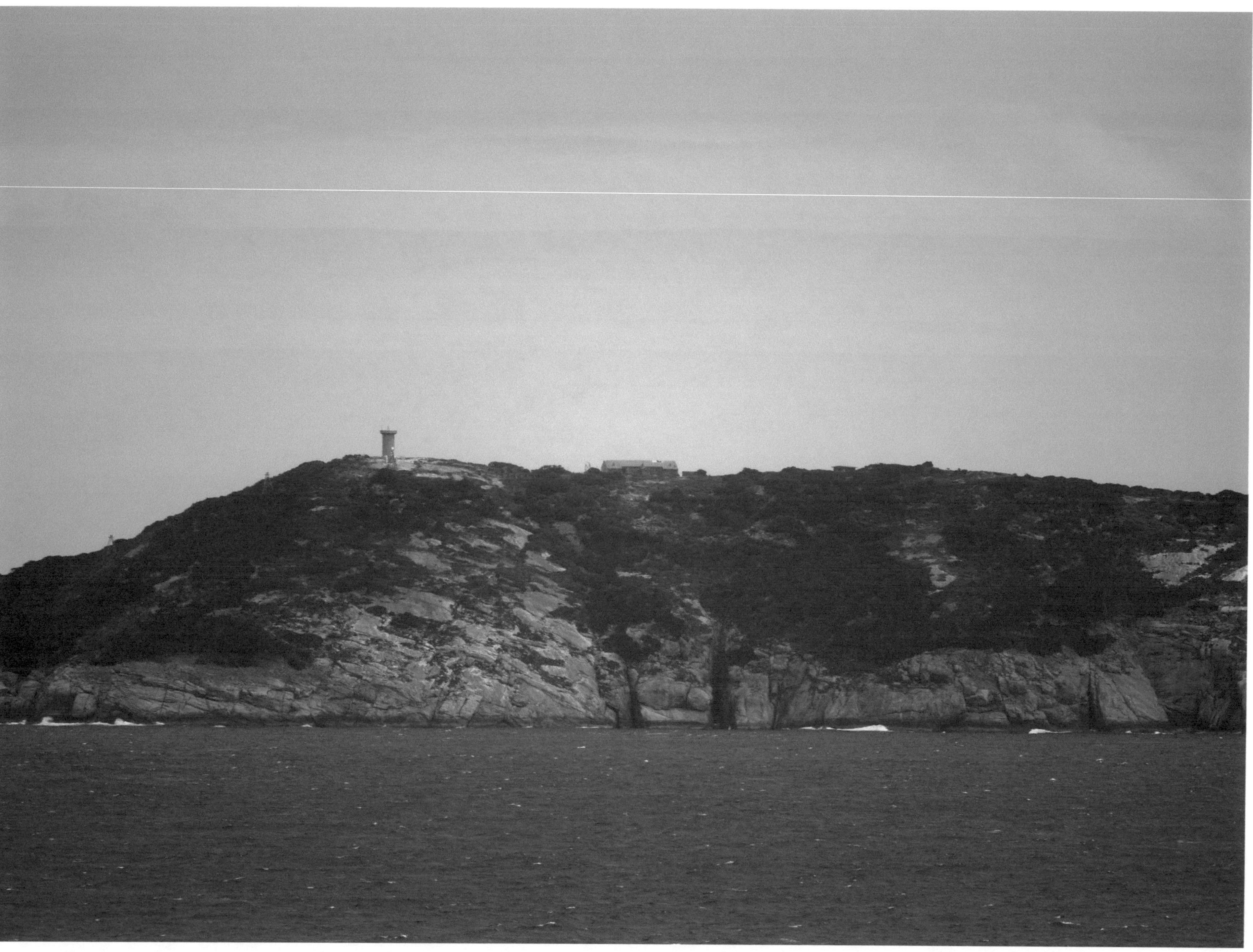

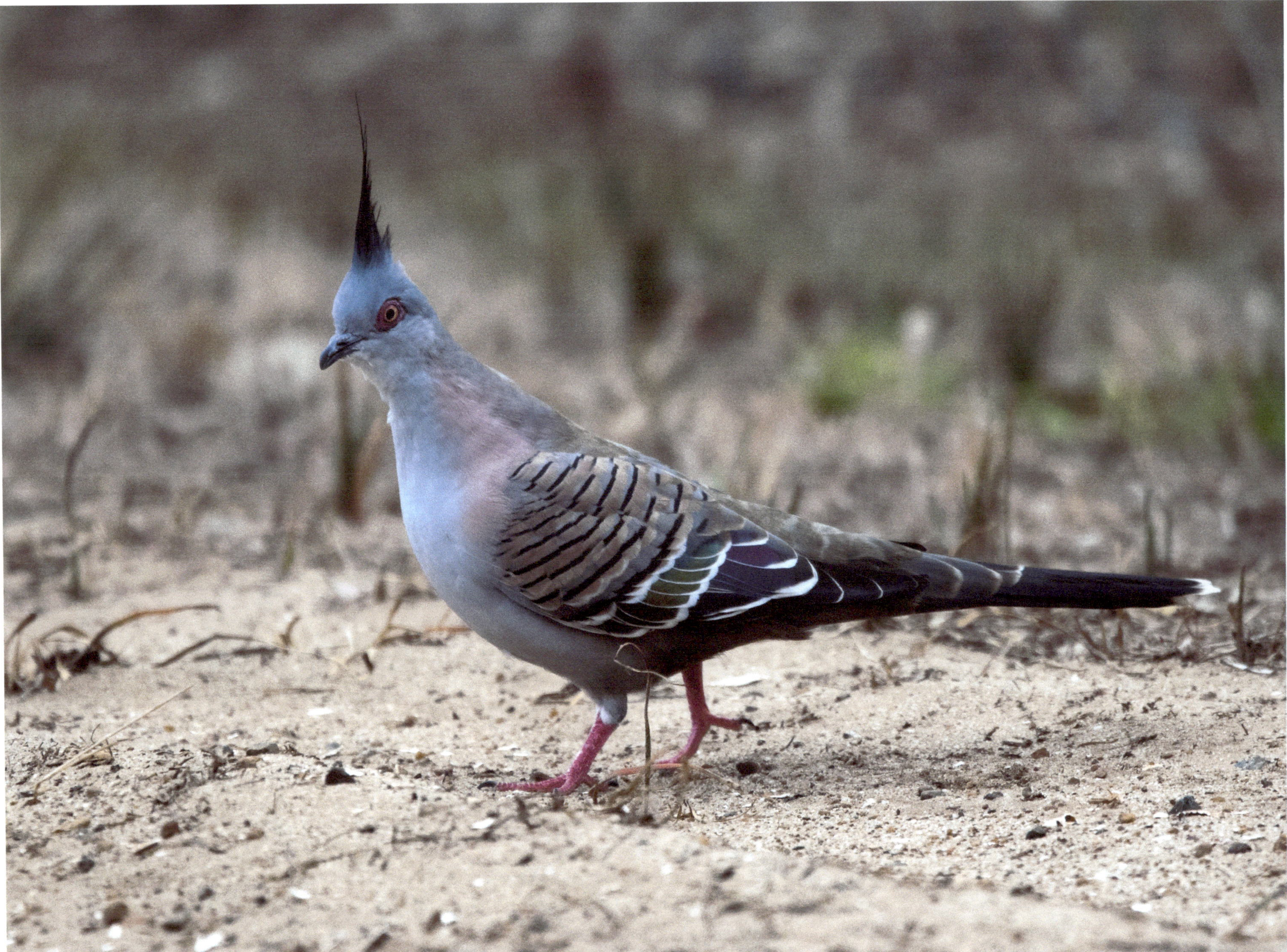

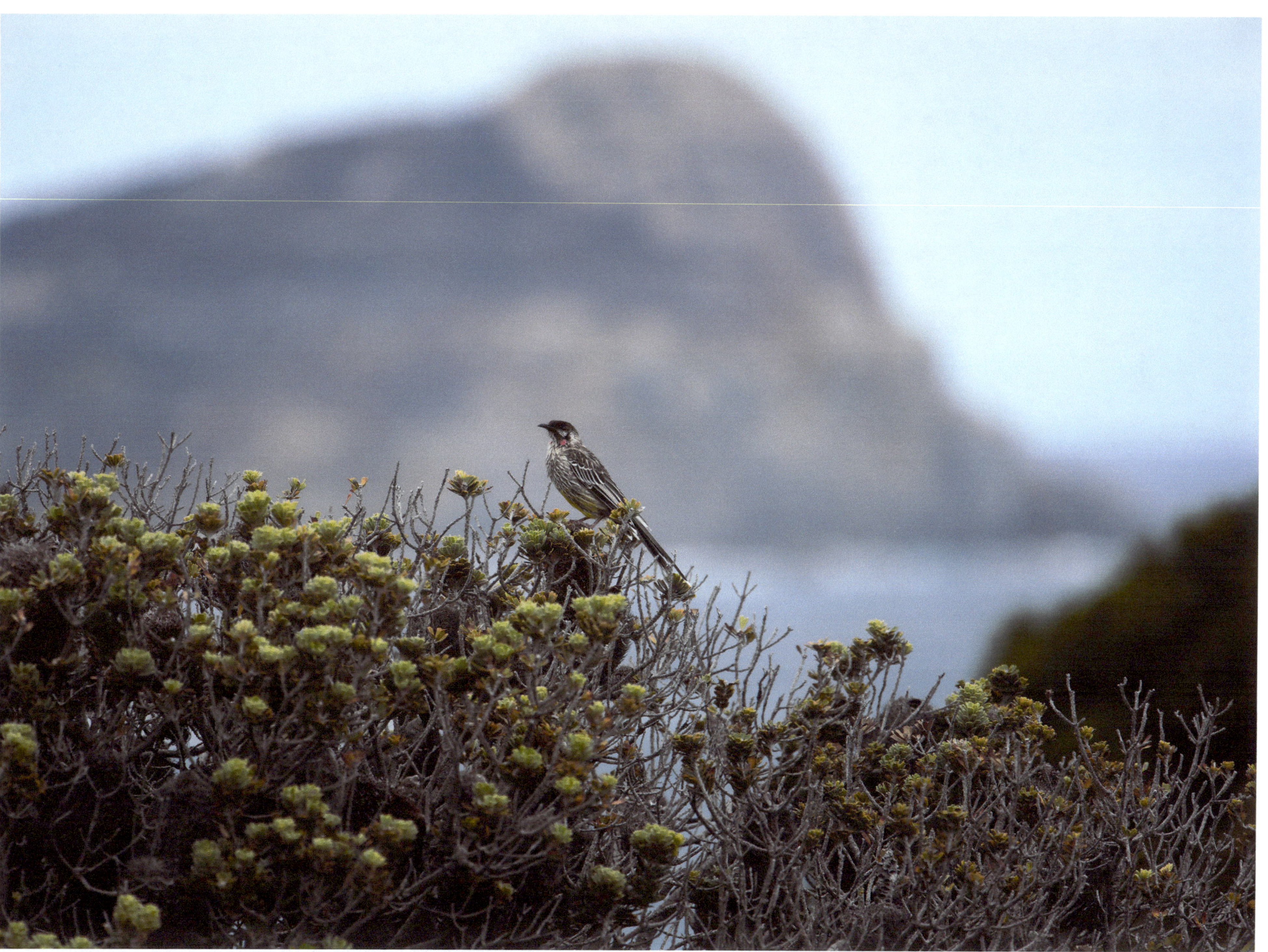

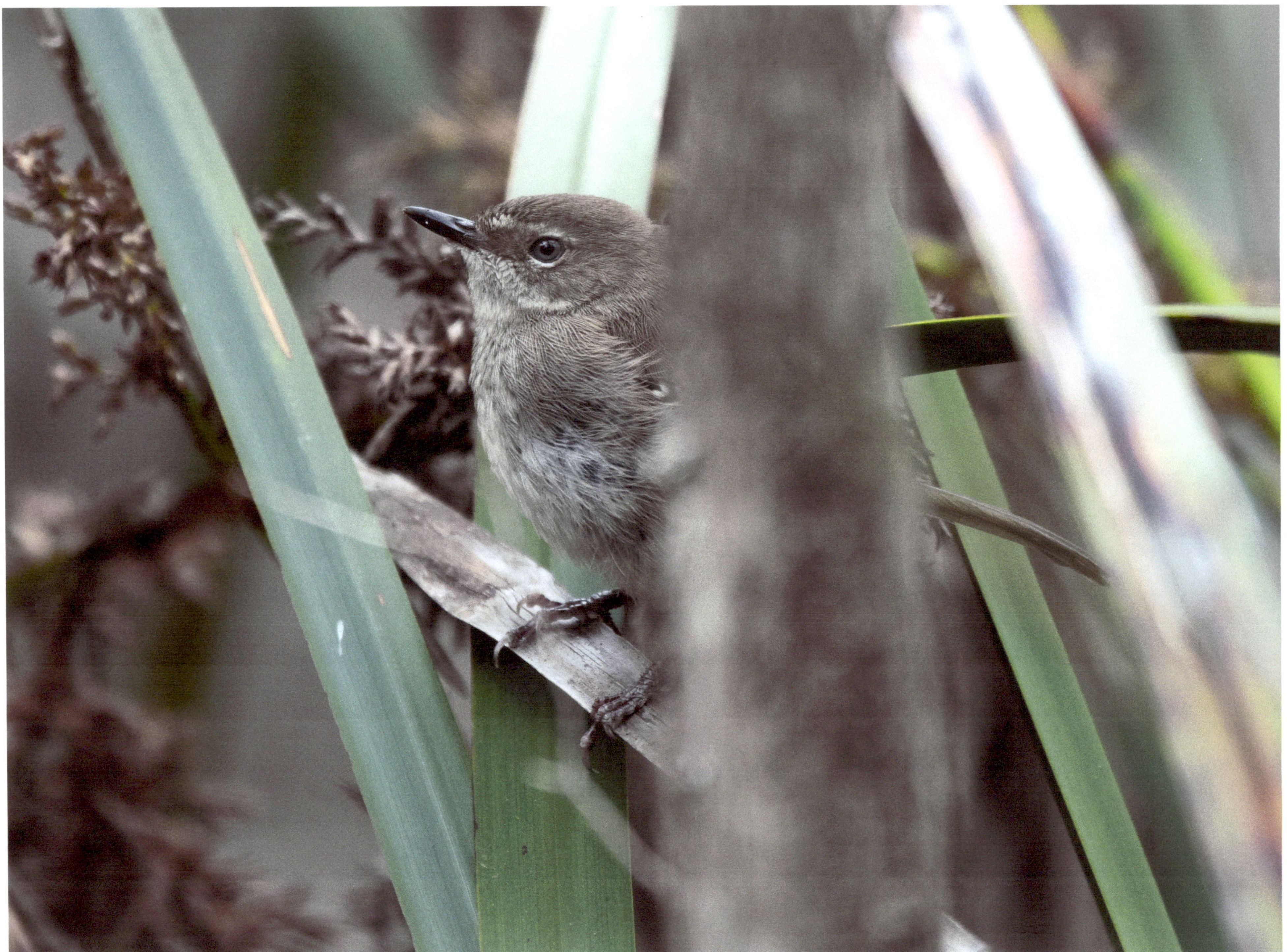

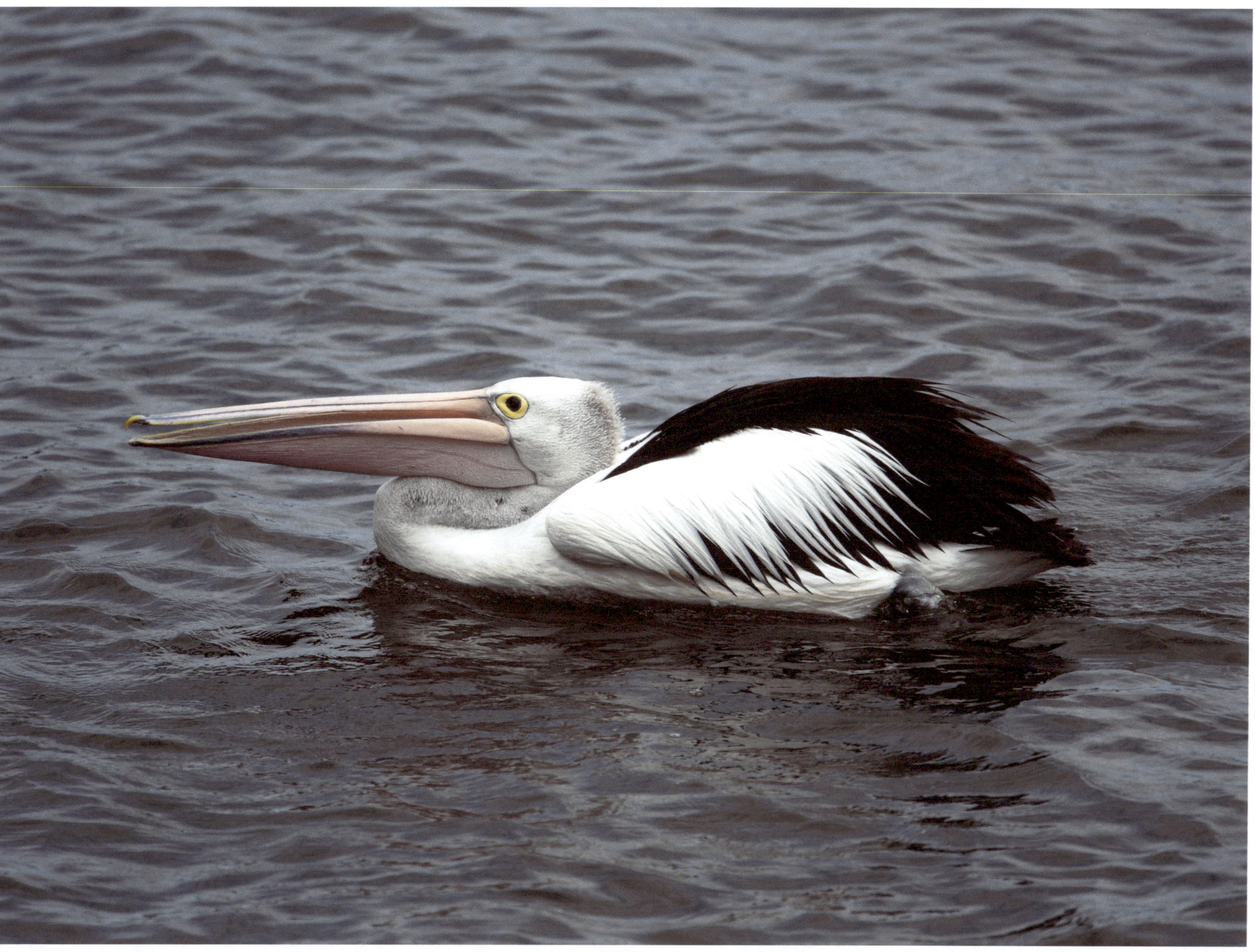

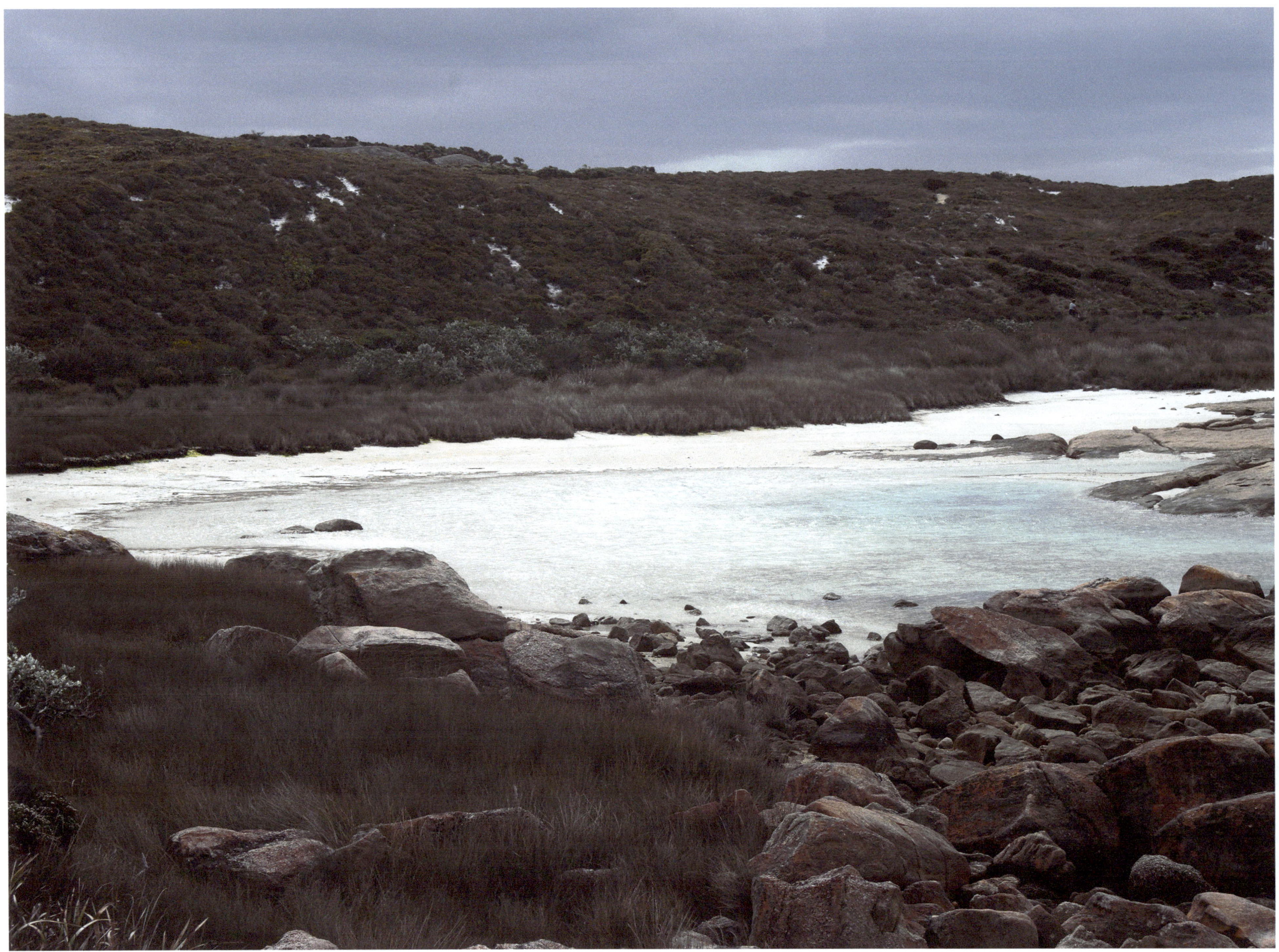

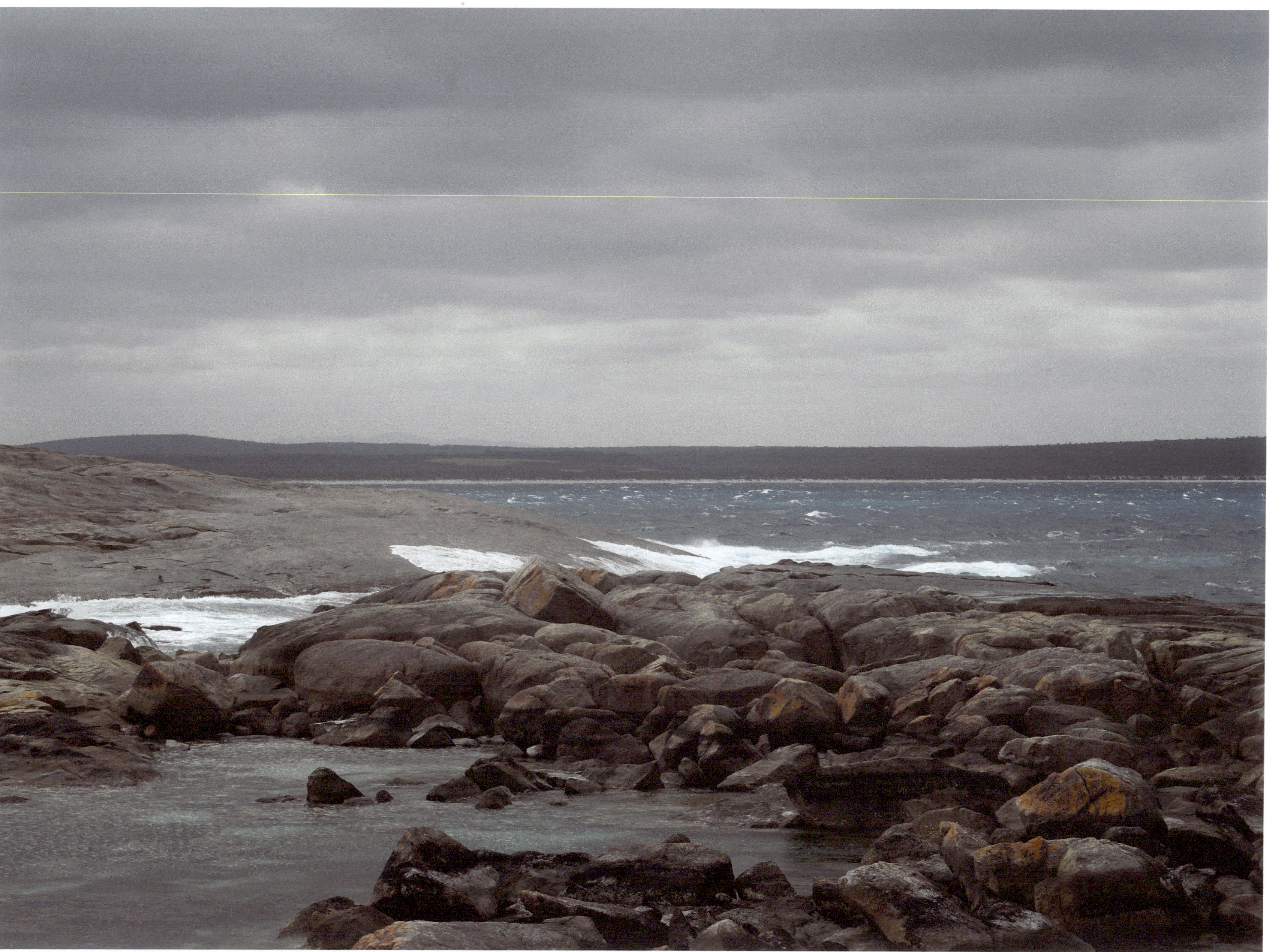

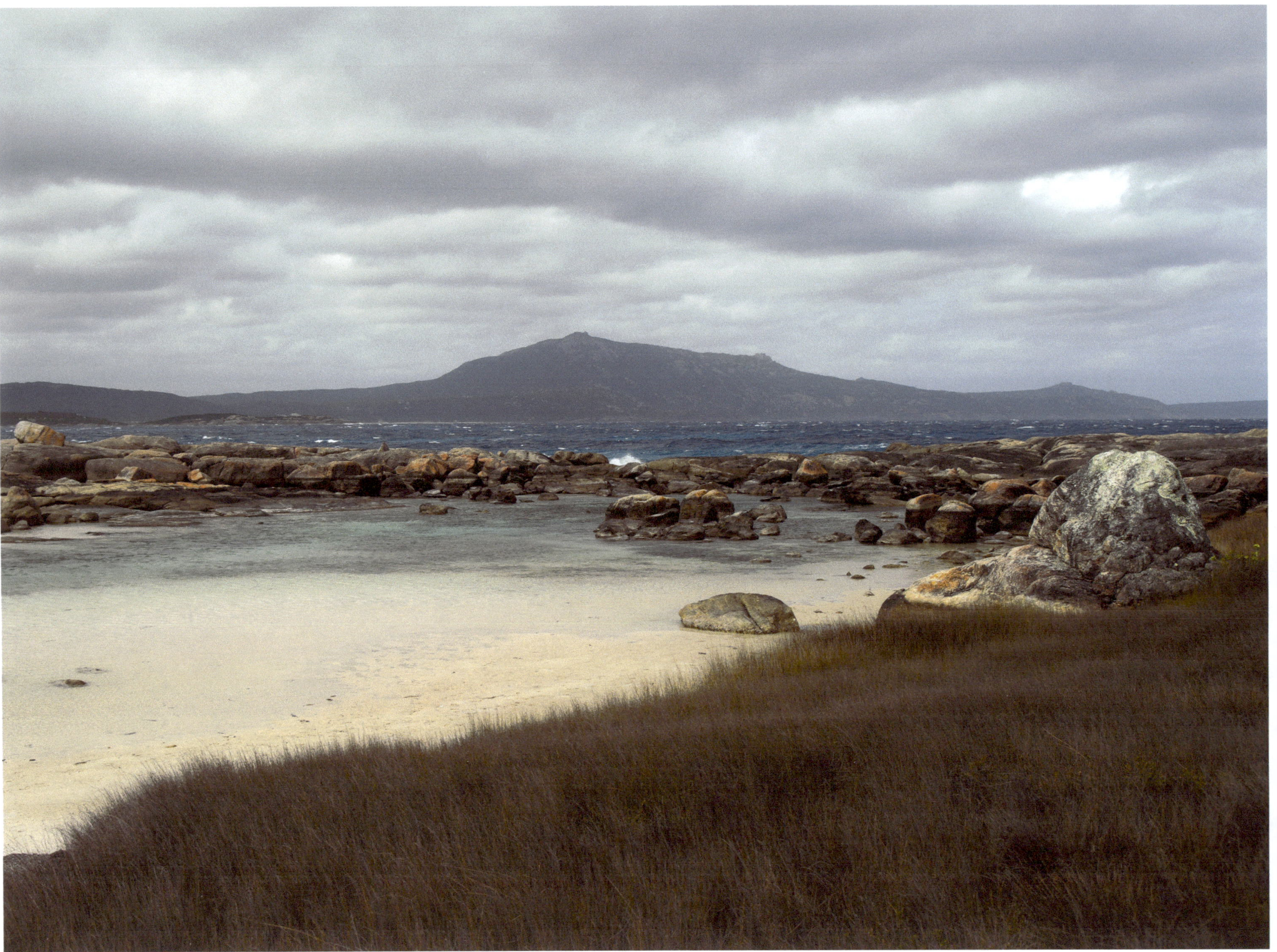

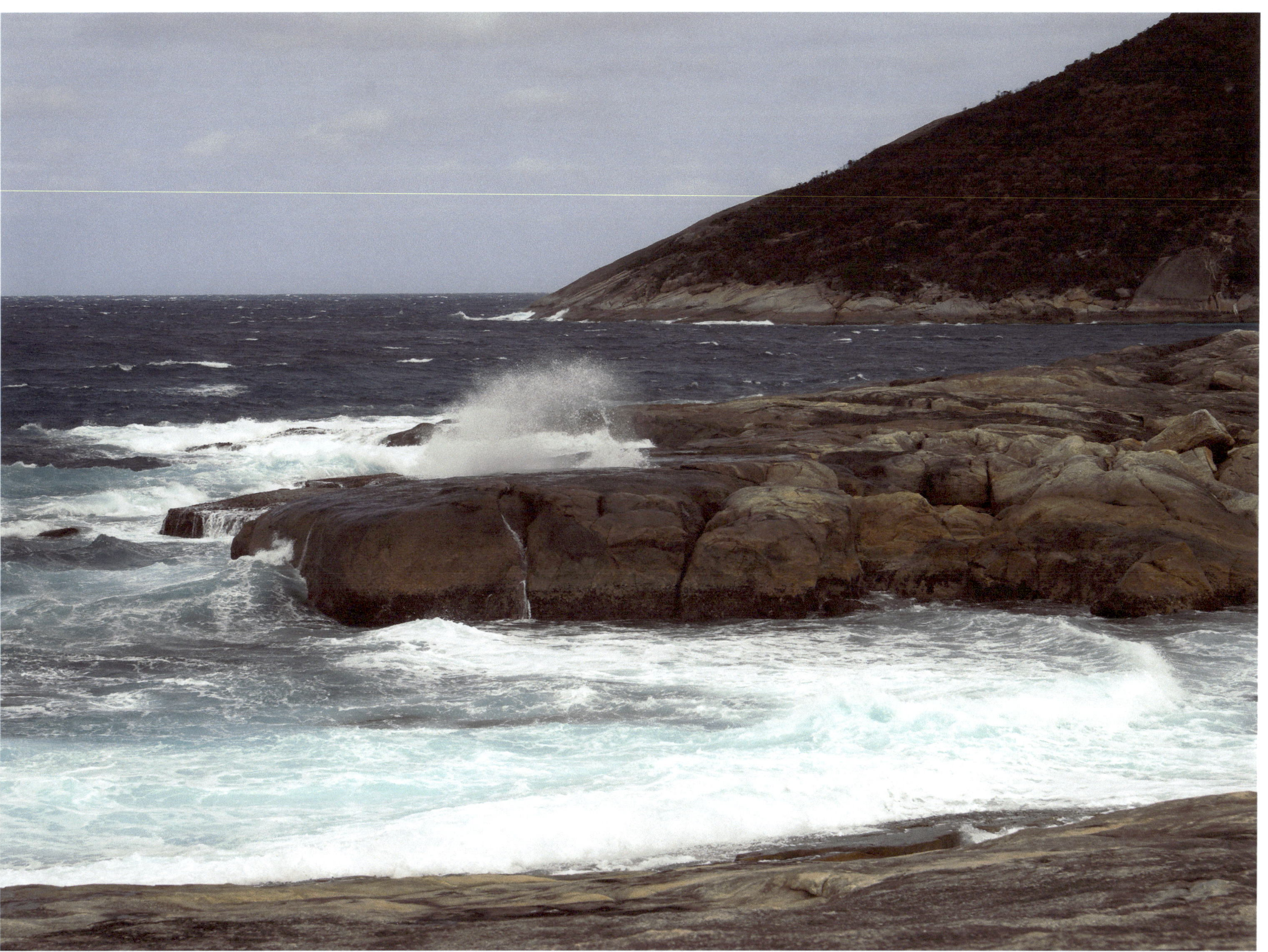

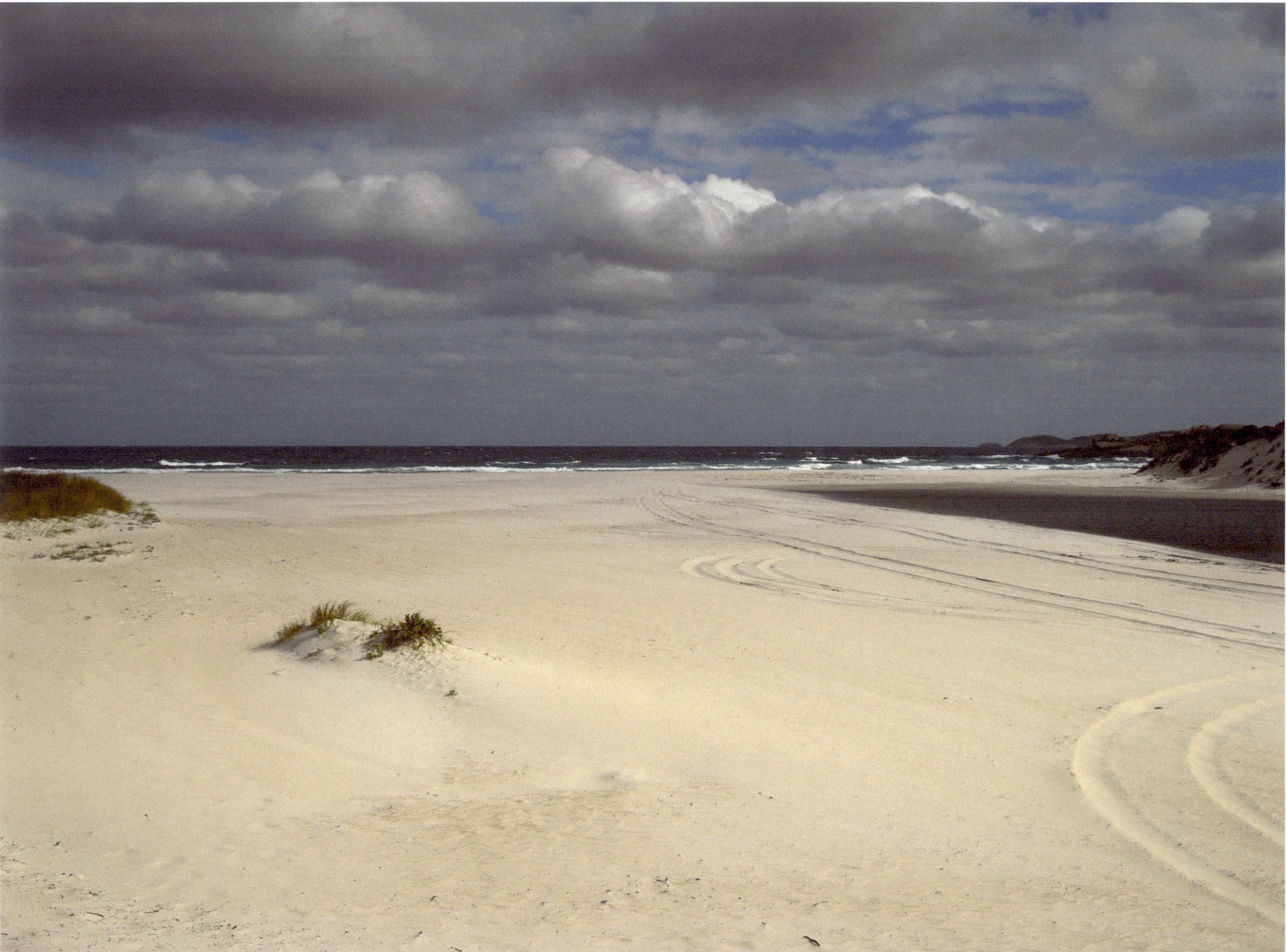

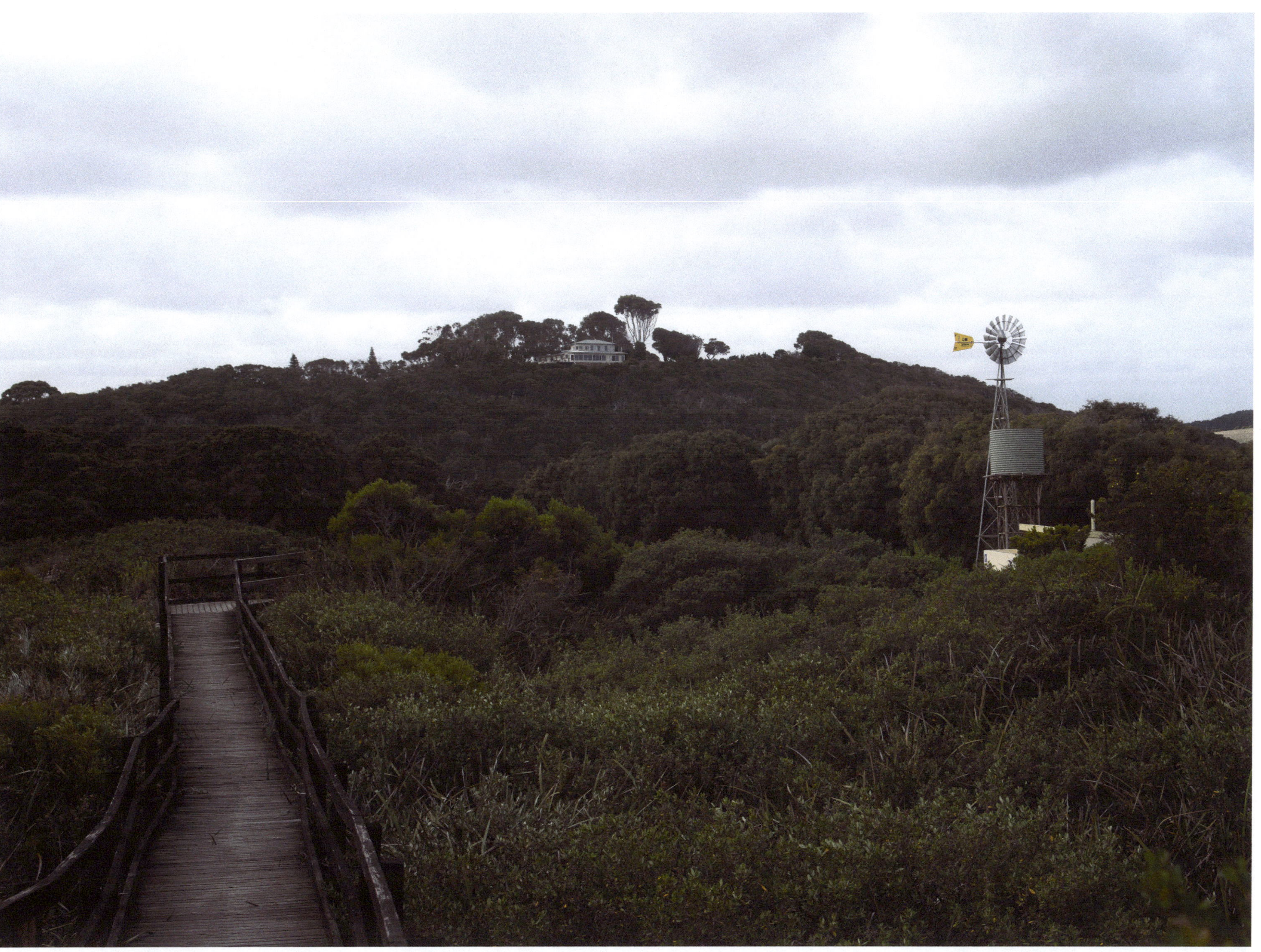

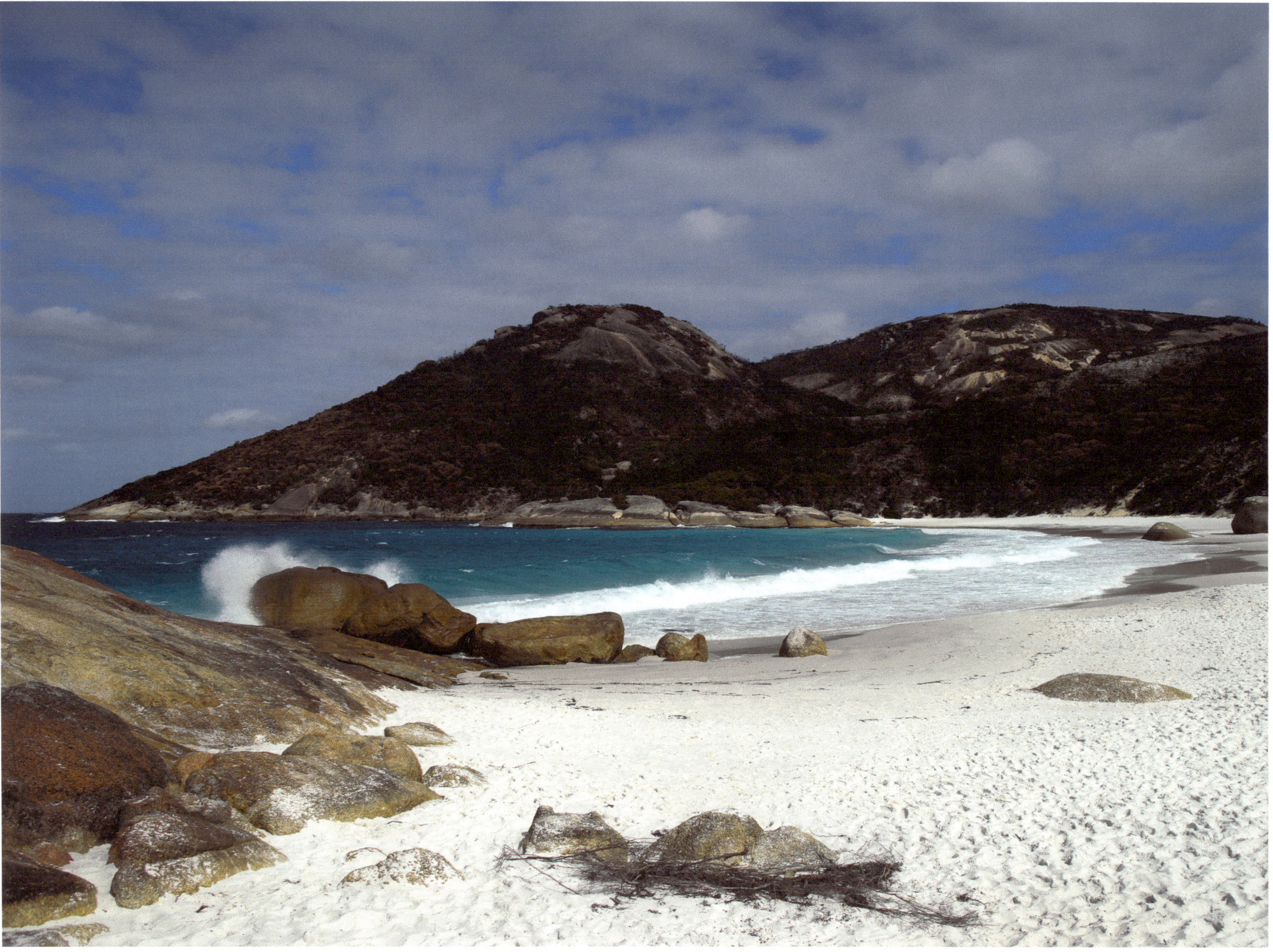

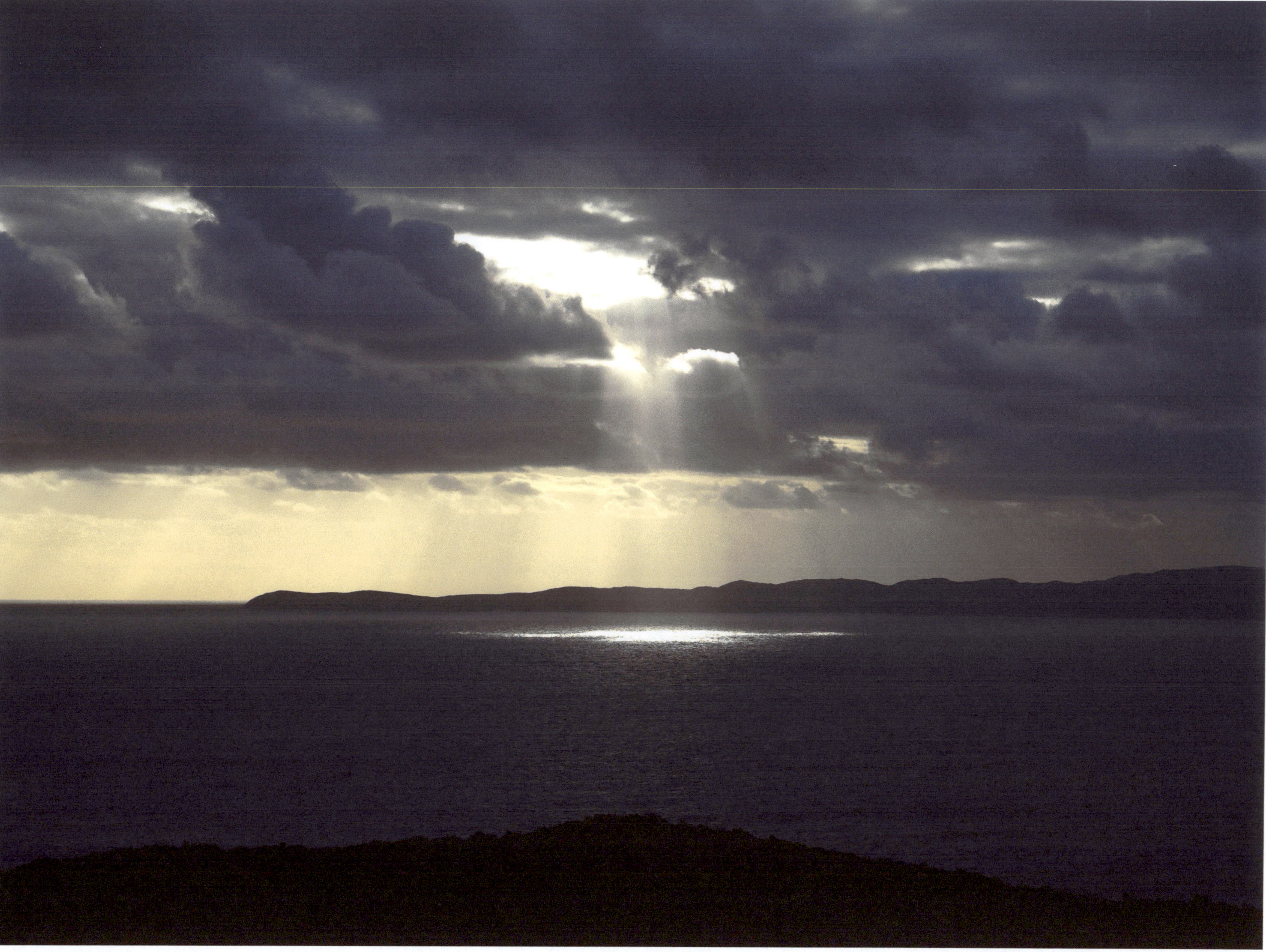

www.ingramcontent.com/pod-product-compliance
Lightning Source LLC
LaVergne TN
LVHW072331100826
845154LV00009B/153